THE BEST OF THE
CLEVELAND BROWNS
Players, Coaches and Games
MEMORIES

by Russell Schneider

Produced and published by
Moonlight Publishing
Hinckley, Ohio
moonlight@clevelandfyi.com

ISBN   0 - 9672056 - 0 - 3

Front cover illustration: Tom Denny
Back cover illustration: Tom Denny
Layout and design: Moonlight Publishing
Published by: Moonlight Publishing
Photographs courtesy of
Browns News/Illustrated
The Cleveland *Plain Dealer*
The Cleveland Browns

Printed in the United States
Phillips Brothers Printing
Springfield, Illinois
First printing: June 1999

Dedication and Acknowledgements

This book is dedicated to my wife and best friend Catherine, for her constant encouragement, patience and support; and to the players and coaches of the Cleveland Browns who, during the past half century, created the mostly good, some not-so-good memories recorded in this book.

Many people contributed to the development of *The Best of the Cleveland Browns Memories*, and heartfelt appreciation is extended, especially to my eldest son and partner Rusty, for his invaluable help in the editing, design and production of the book; and to Tom Denny for his artwork and art direction; and to Ray Yannucci, publisher and editor of *Browns News/Illustrated*, for his willing assistance and for the use of his publication's photographs; and to the world's best public relations man, Dino Lucarelli of the Browns, for his cooperation, research guidance and overall help; and to the Browns for the use of their photographs; and to Browns beat writers Tony Grossi of the Cleveland *Plain Dealer*, and Jeff Schudel of the Lake County (Ohio) *News Herald*, and former Browns beat writer Ed Meyer of the Akron *Beacon Journal*, for their excellent coverage of the Browns over the years; and finally, but absolutely, positively not least of all, to Al Lerner, for giving us a new Browns franchise, and to Carmen Policy, Dwight Clark and Chris Palmer, for making it a good team, and to Cleveland Mayor Michael R. White, for his insistence to the National Football League that the fans of Cleveland, who supported the old Browns so well, deserve a new team.

Russell Schneider
Cleveland, Ohio
June 1, 1999

The Author

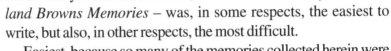

Of the six previous books authored by Russell Schneider, this one – *The Best of the Cleveland Browns Memories* – was, in some respects, the easiest to write, but also, in other respects, the most difficult.

Easiest, because so many of the memories collected herein were personally experienced as a longtime fan of the Browns .

Most difficult because, again as a longtime fan of the Browns, it brought into sharper focus the reality of the fact that the team that was ours the past half century is now the Baltimore Ravens.

But, again, the memories endure and, unlike the team, they cannot be – and have not been - stolen, and for that we should take solace.

Schneider, a Marine veteran and sportswriter for *The Plain Dealer* of Cleveland for 32 years, grew up cheering for the Browns and covered them on a daily basis during their "Kardiac Kids" heyday, from 1978-83. He also covered the Indians, from 1964-77, and wrote a column, *Schneider Around*, prior to leaving the newspaper in 1993.

His six previous books: *Frank Robinson: the Making of a Manager*, 1976; *Lou Boudreau, Covering all the Bases*, 1994; *The Glorious Indian Summer of 1995; The Cleveland Indians Encyclopedia*, 1996; *The Unfulfilled Indian Summer of 1996*; and *The Boys of the Summer of '48*, 1998.

Schneider and his wife Catherine have three children, Russell Jr., who played a major role in the editing, design and production of this book, Bryan and Eileen (Raich).

Introduction

This book, *The Best of the Cleveland Browns Memories*, had its genesis in the wake of the deplorable re-location of the team that played its first game a half century earlier, and thrilled generations of football fans – in Cleveland and throughout the world – with its success (most of the time), and great players.

It begins when the franchise began, with a 44-0 victory over the Miami Seahawks in the old All-America Football Conference which the Browns, under Paul Brown, dominated to the extent that it caused the league to disband after four seasons.

The death of the AAFC, however, also led to the rebirth (should that be the *first* rebirth?) of the Browns who were, along with the San Francisco and Baltimore franchises, invited to join the long-established National Football League.

The Browns' winning tradition continued in the NFL, though the team – and the organization under Art Modell - fell upon hard times in recent years, which contributed to the decision to leave Cleveland and move to Baltimore.

And that, in turn, led to the second coming of the Cleveland Browns under the stewardship of Alfred Lerner and Carmen Policy, along with Dwight Clark, director of football operations, and Coach Chris Palmer.

While the team we all knew and cheered (most of the time) is no longer ours, nobody can take from us the memories of the great players, coaches and games that thrilled us over the past half century.

Many of those memories have been collected in this volume.

Read and relive them, and enjoy … as the glorious tradition of the Cleveland Browns continues.

The Players

Table of Contents

IN THE BEGINNING

In the beginning it was oh-so-easy for Paul Brown and the Cleveland Browns.

At least, they made it look easy as they completely dominated the All-America Football Conference from 1946-49, losing only four games in those four seasons, while winning 52 and tying three others.

With Brown calling the plays and Hall of Famers Otto Graham, Dante Lavelli, Marion Motley, Lou Groza, Bill Willis and Frank Gatski running the plays, the Browns went 12-2 in their first season, losing only to the Los Angeles Dons and San Francisco 49ers; 12-1-1 in 1947, losing only to the Dons and being held to a tie by the New York Yankees; 14-0 in 1948 (extending their unbeaten streak to 23) and becoming the first professional football team to go undefeated in a season; and 9-1-2 in 1949 (running their unbeaten streak to an amazing 28), losing only to the 49ers, while being tied in two games by Buffalo.

They won the championship game each season – against the Yankees, 14-9, in 1946, and 14-3 in 1947; 49-7 against Buffalo in 1948; and 21-7 against the 49ers in 1949, after advancing to the title game with a 31-21 victory over Buffalo.

It was their total domination of the AAFC that led to the demise of the league, and in 1950 the Browns were invited to join the National Football League, which they also dominated the first year, and played for the title each of the next five seasons, winning again in 1954 and 1955.

1946 Cleveland Browns

Front Row: Fritz Heisler, Ray Terrell. Al Akins, Bill Lund, Don Greenwood, Fred Evans, Cliff Lewis, Jim Daniell, Edgar Jones, Otto Graham, Tom Colella, Bob Steuber, Gene Fekete, Lou Saban, Morrie Kono
Second Row: Red Conkright, Marion Motley, Dante Lavelli, Alex Kaptor, George Cheroke, Bob Kolesar, Lin Houston, Len Simonetti, Mike Scarry, George Groves, Eddie Ulinski, John Harrington, Bob Voights, Paul Brown
Third Row: Wally Bock, Allen Coppage, John Rokisky, Bud Schwenk, Ernie Blandin, Mel Maceau, Bill Willis, Frank Gatski, Mac Speedie, George Young, John Yonaker, Lou Rymkus, Lou Groza, Chet Adams, Blanton Collier, John Brickels

The birth of the Browns

It all began with a couple of sportswriters and an entrepreneur named Arthur B. "Mickey" McBride, who was best known for owning a taxicab company in Cleveland. The sportswriters were Arch Ward of the Chicago *Tribune*, and John Dietrich of the Cleveland *Plain Dealer*.

Ward wanted to start another professional football league to compete with the National Football League.

Dietrich told McBride it might be worth looking into as speculation already had arisen that the Cleveland Rams, a member of the NFL since 1937, were thinking about moving.

McBride called on Ward and they quickly reached agreement. McBride, 47, would own the Cleveland franchise in the eight-team league to be known as the "All-America Football Conference."

Formal announcement was made on September 4, 1944, though the AAFC would not begin operations on the field until 1946, after the end of World War II.

McBride, who owned the Yellow and Zone cab companies in Cleveland, and other business enterprises, probably would not be granted a franchise if the situation presented itself today – because of those other enterprises.

Then he was involved in a horse racing wire syndicate and allegedly was linked with organized crime in Chicago.

Arthur B. "Mickey" McBride

But back there in 1944 McBride was welcomed into the AAFC, and set about building and promoting his still unnamed new team.

It was McBride's vigorous promotion, in fact, that finally convinced Daniel R. Reeves, owner of the Rams, to move his team to Los Angeles after winning the NFL championship in 1945.

Records show that McBride first tried to hire Frank Leahy, the Notre Dame coach who was then in the Navy. Leahy intially agreed to join McBride, but changed his mind and stayed at Notre Dame.

Then Dietrich spoke up again, recommending Paul Brown, who'd been eminently successful at Massillon (O.) High School and Ohio State before he, too, went into the Navy.

Brown, 36, was coaching football at Great Lakes Naval Training Station in Chicago and, on February 8, 1945, accepted McBride's offer - a $25,000 a year salary, plus $1,000 a month for the duration of the war, until the AAFC got started.

Otto Graham was signed as the first player, and a contest was held to name the team, McBride chose "Panthers" as the winner. But Brown objected, citing the existence of a mediocre semi-pro team near Cleveland already called the Panthers, and told McBride he wouldn't have his team associated with a loser, even if only by name.

Consequently, another contest was held and "Browns" was declared the winner, partly because of the success at the time of heavyweight champion Joe Louis, whose nickname was the "Brown Bomber," and also as a tribute to the team's coach.

"We decided to shorten the name and call our team the Browns," Brown was quoted in a history of the franchise, although, of course, his name had much to do with it, too.

McBride, who died in 1972 at 85, sold the Browns on June 9, 1953, to a syndicate headed by Clevelander David Jones.

The price was $600,000, the highest ever paid for a pro football franchise at the time.

Hello Browns, goodbye Rams

The birth of the Browns in 1946 coincided with the end of the Rams, whose final game in Cleveland should have been reason for a special celebration – they beat the Washington Redskins, 15-14, on December 16, 1945, to win their first National Football League championship.

But times were different then, at least they were in professional sports, and if what followed the Rams' victory over the Redskins happened today there'd be great grief and consternation among the fans, just as the move of the Browns to Baltimore did in 1995. However, in 1946, when the Rams moved from Cleveland to Los Angeles, the defection was accepted by the fans and the media with slightly more than a yawn.

Bob Waterfield and Adam Walsh

The Rams had drawn just 73,000 fans for their five regular season home games in 1945, and only 32,176 saw them win the title game, the forerunner of the Super Bowl, at the old Cleveland Stadium.

The coming presence of the Browns in the new All-America Football Conference probably was a reason for the lack of concern over the departure of the Rams.

Whatever, the Rams were never a big hit from the time they began in Cleveland in 1937. From then through 1945 (with the exception of 1943 when operations were suspended because of World War II) their overall record for eight years was 34-50-2 and, prior to 1945, the closest they came to a winning season was 1939 when they went 5-5-1.

But in 1945 they were sensational under Coach Adam Walsh, who installed the then-novel T-formation and put rookie quarterback Bob Waterfield at the controls.

Waterfield, better known at the start of the season as the husband of movie actress Jane Russell, led the NFL in passing yardage with 1,609 (88-for-171) in 1945.

However, Waterfield did much more than just pass. The epitome of a triple threat star, he ran the ball, punted, place-kicked and even intercepted six passes on defense.

With Waterfield as their leader, the Rams went 9-1 to win the NFL West Division, losing only to Philadelphia, 28-14, during the regular season in 1945. They played the East Division champion Redskins in the worst weather conditions - the temperature was six degrees Fahrenheit at one point - and the players had to help clear the field of snow before the game could start.

Despite the conditions, Waterfield put on a spectacular show, completing 14 of 27 passes for 192 yards and two touchdowns. Halfback Jim Gillette rushed for 101 yards and one of the touchdowns in 17 carries, and end (as receivers then were called) Jim Benton caught nine passes for 125 yards and the Rams' other touchdown.

But the key to the Rams' victory occurred early in the game.

Sammy Baugh, a future Hall of Famer who was the Redskins' quarterback, threw a pass from his own end zone that struck the goal post and fell out of the field of play. It was ruled a safety, based on the rules in effect at the time, and the Rams were awarded two points – the two points that turned out to be their margin of victory.

The rules have since been changed and Baugh's pass that caromed off the goal post would not be ruled a safety today, simply an incompletion.

But in 1945 it was instrumental in deciding the NFL championship for the Cleveland - soon-to-be-Los Angeles - Rams.

They got more than a football

The Browns and the All-America Football Conference did more than just "get a football" in 1946, as they were advised by Elmer Layden, then commissioner of the National Football League.

They also got five established players who did not want to go west when the Cleveland Rams moved to Los Angeles. They preferred to stay in Cleveland and play for Paul Brown and the Browns.

The five who defected when the Rams pulled out:

• Tom Colella, a running back/defensive back out of Canisius College, who played for the Rams from 1942 through 1945 and was one of quarterback Bob Waterfield's favorite targets;

Paul Brown and Tom Colella

• Don Greenwood, another running back/defensive back from Missouri who was a promising Rams rookie in 1945;

• Gaylon Smith, a fullback/linebacker from Southwestern University who played for the Rams from 1939 through 1942, went into the service during World War II and, upon his discharge, decided to remain in Cleveland;

• Chet Adams, a huge tackle from Ohio University who played for the Rams from 1939 through 1942 before he also went into the service, and remained in Cleveland after the war;

• Mike (Moe) Scarry, a center from Waynesburg College who played for the Rams in 1944 and 1945.

Colella, Greenwood and Smith probably made the most noteworthy contributions to the Browns, primarily because of the high profile positions they played.

Colella led the AAFC with 10 pass interceptions in 1946, punted 47 times for a 40.3 yard average, returned eight punts for 172 yards, and rushed 30 times for 118 yards and two touchdowns.

Greenwood scored six touchdowns for the fledgling Browns as he ran from scrimmage 77 times for 274 yards, returned five kickoffs for 105 yards, and intercepted two passes.

Smith, a tough linebacker who also was good receiver and spelled Marion Motley at fullback, ran for five touchdowns as he gained 240 yards in 62 carries, and caught seven Otto Graham passes for 73 yards.

But there's no doubt Adams and Scarry, while playing in the obscurity of the offensive line, also were key figures in the early success of the Browns, though their longevity was short.

Adams was a starter through the first three seasons with the Browns, helping them win three consecutive titles, and retired in 1949.

Scarry backed up Frank Gatski at center in 1946 and 1947 before he, too, retired.

Among the three backs, Smith retired after that first season with the Browns, Greenwood was a part-time player in 1947, then hung up his cleats, and Colella played through the 1948 season, though his duties were primarily as the Browns' punter.

The Browns probably would have dominated the AAFC even without those five defectors from the NFL and the Rams.

But Colella, Greenwood, Smith, Adams and Scarry all made it easier – and, in particular, helped establish credibility for the AAFC.

A portent of the future

A clairvoyant could have called it a portent of the future, which would have been accurate the way the fledgling Cleveland Browns dominated Arch Ward's All-America Football Conference from its 1946 beginning through four seasons to its end in 1949.

The Browns' domination of the AAFC should have been very apparent the way they played under their novice professional coach, who operated as though he were still teaching a college (or even high school) course in algebra or history.

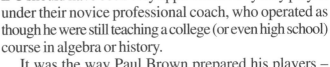

Paul Brown

It was the way Paul Brown prepared his players – and himself – for every game, which is the reason he was eminently successful at Severn (Maryland) Prep School (16-1-1), Massillon (Ohio) Washington High School (80-8-2), Ohio State University (18-8-1), and the Great Lakes (Illinois) Naval Training Station (15-5-2).

The Browns won their AAFC opener in grand style, overwhelming the Miami Seahawks, 44-0, in front of 60,135 fans, in the old Cleveland Stadium on September 6, and went on to capture seven straight, six by shutouts.

They beat the Rockets in Chicago, 20-6, in Game Two, as Marion Motley gained 128 yards in twelve carries; and blanked the Bisons in Buffalo in Game Three, 28-0, as Otto Graham threw two touchdown passes.

Two pass interceptions by Don Greenwood and Mike Scarry set up touchdowns, and Don Greenwood and "Special Delivery" Jones scored twice in the Browns' 24-7 victory over the New York Yankees in Game Four; and defense again was a key as the Browns beat the Brooklyn Dodgers, 26-7, in Game Five, as Lou Saban intercepted two passes and Alton Coppage recovered a fumble, converting them into touchdowns.

The Browns' toughest test came in Game Six, as they were outgained by the Yankees, 237-67, but prevailed, 7-0, on a touchdown pass from Graham to Dante Lavelli and a seventh straight victory was recorded, 31-14, over the Los Angeles Dons, overcoming a 7-3 halftime deficit as Motley scored on runs of 68- and 47-yards.

Motley was held to 22 yards, and Frankie Albert fired three touchdown passes as the San Francisco 49ers handed the Browns their first loss, 34-20, in Game Eight; and they suffered another defeat the following week, 17-16, to the Dons, with the winning points coming on an 11-yard field goal by Joe Aguarre with 18 seconds remaining.

Lavelli and Gaylon Smith scored as the Browns edged the 49ers, 14-7, in Game Ten; Graham hurled four touchdown passes, two each to Lavelli and Mac Speedie, to win Game Eleven, 51-14, over the Rockets, the first of four high-scoring games in which they totaled 193 points to their opponents' 45, beating Buffalo, 42-17, in Game Twelve; Miami, 34-0, in Game Thirteen and Brooklyn, 66-14, in Game Fourteen.

Victory in the AAFC title game didn't come quite so easily – though it was achieved in the final 4:13 – as the Browns beat the Eastern Division champion Yankees, 14-9, in front of 40,496 fans in the Stadium on December 22.

The Browns' winning touchdown came on a 16-yard pass from Graham to Lavelli, though the Yankees mounted one last threat. It was halted when Graham, playing both ways, intercepted a pass at the Browns' 30 yard line. Motley, who scored the Browns' first touchdown, gained 98 yards in 13 carries, as the Browns launched their domination of the AAFC.

The Modell era begins

When Mickey McBride sold the Browns to a syndicate headed by Clevelander David Jones in 1953, the price was $600,000, the most ever paid for a professional football franchise.

But eight years later a young, aggressive and enterprising New York advertising and television executive named Arthur B. Modell came to Cleveland and, on January 25, 1961, he paid more than six times as much for the Browns: $3.925 million.

Arthur B. Modell

The deal, in which Modell risked every penny he owned and every dollar he could borrow, was motivated by his perception that pro football and television would make a perfect marriage.

He proved to be 100 percent accurate.

Modell learned of the availability of the team in October 1960, as the Browns were struggling through an 8-3 season,

Modell aggressively negotiated with Jones and stockholders Homer Marshman and Ellis Ryan, and was able to put together the necessary financing to close the deal.

It was the beginning of a new era in Cleveland's professional football history - and also eventually led to the demise of Paul Brown as general manager and coach of the team bearing his name. It lasted through 1995 when Modell moved the franchise to Baltimore.

After taking over in 1961, Modell made clear the areas of responsibility he expected to share with Brown: the coach was to run the football end, and Modell would handle business.

But it wasn't long before their "partnership" deteriorated, for a number of reasons, not all of which were made public.

One reportedly involved Ernie Davis, the 1961 Heisman Trophy winner from Syracuse, who died tragically of leukemia.

The Browns acquired the right to draft Davis in a December 14, 1961 trade with Washington in which the Redskins got veteran running back Bobby Mitchell. The deal was made by Brown, without consulting Modell. In fact, Modell didn't learn of it until he was informed by Redskins owner George Preston Marshall.

It was the beginning of the end of Modell's and Brown's relationship, though they publicly co-existed peacefully through the 1962 season as the Browns were going 7-6-1.

Finally, on January 7, 1963, Modell called Brown into his office and told the coach he was through. Blanton Collier would take over the team, though Brown would remain as a vice president and continue to be paid his $82,000 annual salary for the next six years.

Modell called it simply a move "in the best interest of the Browns," and never really elaborated further.

Brown called himself "a vice president of I-don't-know-what."

It was an unpopular move then, and Modell continued to be criticized by diehard fans for firing Brown as the team managed to win only one NFL championship, in 1964, after Brown's dismissal.

During Modell's tenure as owner of the Browns the team compiled a 277-242-6 record (a winning percentage of .534), won the NFL once (1964), two conference championships and nine division titles in 34 years.

THE PLAYERS

More than 800 men have worn the orange, brown and white uniforms of the Cleveland Browns at one time or another from 1946-95, although, to be sure, less than half of them actually played in regular season games.

The list begins with Bobby Abrams, a linebacker from the University of Michigan who was with the Browns briefly in 1992, and ends with Lance Zeno, a center from UCLA who was on the roster in 1992 and 1993.

Of those fewer-than-400 who did play for the Browns, thirteen have made it to the Hall of Fame – Jim Brown, Len Ford, Frank Gatski, Otto Graham, Lou Groza, Leroy Kelly, Dante Lavelli, Bobby Mitchell, Mike McCormack, Marion Motley, Ozzie Newsome, Paul Warfield and Bill Willis - as well as Paul Brown, the team's first coach.

There also have been fourteen former Browns who, after ending their playing careers, became head coaches in the National Football League – Monte Clark, Bill Cowher, Abe Gibron, Otto Graham, Mike McCormack, Walter Michaels, Dick Modzelewski, Chuck Noll, Lou Rymkus, Lou Saban, Jim Shofner, Don Shula, Mac Speedie and Paul Wiggin.

All are profiled in the stories that follow, though *The Best of the Cleveland Browns Memories* are not limited to the players who were the best or the toughest or the most honored, they are, simply, those who are among the most memorable players who wore the brown, orange and white of the Cleveland Browns – the all-time champion of the All-America Football Conference, and one of the premier franchises in the National Football League, beginning in 1950.

Football's greatest quarterback

Anybody who saw him play could have no doubt.

Otto Graham was the greatest quarterback in the history of professional football.

Some had a stronger arm or ran faster or scrambled better.

But nobody did more for his team, physically and emotionally, than Otto Graham did for the Browns from their inception in 1946 until he retired after the 1955 season.

In those 10 seasons, Graham took the Browns to four All-America Football Conference titles, and into the National Football League championship game the next six years, winning three of them.

Graham was named to the AAFC and NFL all-league teams in nine of his ten seasons as a professional, during which he passed for 23,584 yards and 174 touchdowns.

An All-America tailback in the old single wing at Northwestern University, Graham went there on a basketball scholarship. He actually played professional basketball for a year before entering the Navy in World War II.

As the first and highest paid player signed by the Browns, Graham received a salary of $7,500 in 1946.

By 1955, Graham's final season with the Browns, he was making $25,000, then the NFL's largest salary.

Otto Graham

Paul Brown and Graham made a great combination, though their relationship was strained at times because of Brown's dogmatic insistence upon calling plays.

"There were only a few times I ignored what he sent in and called my own, because if it didn't work, look out," Graham was quoted in a book that chronicled the history of the team.

"Paul was the boss, there was no question about that."

Still, Graham said he considered himself "very fortunate to have played for Paul Brown because I personally think he (was) probably the finest football coach that ever coached the game."

There were too many highlights in Graham's sensational career to detail, but one performance in particular speaks eloquently of his intensity and fierce determination to excel.

It took place on November 15, 1953, in a game against the San Francisco 49ers in front of 80,698 fans in Cleveland Stadium.

Players in those days didn't wear facemasks and Graham, on a play near the end of the first half with the Browns losing, 10-7, ran with the ball when his receivers were covered.

Graham was knocked out of bounds and hit in the mouth with an elbow thrown by 49ers linebacker Art Michalik.

Graham got to his feet, groggy and bleeding profusely. He half walked and was half carried off the field.

"The inside of his mouth was cut all the way back to his tonsils," Dr. Vic Ippolito, the Browns' physician, described Graham's injury.

"It took about 20, 21 stitches to sew him up and, though he insisted on going back to the field, I never thought he'd play anymore that day.

"But he did, and he played great. So great, we won the game (23-21). It was amazing."

That was Otto Graham. The greatest of them all.

'Nobody ... can kick my ass'

During the week prior to Super Bowl XVIII in 1984, Lyle Alzado, who'd played for the Browns from 1979-81, was - by his own admission - at his all-time loudmouth best.

Then a member of the Los Angeles (nee Oakland) Raiders, the team to which he was traded for an eighth round draft choice on April 8, 1982, Alzado told the scribes surrounding him that he knew why he was so popular with them that day.

"It's because I've got such a big mouth," said the often-intimidating defensive end.

Then, conceding that the build-up for the Super Bowl is overdone, Alzado said, "A lot of this (bleep) is hype, like when I say our defense is good, that it's the best in the league, and that we're going to kick the (Washington) Redskins' ass. What I mean is that I *think* we will, that I *expect* we will, though it's not reality until we do.

"But one thing that's not hype is that there's nobody in this world can kick my ass - and that's reality," he said. "If me and King Kong went into an alley, it wouldn't be the monkey coming out."

As it turned out, nobody - including the Redskins in Super Bowl XVIII, won by the Raiders, 38-9 - kicked Alzado's ass, at least not that anybody knew.

Not even then-heavyweight champion Muhammad Ali, whom Alzado fought in an eight round exhibition in 1979.

Lyle Alzado

Oh, Alzado left the ring bloodied and, certainly, sore. But he never backed up against Ali, and stayed on his feet throughout. the bout.

Alzado played for the Raiders through 1984, ending a 15-year NFL career that began in 1971. He was Denver's fourth round selection in the draft out of Yankton College in South Dakota, the enrollment of which was 225. When asked, "Why Yankton?" Alzado replied, "Because nobody else would take me."

Finally, as it does to everyone, there came a fight he couldn't win, though it arrived much sooner than anyone expected. Alzado was only 43 when he died in 1992, his once powerful body ravaged by the effects of his use of body-building steroids.

A product of the teeming, often violent streets of the Brooklyn Brownsville section of New York, Alzado, one of 13 children whose father, he said, "used to beat the crap out of me," always was obsessed with playing football at its highest level.

Alzado, a two-time All-Pro and Pro Bowler in Denver, helped the Broncos reach the Super Bowl twice, including 1977 when he was NFL's "Defensive Player of the Year." When he held out for a pay raise in 1979, he was traded to the Browns for two future draft choices.

He was a team leader during the exciting days of the "Kardiac Kids," but - in what proved to be a huge mistake - Alzado was dealt to the Raiders for an eighth round draft choice.

"It was embarrassing," Alzado said of the deal. "(The Browns) told the Raiders I had mental problems, which I admit I had a few. Doesn't everybody? They said I couldn't run anymore, I couldn't pass rush anymore, I couldn't do this, I couldn't do that."

But he proved that he still could, and going to the Raiders revitalized his career, if only briefly, and in his euphoria he vowed, "I'll never quit. They'll have to kill me."

However, after three seasons with the Raiders, Alzado had to quit as his illness began to destroy his once-powerful body, finally finding a fight he couldn't win.

Much more than just 'The Toe'

They called him "The Toe" because he was such a great kicker, one of the best - perhaps THE best - ever.

But Lou Groza was more than a kicking specialist.

He also was an offensive tackle, again one of the best, for 13 of his 21 seasons with the Browns in the All-America Football Conference and the National Football League.

Groza was the Browns' leading scorer in 13 seasons and his 1,608 points (1,349 in the NFL) are the most in the history of the franchise. He also was an All-Pro tackle six times before he retired for good in 1968.

Lou Groza

"You have to remember," Groza said about his double duty with the Browns early on, "there was no area of specialization in those days. Kicking was incidental to playing football."

It was Groza's field goal with 28 seconds remaining that gave the Browns a 30-28 victory over Los Angeles in their first NFL championship game in 1950, their first year in the league.

And he came through on numerous other occasions to more than earn his 1974 election to the Hall of Fame.

Still, by Groza's admission, "The biggest pressure situation was in 1961 when I was doing nothing but kicking.

"Under those conditions you are living the situation; you've got to come up and kick the field goal.

"Here's where I really had to try to put out of my mind, 'What if you miss?' So I tried never to think that I was going to miss, always that I was going to make it."

What's so amazing about Groza's career is that he came to the Browns out of the Army after serving three years in World War II at Leyte in the Phillipines and Okinawa without having played any football.

In fact, Groza played only three games on the 1942 freshman team at Ohio State, then coached by a fellow named Paul Brown, before going off to war.

Groza retired twice, the first time in 1960, after suffering a back injury, and the Browns acquired punter/placekicker Sam Baker from Washington where he had played since 1956 and scored 253 points (on 54 field goals in 96 attempts).

Baker made 17-of-20 field goals and 44 extra points for 95 points in 1960, but Brown heartily welcomed Groza back.

Baker did the Browns punting in 1961, averaging 43.3 yards on 53 kicks, and was traded to Dallas after the season.

Groza picked up where he left off and kicked for the Browns through 1967, then retired again.

And what was the highlight of Groza's career? That 1950 championship game leading the NFL in scoring? Making All Pro? There were too many to rate them, Groza has said.

But one Groza will long remember was the time he scored the only touchdown of his career. It was against Washington in 1951 on a tackle-eligible play.

"I caught a pass for about 20 yards ... they legislated against it the next year because they didn't want tackles making as much money as receivers," he quipped.

When Lady Luck was disguised

While it was the loss of two coin flips that led to the Browns drafting Jim Brown in 1957, credit for finding the greatest running back in history must go to Dick Gallagher.

Gallagher, the Browns chief scout, had been paying close attention to the Syracuse University team featuring Brown, as it was Cotton Bowl bound with a 7-2 record in 1956.

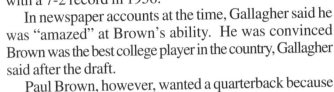

Jim Brown

In newspaper accounts at the time, Gallagher said he was "amazed" at Brown's ability. He was convinced Brown was the best college player in the country, Gallagher said after the draft.

Paul Brown, however, wanted a quarterback because he was dissatisfied with Tommy O'Connell and Babe Parilli.

But the Browns were unable to pick any of the quarterbacks Paul Brown coveted - Paul Hornung, John Brodie and Len Dawson - so he selected Jim Brown sixth overall. Neither Hornung, Brodie, nor Dawson was available because the Browns lost two coin tosses with Green Bay and Pittsburgh.

In an interesting footnote, Jim Brown deserves some credit, along with Gallagher, for the second round choice of Penn State quarterback Milt Plum, who became the Browns starter in 1958.

Gallagher had seen, and was greatly impressed by Plum when he scouted Jim Brown in a Syracuse-Penn State University game that season.

Plum went on to have a decent, if brief pro career.

But it was Jim Brown who established himself as the National Football League's all-time rushing leader, a star of the first magnitude whose exploits on the field are legendary.

His fabled twice-a-season battles with New York Giants linebacker Sam Huff were something to behold, and Huff called Brown the best athlete he ever saw.

Another All-Pro linebacker, Chuck Bednarik of the Philadelphia Eagles, paid Brown an even greater tribute. "The man is super human," Bednarik was quoted in an assessment of Brown after both had retired.

"(Brown) has finesse, ability, power - sheer power - and desire; above all, he had desire.

"He didn't play as an individual, although he did a lot of things on his own. He was strictly a team player. He didn't just worry about Jim Brown."

In his nine year career through 1965, Brown rushed for 12,312 yards in 2,359 attempts, an average of 5.22 per carry and 106 per game, scored 126 touchdowns (including 21 in his final season), gained 1,000 yards in seven seasons (including 1,863 in 1963), and 100 yards in 58 games.

Some of Brown's records have been surpassed, and others probably also will be broken.

But nobody was greater. As Bednarik said, Brown had everything, including a fierce determination to excel.

After the Browns lost those two coin tosses and picked Brown because they couldn't draft the quarterback they wanted, Bob August wrote in the Cleveland *Press*: "Time could prove that this apparent misfortune was Lady Luck in disguise."

Which it most certainly did.

Between Motley and Brown

Everybody knows that the two greatest fullbacks in Browns history were Jim Brown, who played from 1957 through 1965, and Marion Motley, 1946 through 1953. Both made it to the Hall of Fame, Brown in 1965 and Motley in 1968.

But - quickly now - who was the team's fullback between Motley and Brown, from 1954 through 1956?

It was Maurice Bassett, after whom the Browns' "Outstanding Rookie in Training Camp" award was named.

Bassett, then a 6-1, 230-pound battering ram, was the leading rusher with 588 yards as a rookie in 1954 when the Browns went 9-3 and beat Detroit, 56-10, to win their second championship in only their fifth year in the National Football League.

The Browns also won the NFL championship in 1955, when Bassett alternated at fullback with Ed Modzelewski, and defeated the Los Angeles Rams, 38-14, in the title game.

Those back-to-back championships are memories that Bassett said he'd always cherish.

"The thing that gives me the greatest pride," he once said, "is that I played between the two greatest fullbacks the Browns ever had, and I played on two world championship teams, but they only played on one each."

Maurice Bassett

The Browns won with Motley their fullback in 1950, when they beat the Rams, 30-28, and with Brown in 1964, when they defeated Baltimore, 27-0.

It has been 31-plus seasons since their last NFL championship although, to be sure, they came close in 1965, 1968, 1969, 1986, 1987, and 1989.

Bassett grew up in Chickashaw, Oklahoma and played his collegiate football at Langston University after a year in the service, during which he was a star on a team representing the Naval Amphibious Base in San Diego.

The Browns picked him in the third round of the 1954 draft, and he competed with Fred "Curley" Morrison, who'd been a star at Ohio State, to take over for Motley, who retired.

Bassett won the job, not only because of his battering ram running ability, but also because he was a better pass blocker for quarterback Otto Graham than Morrison, although both played as running backs in the same backfield the following season.

Modzelewski, who came to the Browns in a 1955 trade with the Pittsburgh Steelers, replaced Bassett as the starting fullback in 1956.

Then the arrival of Jim Brown, who was drafted in the first round, sixth overall in 1957, spelled the end for Bassett in Cleveland.

But not the end of his professional football career.

Upon leaving the Browns, Bassett went north and, for the next three seasons (1957-59) played in the Canadian Football League.

In 1960, when the American Football League came into existence, Bassett signed with the Buffalo Bills, but retired as a player after that first season.

He returned to Cleveland, completed work on his college degree, and became a high school football coach and teacher.

'How can a guy like that die?'

June 27, 1986, one of the worst days in Browns history.

It was the day they lost one of their best, and most highly respected players, free safety Don Rogers.

The cause of Rogers' death at 23, the night before he was to be married, made it even worse.

Don Rogers

A Sacramento (California) County coroner's investigator was quoted in the Lake County (Ohio) *News-Herald* as saying; "The toxicologist told me (Rogers) had enough drugs in him to kill an elephant."

Reportedly, the drugs were ingested by Rogers during a bachelor party the night before he died.

His was the third tragic death of a Browns player since the franchise was founded in 1946. Earlier, Ernie Davis, a former All-American running back at Syracuse and the 1961 Heisman Trophy winner, died of leukemia on May 16, 1963, and less than three weeks later Don Fleming, who'd been acquired in a 1960 trade and quickly established himself as one of the NFL's premier defensive backs, was electrocuted in an industrial accident on June 4, 1963.

Rogers, the Browns' No. 1 selection (18th overall) in the 1984 college draft out of UCLA, where he'd been an All-American, had made an immediate impact in the NFL with his size, speed and fierce tackling.

Rogers, 6-1 and 210 pounds, won the AFC "Defensive Rookie of the Year" award in his first season, and in his two years with the Browns, had three interceptions for 87 yards in returns. He also led the team in tackles with 154 in 1985.

In four years at UCLA, Rogers averaged over 100 tackles per season, and was second in the PAC-10 with seven interceptions as a senior.

"Having him is like having a linebacker in the secondary," said then-Coach Sam Rutigliano, referring to Rogers' speed and toughness. "It's going to cause a lot of receivers to hear a cat sipping milk at 100 yards."

It was after his second season with the Browns that Rogers promised even more. "You've seen the best of me the last couple of years, but there's more to come. I want my presence out there to be a big factor."

Unfortunately, he never had a chance to live up to that pledge.

Modell said Rogers' death was more difficult to accept than that of Davis or Fleming. "You never get conditioned to death in any form. Even a parent in their nineties, an aged person you know is going to die, it's still a blow when it happens.

"It's worse when you have a 23-year old boy in the picture of health the day before his wedding, to collapse and die. I feel the same sadness as I did for Ernie Davis and Don Fleming, though the news of the deaths were dissimilar."

Speaking for Rogers' teammates, Bob Golic said, "It's such a loss, it's unbelievable. Not only was he a great player, he was really a nice guy. His personality added a lot to the team.

"This really hits home. You see a guy every day and all of a sudden he's not around. It's scary in a way. Here's a guy in top physical condition ... how can a guy like that die?"

Rejected twice, and twice wronged

It happened twice to Mike Baab, and each tine he was shocked. So were Browns fans, the media and Baab's teammates. Especially his teammates.

First, Baab, who'd been a 1982 fifth round draft choice out of the University of Texas, was sent away, traded to the New England Patriots on August 30, 1988, six days before the NFL season opener.

Mike Baab

Then, according to newspaper accounts, the deal was made by Coach Marty Schottenheimer who had decided (wrongly, as it turned out) that the Browns would be a better team with Gregg Rakoczy starting at center instead of Baab.

Browns players reportedly were so upset by the deal that Schottenheimer called off practice that day to placate them. Particularly angered by the move was quarterback Bernie Kosar, who was said to have thrown down his playbook and directed "heated comments" at the coach.

Four years later, after he'd been re-signed as a Plan B free agent by the Browns in 1990 and had resumed his job as their starting center for two seasons, Baab was dumped again. This time he was released on August 17, 1992 by then-coach Bill Belichick, again amidst howls of protest from his teammates, fans and media.

It was charged in the Akron *Beacon Journal* that the popular, 6-4, 275-pound center was cut for financial reasons, though it was hotly denied by Browns vice president David Modell, son of then-owner Art Modell.

Baab was scheduled to be paid about $600,000 in 1992, and by waiving him and giving his job to free agent Chris Thome (whose salary was $76,500), the Browns would save about $525,000, which the team desperately needed to satisfy holdout receiver Webster Slaughter.

"Rob Peter to pay Paul?" David Modell reportedly lashed out in response to the charge that Baab was cut to save money. "This football team is committed to fielding a team that's going to compete for the world championship, and our player personnel moves are pointed toward that goal exclusively," he was quoted in the *Beacon Journal.*

Whatever, that move also proved to be an unwise one for the Browns as Thome was found wanting. Eleven days after Baab was waived a deal with the Chicago Bears was made to acquire veteran center Jay Hilgenberg, who also left much to be desired and ended his NFL career the following season with New Orleans.

As for Baab, an admitted devotee of comic book hero "Conan the Barbarian," he was "relieved" in 1988 to be sent to the Patriots by Schottenheimer (though he quickly re-signed with the Browns after two seasons in New England). Upon joining the Patriots, Baab was quoted in the Foxboro (Massachusetts) *Enterprise* as saying:

"Marty Schottenheimer is a very intense person by nature. Every game he coaches is like the seventh game of the World Series. Being competitive on the football field is one thing. (But) playing under the kind of intensity the Browns play under is unbearable."

Ironically, after he was cut by Belichick and the Browns in 1992, he signed as a free agent with the Kansas City Chiefs, whose head coach was the same Marty Schottenheimer whose "intensity" was a problem for Baab during his first six seasons in Cleveland.

The Assassin's loyalty prevailed

He was nicknamed "The Assassin," and Eddie Johnson loved it - just as he loved Cleveland from the time he was picked by the Browns in the seventh round of the 1981 draft out of the University of Louisville.

The trouble is, the nickname was something the sportswriters and fans gave the 6-1, 220-

Eddie "The Assassin" Johnson

pound linebacker and, almost annually, Johnson had to fight for a place on the roster which, to his credit, he usually won. For ten years, in fact, through 1990.

Then he retired gracefully after playing in 148 NFL games for the Browns, 70 as a starter.

For four straight seasons, beginning in 1987 under Marty Schottenheimer, and then Bud Carson, the Browns brought in rookies and veterans from other teams and lined them up to take Johnson's job.

Characteristically, Johnson didn't pout or complain, he just stayed ready and continued to play like … well, like an assassin.

One of the potential replacements for Johnson was Mike Junkin, who was the Browns' first round draft choice in 1987 and was advertised as playing like "a mad dog in a meat market." After Junkin was handed Johnson's inside linebacker job by Schottenheimer, he was injured in the fourth game of the season and never started again.

Another was Barry Krauss, a ten year veteran who'd played for the Baltimore-Indianapolis Colts and was signed as a free agent in 1989. He was expected to replace Johnson, but didn't even survive training camp (and went to the Miami Dolphins later that season).

"I can't worry about Barry Krauss or Mike Junkin or anybody else," the indomitable "Assassin" was quoted in the Lake County *News Herald*. "The only person I have control over is Eddie Johnson," and control himself he did.

Johnson also made clear in a most forceful manner his enduring love affair with the city of Cleveland and fans of the Browns.

As one of the team's unprotected free agents in the spring of 1989 – when the Browns were trying to replace him with Krauss – Johnson turned down a contract offer from the Indianapolis Colts that reportedly would have paid him close to $1 million dollars for two years. The Colts were said to be one of nine teams interested in Johnson.

Instead, he re-signed with the Browns for about $850,000 in 1989 and 1990.

Why? "I talked to Bud Carson and he convinced me I'm in his plans somewhere," Johnson said. "I want to play for two more years. I think it would be a tremendous honor to finish my career in Cleveland.

"I thought about playing with those guys (the Colts)," he admitted. "But I love the Browns and the 'Dawg Pound.' I think we can all have fun and win some ball games this year. I'm glad this is all over. It was nice to find out there are nine teams that know Eddie Johnson can play."

Which he did, on numerous occasions, though neither he nor the Browns – or their fans – had as much fun as they would have liked.

After winning the AFC Central Division in 1989, the Browns lost to Denver, 37-21, for the conference championship and a berth in Super Bowl XXIV, and fell to a 3-13 record in 1990, after which Johnson walked away from the game, his head held high.

A little guy with a big heart

Dino Hall was a little guy, at 5-7 and 165-pounds, the smallest player in the National Football League during most of his five year career with the Browns from 1979-83.

But what Hall lacked in size he made up for in heart, desire, courage, spirit - and any other intangibles along that line you can find in a dictionary.

Hall was listed on the roster as a running back, though he seldom ran from scrimmage. He was employed primarily as a kickoff and punt returner.

To further establish his gutsy style of play, Hall also was a member of the "suicide squad," the kickoff and punt coverage teams, and never was averse to bravely throwing his body into the first wave of blockers.

He wasn't drafted, but signed as a free agent after graduating from - and starring for - Glassboro (New Jersey) State College.

Dino Hall

As a senior, Hall was the Division III rushing champ, averaging 133 yards per game. Hall had a single game high of 255 yards and was selected to the Kodak All-America team.

Despite his stature, Hall is listed frequently in the Browns' record book. He is the team's career leader in kickoff return yardage, with 3,185, as well as the second most in a season, 1,014 (1979), and the most in a game, 172 (1979); returned the most kickoffs in a career, 151, in one game, nine (1979); and second most in a season, 50 (1979).

Hall also is fourth in the record book in punt return yardage, with 901 for his five year career with the Browns.

In his very first game as a pro, against Pittsburgh on October 7, 1979, Hall tied an NFL record by returning nine Matt Bahr kickoffs for 172 yards.

It was primarily Hall's speed - he also was a sprinter as well as an outstanding baseball player (second baseman) at Glassboro State - and elusiveness that made him so proficient in returning kickoffs and punts, though he always maintained that there was much more involved.

"It's true that a good return man has to be fast, but sure hands are equally important," said Hall, who seldom fumbled a punt or kickoff.

He often admitted that the constant reference to his small stature bothered him before he proved himself with the Browns.

"It used to really get to me," he said in a 1982 article in the Cleveland *Plain Dealer*. "Most of my life people were always telling me I was too little to do this, too little to do that.

"And the sportswriters, most of you guys still refer to me as 'Little Dino' in the papers. It's almost like my mother named me 'Little,' when I was born, instead of just plain 'Dino.'

"But I don't let it bother me anymore. Not since I've been able to prove that I could play with the big guys here."

Which he did.

He proved it for five seasons, including 1980, when the Browns, then known as the "Kardiac Kids," won the AFC Central Division of the NFL, and came within 49 seconds of playing for the conference championship and a trip to Super Bowl XV.

Which they would have done with "Little Dino" Hall their return man.

The costly quarterback mistake

It was a deal that was supposed to solve the Browns' impending quarterback problem that appeared to be imminent because of the deteriorating condition of Bill Nelsen's knees.

On paper, it made sense – at least at the time.

The Browns would get Mike Phipps, then the heralded, All-American quarterback from  Purdue University who'd set a remarkable total of 24 career, season, single game and Big Ten records for the Boilermakers.

Included were 375 pass completions in 733 attempts for 5,423 yards and 37 touchdowns in leading Purdue to victories in 22 of the 27 games Phipps started.

To get the 6-3, 207-pound quarterback as the third player selected in the 1970 college draft, the Browns traded sixth year wide receiver Paul Warfield to the Miami Dolphins.

It was a costly acquisition – and would prove to be even *costlier* down the road.

Warfield, the former Ohio State star, had caught 215 passes for 4,346 yards and 44 touchdowns in his six seasons with the Browns, including 42 for 886 yards and 10 touchdowns in 1969.

But the Browns were desperate. Nelsen was, literally, on his last legs, though he did manage to play three more

Mike Phipps

seasons, through 1972.

The Browns promptly signed Phipps to a five-year contract that reportedly was worth $250,000, but which turned out to only worsen the deal.

Phipps was a major disappointment, while Warfield became one of the NFL's brightest stars and was elected to the Pro Football Hall of Fame in 1983. He played for the Dolphins from 1970-74, and returned as a free agent to play for the Browns in 1976 and 1977, then retired.

Phipps played behind Nelsen in 1970 and the first half of 1971, and was the starting quarterback through 1975 with only moderate success. The Browns failed each season to make the playoffs with Phipps at quarterback, though their won-lost record was a creditable 10-4 in 1972 when they finished second in the AFC Central Division.

The end of the Phipps era came in 1976 when he suffered a separated shoulder in the opening game. Phipps was replaced by Brian Sipe and never regained the starting job. At the end of the season Phipps was traded to the Chicago Bears in a deal that partially – but definitely not fully - atoned for the costly mistake made seven years earlier.

The Browns received a fourth round draft choice in 1977 for Phipps, which they used to select defensive tackle Mickey Sims.

And, of course, they also re-acquired Warfield who, in 1975, had jumped from the Dolphins to the Memphis Grizzlies of the ill-fated World Football League.

In his final two seasons with the Browns, Warfield caught 56 passes from Sipe for 864 yards and eight touchdowns.

Phipps closed out his NFL career with the Bears, from 1977-81, during which he was the starting quarterback for only part of the 1979 season, and finished with a passing record of 886 completions in 1,799 attempts (49.2%), for 10,506 yards and 55 touchdowns, with 108 interceptions.

'You have to be unemployed or crazy'

It was the worst day of Bob Golic's life. In his words, he "died" when the New England Patriots cut him on August 31, 1982, apparently ending his three-year NFL career.

But Golic's "resurrection" came quickly. Seventy-two hours later, in fact, when he was claimed on waivers by the Browns, a move that turned out great for both parties.

Switched to nose tackle by the Browns from linebacker, a position the Patriots thought Golic was too slow to play, he flourished, becoming one of the best in the NFL, extending his career – or "football life," as he called it – for eleven more seasons.

Golic was a starter for all but two of the 89 games he played for the Browns from 1982-88, during which he won All-Pro honors in 1986 and was named to the Pro Bowl three times (1986-88). He joined the Los Angeles Raiders in 1989, and when he retired after the 1992 season, became a television analyst on NFL games.

Browns fans were almost as happy to have Golic back "home" as he was to be in Cleveland, where he'd grown up. He was a football and wrestling star at St. Joseph High School, went on to Notre Dame and was selected by the Patriots in the second round of the 1979 draft.

Looking back on the day he was informed by the Patriots that they were cutting him, Golic said, "I remember thinking, 'My God, is this all? Am I finished?'" he was quoted in a Buffalo *News* article.

Bob Golic

"When I started playing football as a kid, one of the first things my father did was make me promise that, once I stopped enjoying playing the game, I would walk away from it. Otherwise I'd be cheating myself and the team I was on. There was no enjoyment for me with New England, so I contemplated walking away from the game," although the Patriots beat Golic to the punch.

He also admitted, "I wasn't sure I wanted to play nose tackle (for the Browns), though I knew I wanted to continue playing football."

Which Golic did. Very well. As Marty Schottenheimer, then-coach of the Browns, was quoted in 1985: "I wouldn't trade (Golic) for another nose tackle in the National Football League."

Always quick with the quip, which made him a natural for television, Golic said of his position with the Browns, "To play nose tackle you have to be unemployed or crazy. I was unemployed. The other part is still up in the air."

The fact is, however, that Golic immediately fell in love with his new job, which first entailed backup duty but soon saw him become a starter when Henry Bradley's sore knees forced him out of the Browns lineup.

"I was excited by it," he said. "I found more enjoyment playing nose tackle than I found at linebacker. At linebacker, you kind of run around, and every now and then you make a tackle.

"At nose tackle, you're one-on-one every play, and you know whether you won or lost. It reminded me of my years as a wrestler (he was an All-America heavyweight at Notre Dame). You get hit by everybody but the water boy and are a sacrificial lamb.

"But it's great. I find myself having a lot of fun."

Something like a guy who "died" and went to football heaven – which Golic believed he did when he came to the Browns.

A career saved by Rutigliano

When he came to the Browns in 1975, in exchange for a fourth round draft pick, Reggie Rucker brought with him a reputation – a *false* reputation, he insisted, and subsequently proved – for being a malcontent, a troublemaker.

He'd been with three teams previously, beginning with Dallas, which signed him as a free

Reggie Rucker

agent in 1970, the New York Giants and New England, and the deal that brought him to Cleveland was not considered a major one, though that's what it turned out to be for the Browns.

And because it did, Rucker, who played seven seasons for the Browns, through 1981, credits one man in particular, former head coach Sam Rutigliano.

"There is no doubt in my mind that Sam saved my career," Rucker said in a 1979 article that appeared in the Cleveland *Plain Dealer*. "(Rutigliano) taught me so many things, on the field and off. I owe him so much. I'm doing my best to show him I appreciate his influence."

Which Rucker did, very well, especially during the thrilling days of the "Kardiac Kids." That was Rutigliano's never-say-die team of 1980 that won the AFC Central Division, but lost in the first game of the playoffs to eventual Super Bowl XV champion Oakland.

Rutigliano's influence on Rucker began in 1971 when Sam was an assistant coach of the Patriots and Reggie was one of their receivers. They were together with New England through 1973, after which they temporarily parted company.

When Rutigliano was named head coach of the Browns in 1978, Rucker had already established himself as one of Brian Sipe's favorite and most dependable targets.

And, just as Rucker credited Rutigliano for resurrecting his playing career, the former coach was equally generous in his praise for the swift and elusive, sure-handed, 6-2, 195 pound receiver.

"Reggie is an accomplished receiver who helps create a lot of things," Rutigliano was quoted in another *Plain Dealer* article in 1981. "He reacts well to all the pressure situations, and is a leader by example, in a quiet reassuring manner.

"I've known Reggie for a long time and I think he's better now than ever because he makes more difficult catches. He makes the key catches. Who cares if a guy catches 70 balls and his team goes 2-14?

"In my opinion, Rucker is very much underrated, primarily because of all the good receivers in our division, guys like Lynn Swann, John Stallworth, Isaac Curtis, and Ken Burrough."

Rucker more than justified Rutigliano's confidence. In his seven seasons with the Browns, Rucker caught 310 passes for 4,953 yards and 32 touchdowns, paired up as he was with Dave Logan, the team's other wide receiver, and Hall of Fame tight end Ozzie Newsome - as well as Sipe, the trigger-man of the "Kardiac Kids."

Rucker was signed originally as a free agent out of Boston College by the Cowboys in 1970, and started in place of Lance Retzel in Super Bowl V.

He played for three teams in 1971 - two games for Dallas, four for the New York Giants, and five for New England – and the following season, by his own admission, Rucker's career was "saved" by Rutigliano.

A stroke of genius – or luck

Until Jim Brown came along in 1957 there never was a more punishing, harder running fullback than Marion Motley, another one of the original Browns.

Motley had played high school football in the early 1940s at Canton (Ohio) McKinley, the archrival of Massillon Washington High, which was then coached by Paul Brown.

A few years later Motley played for Brown at Great Lakes Naval Training Station during World War II, after briefly attending the University of Nevada (though he did not play a full football season there).

But still, according to Motley in a history of the early Browns, his request for a tryout in 1946, when the team was formed, was rejected.

"I wrote Paul ... but he wrote back and said he had enough backs," Motley was quoted in the book

"But awhile later I got a telephone call and was asked to report to Bowling Green," which was where the Browns were holding their first training camp.

Motley never found out for sure, but surmised the invitation was tendered to help alleviate what might have been a sticky racial situation.

At the time there were only a couple of black players in professional football and, bear in mind, Jackie Robinson had not yet broken the so-called "color-barrier" in major league baseball.

Marion Motley

But, Motley said, "Bill Willis had reported (to the Browns) for a tryout, and I think they felt he needed a roommate."

If that was the reason, it proved to be a stroke of luck - or a stroke of genius by Brown.

Motley, a huge, 6-1, 238-pound power runner with surprising speed, recalled, "I was 27 years old, married with four children and working in a steel mill.

"I knew this was the one big chance in my life to rise above the steel mill existence and I really wanted to take it.

"I had no doubt that I could make the team because I had played against some of the best competition around during the war and I measured up pretty well in my own mind."

In everybody's mind, as it turned out.

Motley played eight seasons, through 1953, and was, without a doubt, the greatest fullback of his time.

In his career, which was cut short by knee injuries, Motley rushed for 4,732 yards, an average of 5.65 per carry, and scored 234 points. Not only was he the leading ground-gainer in the history of the All-America Football Conference, he also played linebacker his first two years with the Browns.

When they went into the National Football League in 1950, Motley immediately took over as the leading rusher with 810 yards in 140 carries in just 12 games.

Motley also was a devastating blocker and pass protector for Otto Graham.

So much so, in fact, he often was credited for being a key to the Browns' aerial armada because of his blocking ability.

Motley's career was capped in 1968 when he was elected to the Hall of Fame.

And it all began because the Browns felt they needed a roommate for Bill Willis.

Absolutely, positively the best

The opinion was unanimous, beginning with Blanton Collier and continuing through every coaching regime thereafter: Nick Skorich, Forrest Gregg and Sam Rutigliano.

Without a doubt, Jerry Sherk was the best defensive lineman in the history of the Browns.

"Absolutely," Collier said before his death in 1983. "Nobody was better than Jerry Sherk."

Jerry Sherk

Unfortunately, Sherk was forced into retirement in 1982 when he should have been at the peak of his career.

Sherk was the victim of a staph infection incurred in a game in Philadelphia late in 1979. The infection settled in his left knee and Sherk was hospitalized for three months.

It cost Sherk all of the 1980 season - and almost his life. The ruggedly handsome, 6-5, 250 pound tackle was never the same, though he tried valiantly to regain his All-Pro form in 1981.

But Sherk wouldn't lament his misfortune, or whine his way off the playing field.

Always the consummate professional, Sherk said in his valediction: "I leave the Browns knowing that the biggest prize was not any one trophy, but the special relationship that I have with the people of Northeast Ohio."

The staph infection that shelved Sherk, which was compounded because of other knee injuries he'd suffered earlier, ravaged his strength and impaired his speed, the two attributes that made him something extra special.

A second round draft choice in 1970 out of Oklahoma State where he also was an outstanding wrestler, Sherk won numerous awards with the Browns: He was named to the Pro Bowl four consecutive seasons, 1974 through 1977, and was picked as the best defensive lineman in the National Football League by the players in 1975.

The "high point" of his career, Sherk said at the time he announced his retirement, "were four games in 1975 when I made 10 unassisted tackles in each game and I kept wondering why everybody else seemed to be slowing up so much."

Which was a typical statement for the unassuming Sherk.

Art Modell, then owner of the Browns, was right when he said, "What Jerry has accomplished on the field are achievements that made him the best tackle in the Browns' history.

"(Sherk) has meant so much to this organization and this city. Those who have had a chance to know Jerry realize what a special person he is."

The Browns almost lost Sherk once before when he was drafted and wooed by the Portland Storm of the then-World Football League in 1974.

But the Browns countered with a better offer and Sherk signed a three year contract that kept him in Cleveland.

It was a decision Sherk said he never regretted.

"My goal when I first came into professional football was to play," Sherk recalled his days as a rookie with the Browns.

"Then my goal was to be a starter. And when I became a starter, my goal was to be called the best."

All of which Sherk achieved.

Including the latter.

Brennan recalls 'The Drive'

He was undersized by professional football standards, and didn't have blazing speed, though the report on Brian Brennan was that he was "quick," "intelligent" and had "good hands."

It was a positive recommendation, if not the credentials of a future Hall of Famer.

And so, Brennan, who'd teamed with Doug Flutie during their collegiate careers at Boston College and set all the Eagles' receiving records, was picked by the Browns in the fourth round of the 1984 draft. It was a decision the Browns never regretted.

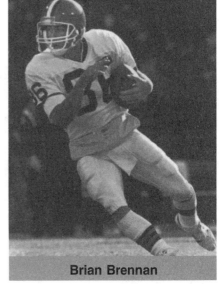

Brian Brennan

Neither did Brennan, who told in a *Browns News/ Illustrated* article how he had waited ... and waited and waited ... on draft day before the phone finally rang. On the other end of the line was Browns executive and Hall of Fame receiver Paul Warfield.

"I was elated to be a Brown, and thrilled to have the opportunity to play in the NFL," said Brennan.

He went on to lead Browns receivers in each of his first three seasons, from 1984-86, and when he retired after the 1991 season, was the team's fifth leading pass catcher all-time, behind Ozzie Newsome, Gary Collins, Greg Pruitt and Reggie Rucker.

Brennan also told about his "most significant" - not most pleasant - memory of the game in which the Browns came within a minute of reaching Super Bowl XXI.

The date was January 11, 1987, and the Browns were locked in a 13-13 tie with the Denver Broncos in the AFC championship game at the Stadium.

With nearly six minutes remaining and the Browns on the Denver 48 yard line, they huddled and Bernie Kosar called the play. It was a pass and Brennan said he knew it would go to him. "I knew for two reasons. First, Dennis Smith, the defensive back lined up over me, wasn't a good coverage guy and, second, Bernie looked at me and nodded."

Again, in Brennan's words, "As I released off the line of scrimmage, I knew Smith was dead. He was playing off me, using an inside technique. All I had to do was make him think I was headed to the post (inside) and run my corner route (to the outside).

"Kosar was pressured but made a nice throw. I needed to slow down slightly and catch the ball. As I caught the pass, Smith was way off balance. I made a little sidestep, and was headed for six points."

The touchdown and extra point put the Browns ahead, 20-13, with 5:43 remaining, and as Brennan said - and 79,915 fans in the Stadium agreed - "We were headed for the Super Bowl."

But they failed to consider John Elway. In what would forever be known with distress to all Browns fans as "The Drive," Elway marched the Broncos 98 yards in 15 plays to a touchdown and extra point that tied the score at 20-20 with 37 seconds left.

The game went into overtime and the Browns, after winning the coin toss and receiving the kickoff, were forced to punt. The Broncos took over on their own 24 and drove 60 yards to set up a 33-yard field goal by Rich Karlis. It gave Denver a 23-20 victory, depriving the Browns of what would have been their only appearance in a Super Bowl.

Brennan played for Cincinnati (nine games) and San Diego (six) in 1992, then retired from football, becoming a stock broker and, as he said, relishes most of his memories with the Browns – though, certainly, not all of them.

'Almost like ... a twilight zone'

Considering how well he played for eight-plus seasons for the Browns, it seemed that Kevin Mack deserved more than he got from them when he made his final appearance in Cleveland on December 19, 1993.

As reported in the Cleveland *Plain Dealer*, "Mack's purgatory continued when he was denied the chance to run the ball one last time in a Browns uniform at the Stadium.

Kevin Mack

"Chants from the crowd of 'We want Mack, we want Mack,' went unheeded by the Browns' coaching staff. All he did was play on special teams.

"'I'm a little disappointed I didn't get in,' Mack said. 'But I'm pretty sure the coaches were pretty confident that what they were doing was going to be successful. So I can't fault anybody, at least, not at this time.'"

It also would seem that the Browns could have used Mack, the franchise's fifth leading rusher, in the 20-17 upset loss to the New England Patriots.

The 6-0, 224-pound, former Clemson University running back had been inactive for nine consecutive weeks that season, after un-retiring and rejoining the team prior to the fourth game. The week before the Patriots game he gained 16 yards in four carries in a 19-17 loss to Houston, which gave rise to speculation he'd see more action.

Perhaps it went back five months earlier, to July 19, when Mack first announced his plan to retire, saying he'd lost his desire to play. He returned to the team in August, admitting he'd made a mistake – although he never expected to pay for that mistake by being demoted to the role of a practice player by then-coach Bill Belichick.

"There's some resentment and some frustration," Mack admitted after sitting out the entire Patriots game. "(But) right now I'd rather not say anything about it because the season's not over with and I don't want to be a distraction to this team in any way."

Earlier in the season Belichick released Bernie Kosar, which also bothered Mack. As he said, "That was real difficult for me because Bernie and I were good friends.

"There's a lot of things happened that I don't think really came out and probably never will ... you know. I can't say (more)" – though he added in a final comment on the 1993 season, when they went 7-9 under Belichick, that it was "almost like being in a twilight zone, another world."

His acquisition in 1984 was one of the best moves ever made by the Browns. They traded three late round picks in the 1984 draft to Chicago for the Bears' three selections in the Supplemental Draft, one of which was used to claim Mack. He had played for the Los Angeles Express in the defunct United States Football League in 1984, and began his career with the Browns in 1985. It was interrupted, however, in 1989 when Mack was incarcerated for 30 days after pleading guilty to illegal substance use.

He played only four games that season, including the finale, won by the Browns over Houston, 24-20, when Mack bulled four yards into the end zone for a touchdown with 39 seconds remaining. It clinched the AFC Central Division championship.

Mack often said that game was the highlight of his football career.

He didn't, but undoubtedly would have said that his final season with the Browns was the lowlight.

The not-so-good old days

For a guy who played but one season for the Browns, Jim Daniell established quite a reputation and legacy.

As captain of the Browns in 1946, their first year as a charter member of the All-America Football Conference, Daniell was their first regular left tackle, of which there were only three who followed in the next 38 years, until 1985.

Daniell's immediate successor was Lou (The Toe) Groza, who played the demanding position from 1947 through 1958 when he gave up his offensive line duties to concentrate on kicking.

Dick Schafrath took over from 1959 through the first nine games in 1971, and Doug Dieken was the starter from the tenth game in 1971 through 1984.

All played with distinction, though Paul Brown, the original coach who was fired by owner Art Modell after the 1962 season, probably would disagree with the assessment of Daniell.

Daniell, who was awarded the Silver Star and a presidential citation for valor while serving with the Navy in World War II, played for Brown at Ohio State, and then with the Chicago Bears in the National Football League in 1945.

Jim Daniell

He was paid only $300 a game by the Bears, which is the reason Daniell quickly accepted Brown's offer of $9,000 a season to jump to the Browns.

Daniell was paid another $1,000 to serve as captain of the Browns, a position which he lived to regret taking.

On December 14, 1946, six days after the Browns completed a 12-2 season, and eight days before they were to play the New York Yankees in the AAFC championship game, Daniell and two teammates were arrested and thrown in jail for the night.

Daniell was cited for intoxication, and his companions, offensive lineman Lou Rymkus and receiver (then called "end") Mac Speedie, were charged with disorderly conduct.

Brown was furious and promptly fired Daniell.

"As captain, (Daniell) is supposed to set an example," Brown was quoted at the time, which presumably was the reason he didn't similarly discipline Rymkus and Speedie.

Brown's rules in those days did not allow players to drink or smoke – "And no sex, not even with your wife, during the season," Daniell was quoted in 1983, before his death at 65.

Daniell, though embittered, later called his dismissal "the best thing that ever happened" to him, because he became a very successful businessman after leaving football.

"I was motivated because I wanted to make enough money to buy the Browns," Daniell said in 1978. He wanted to get back into football on a management level because, "as a player your future too often is dictated by somebody else."

Though the defrocked captain failed in his ambition to buy a team, Daniell swiftly rose to the top in the business world.

From 1974 until his retirement in 1982, Daniell - a multi-millionaire by then - was chief executive officer of the RMI Co. and also was assistant to the chairman of U.S. Steel.

It is a fascinating story that offers an insider's view of the way pro football was played in the not-so-good old days.

Another Lombardi or Brown?

With the Browns as a linebacker and special teamer in 1980 and 1982, and the Philadelphia Eagles from 1983-84, there was nothing spectacular about Bill Cowher - except his tenacious competitive spirit.

And it's that tenacious competitive spirit, coupled with a fierce desire to excel that established Cowher as one of the best young coaches in the National Football League.

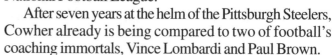
Bill Cowher

After seven years at the helm of the Pittsburgh Steelers, Cowher already is being compared to two of football's coaching immortals, Vince Lombardi and Paul Brown.

The Browns signed Cowher after he failed a training camp trial as an undrafted free agent with the Eagles in 1979. They traded him back to Philadelphia in 1983, and he was waived by the Eagles again in 1984, ending his playing career.

But not his football career.

Cowher joined Marty Schottenheimer's staff as the Browns special teams coach in 1984, was promoted to secondary coach in 1987, and remained through 1988 when both went to Kansas City.

With the Chiefs, Cowher was Schottenheimer's defensive coordinator and linebackers coach for three seasons (1989-91), then was hired by the Steelers to replace another former Browns player, retired Hall of Fame coach Chuck Noll.

With that appointment Cowher's coaching career took off. Actually, it soared. In the next seven years (1992-98) Cowher became the Steelers second winningest coach, behind Noll (193-148-1), as his teams won 71 regular season games, losing 41.

In fact, it wasn't until 1998 when the Steelers went 7-9 that a team - any team - with which Cowher was affiliated as an assistant or head coach suffered a losing record.

In his seven seasons at Pittsburgh, the Steelers reached the playoffs six times. They won the AFC Central Division in 1992, 1994, 1995, 1996 and 1997, went to Super Bowl XXX in 1995, losing to Dallas, 27-17, and were an AFC wild card in 1993.

Now Cowher is under contract with the Steelers through 2003, reportedly at a salary of $2 million a year, making him one of the highest paid coaches in the NFL.

"I look at what he has done in Pittsburgh and I think, in many cases, he simply willed (the Steelers) into the playoffs," former Browns general manager Ernie Accorsi was quoted in a story about Cowher in the July 27, 1998 issue of *The Sporting News*.

"A lot of guys can mesmerize you with chalk on a blackboard, but he has mastered the essence of the game. He can translate his incredible passion to his players. I'll tell you this, if I am going onto Omaha Beach (in World War II), I want him taking me in."

And as sportswriter Paul Attner said in that article: "The good Lord blessed Bill Cowher. He gave him the ability to inspire others, and Cowher has used that gift well. Not since Lombardi have we seen such a motivator in the NFL - a mesmerizing speaker and emotional firebrand, a whirlwind of clichés and anecdotes, who can seize the moment and devour it in one chunk."

And this, also by Attner: "Only football god Paul Brown can match Cowher's streak of producing six playoff clubs in his first six years as coach - and they couldn't wait to roll out the red carpet so Brown could walk regally into the Hall of Fame."

'It was the greatest thing'

Monte Clark was traded to the Browns by Dallas in the winter of 1962-63, which didn't please the then-defensive lineman who'd been a four-sport star at the University of Southern California, and a fourth round draft choice of the San Francisco 49ers in 1959.

Several years later, however, before he ended a seven year career in Cleveland to become an assistant coach of the Miami Dolphins in 1970, Clark's mind had changed.

"It (being traded to the Browns) was the greatest thing to happen to me," said Clark, who was switched to offensive right tackle where he replaced retiring future Hall of Famer Mike McCormack.

With Clark as a mainstay on the line, the Browns won the NFL championship in 1964, the Eastern Conference in 1965, and the Century Division in 1967, 1968 and 1969.

"I was very fortunate to play for Blanton Collier," head coach of the Browns from 1963-70. "Not only did Blanton make me a better football player, he also helped make me a good coach," said Clark.

He was an assistant under Don Shula with the Dolphins for six seasons, helping them go undefeated in 1972 and win three AFC championships and Super Bowls VII and VIII.

Monte Clark

Clark was a candidate to coach the Browns in 1975, after Nick Skorich was fired, but Art Modell subsequently chose Forrest Gregg, who at the time was a Browns assistant coach.

A year later Clark, then 38, became the youngest head coach in the NFL when he was hired by the 49ers, though he was there only one season, 1976, when their record was 8 - 6. He was head coach of the Detroit Lions from 1978 - 84, taking them into the playoffs in 1982 and 1983. His seven year record with the Lions was 43 - 63, including two playoff game losses.

In his tribute to Collier, Clark said, "Blanton had a great approach to preparing for games. Also, he had so many deep-rooted beliefs that I accepted and took on. Things like his philosophy of a squad being a family. I thought of him many times and talked to him every chance I got."

Clark, who was 6-6 and 265 pounds during his NFL playing days, was the captain of the USC Trojans in 1958 and, after being drafted by the 49ers, was a regular on the defensive line for three seasons, then was traded to Dallas.

The Browns got Clark from the Cowboys in a deal for veteran guard Jim Ray Smith, who had announced his intention to retire unless he could be traded closer to his home and real estate interests Dallas.

The Cowboys were interested and invited the Browns to pick a player they'd take for Smith. Collier and offensive line coach Fritz Heisler scrutinized the Dallas roster and finally decided on Clark.

"Knowing that McCormack was talking about retirement, and also being aware that (offensive left tackle) Dick Schafrath was coming back from a major shoulder injury, we concentrated on their (Cowboys) linemen," Collier was quoted at the time.

"Although Clark was a defensive lineman, we felt he could be switched to offense and we needed to improve our pass protection."

As Clark said, it was a great deal for him. It also was great for the Browns.

Plenty tough ... and courageous

When Cody Risien held out for 28 days in 1987, a member of the Browns hierarchy – who was never identified – questioned the veteran offensive tackle's "toughness."

Without identifying the source of the remark, Risien's agent, Randy Hendricks, said he was told that Risien was "mentally soft" and that he wasn't in training camp "because he'd rather be home with his pregnant wife, Kathy," according to a story in the Lake County *News Herald*.

When informed of the accusation, an understandably angry Risien said, "I wouldn't talk to my dog the way they've talked to me."

Not only was it an unkind remark by someone who didn't have enough courage to speak for attribution, it also was totally inaccurate, as Risien proved time after time. He did so, not only after ending his holdout, but long before, ever since he was a seventh round draft choice out of Texas A&M in 1979.

A leader on the field and off as one of the Browns' members of the Fellowship of Christian Athletes and Athletes In Action, Risien became a starter at right guard in the seventh game of his rookie season, then was switched and took over as the regular at right tackle in 1980.

Cody Risien

Risien started at right tackle through the end of his career in 1989, with the exception of 1984, when he was on Injured Reserve after undergoing knee surgery, and for four games in 1985 when he was sidelined with another knee injury.

A two-time Pro Bowler and three-time All-AFC selection, Risien played a total of 146 games for the Browns, all but six as a starter, and it's hard to believe that anyone could question his toughness or courage. Consider, for example, that Risien underwent eleven operations in his eleven years in the NFL - seven on his elbows, three on his knees and one on an ankle.

Furthermore, in 1989, Risien was the winner of the prestigious "Courage Award," an annual NFL honor bestowed upon one player from every team as selected by his teammates.

It was during his fifth year with the Browns, that Risien received another "honor," this one given by just one person – but certainly one whose opinion was to be valued.

Doug Dieken, the Browns' starting offensive left tackle from 1971-84 said the 6-7, 270-pound Risien had become the best offensive tackle in the NFL.

When Risien decided in training camp in 1990 to retire, to everybody's surprise, several players questioned how the 33-year old tackle, still one of the best in the NFL, could walk away from his base salary of $625,000.

Risien, making clear his priorities and principles, was quoted in a Cleveland *Plain Dealer* story, "Certainly, money's important. I'm not in a position (financially) where I never have to work again. But I felt if I played any more, I would play primarily for the money. I would feel like I was a slave to that. There's no freedom in that."

Looking back, Risien said, "I wouldn't trade anything. The things the Lord has taught me, the things He built into my life by helping to pull me through the adversities of the last several years, have been invaluable.

"Those things will last an eternity. That's what has been so overwhelming, how God has played a part in my career."

30

When 'bigotry' split the team

It is one of the ugliest memories in Browns history and Ross Fichtner, who'd been the team's third round draft choice out of Purdue University in 1960, was the focal point, the target of "bigotry" charges leveled by teammate John Wooten.

The highly-publicized quarrel, which erupted on July 3, 1968, in an article in the Cleveland *Plain Dealer*, cost the Browns both Fichtner, a starter at safety, and starting left guard Wooten, a fifth round pick out of Colorado University in 1959.

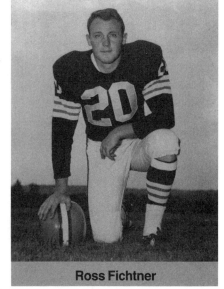

Ross Fichtner

Fichtner responded to Wooten's accusation, saying, "I don't see how I can continue my career in Cleveland if 15 colored boys out of a football team of 40 hate my guts." He was right.

Less than three weeks later, on July 19, the Browns placed both players on waivers and, when neither was claimed, Fichtner and Wooten were released.

Browns owner Art Modell said the action was taken "in the best interests of both the club and the players."

Fichtner subsequently joined the New Orleans Saints and played for them in 1968, but then retired and took a job as an assistant coach of the Florida Blazers of the ill-fated World Football League. In 1977 he was defensive backfield coach for the Chicago Bears.

Wooten became a player agent and later a scout for the Dallas Cowboys.

The controversy exploded when Wooten accused Fichtner of discriminating against black players by not inviting them - as Fichtner had done the previous three years - to play in a celebrity golf tournament at the Country Club of Ashland.

"All of a sudden we're not invited because we're black," Wooten was quoted. "Don't tell me I should understand, because I don't. Who were the guys that were invited? Fichtner and all his bigoted friends. Everyone tries to cover everything up because of the Browns. But he's not going to hide. I'll jerk the covers off him every chance I get."

Fichtner denied Wooten's accusations, but the damage was done. The story was picked up by newspapers all over the country and Fichtner's reputation was badly tarnished.

Fichtner said that the invitation list was cut from 30 to 18, and that it was not strictly a Browns party. "I sat down with Art Modell and (then-coach) Blanton Collier and tried to explain the whole situation, but they said they know the Browns have been greatly scarred. They said they know we have a problem and that it had to be faced."

Fichtner also pointed out in the story, "Two years ago when Leroy Kelly was given ... an award as our outstanding player, all the Negro players were there.

"(But) last year (1967) when Paul Wiggin won it, none of them (Black players) were there. And (Wiggin) was one of the best liked guys on the club. The Negro players hardly ever showed up at our team parties. Few of their wives ever get together with our wives, even though they always are invited. In fact, I've never been invited to a Negro party, but I haven't said anything."

Not only did the quarrel cost the Browns two starters, it also tended to split the team into two factions, which was the reason Modell was compelled to take swift action.

Fichtner, a starter in 1962-63 and 1965-67, was replaced at safety by Mike Howell, while John Demarie, who was shifted from center to left guard, took over for Wooten.

'He brightened ... the room'

Maybe it was because he'd been a journeyman linebacker himself that Marty Schottenheimer, then coach of the Browns, admitted his affection for Johnny Davis when he announced on August 26, 1986, that the journeyman fullback was being waived.

"This is always a tough day for me," Schottenheimer said, his voice choking with emotion. "I guess one of the reasons it's so tough is because I went through it several times myself."

Johnny Davis

As he talked about cutting Davis, Schottenheimer said, as reported in the Dayton *Daily News*, "He'll be sorely missed by all of us. We haven't been able to give Johnny as much as he has given us ... he is quite a person," and anyone who knew Davis would readily agree.

A 6-1, 235-pound fullback – though he was more a blocker than a running back during most of his nine-plus years in the NFL – Davis was a second round draft choice of the Tampa Bay Bucaneers out of the University of Alabama in 1978, played for the Super Bowl XVI champion San Francisco 49ers in 1981, and joined the Browns in 1982.

Davis, or "B-1," as he was nicknamed (though nobody ever explained why), was never a featured ball carrier, though he rushed for 370 yards as a rookie with the Bucaneers, and scored seven touchdowns and gained 297 yards – third most on the team – in 94 carries for 49ers in 1981.

Typically, the unassuming Davis smiled and answered reporters' questions forthwith and forthrightly as they sought his reaction to being cut by the Browns.

"I didn't fit into the Cleveland Browns' plans for this year," Davis said without rancor, "but I'm not going to drown in my sorrow. There are other teams and other plans I can fit into.

"I can't tell you what I'm going to do now, but I can tell you what I'm going to do tomorrow. I'm going to get up and work out. Somebody is going to need a good football player, and when they do, I'm going to be ready."

As it turned out, the Browns did, if only briefly later that season.

On September 11, after starting fullback Kevin Mack was sidelined with a deeply bruised left shoulder, Davis was re-signed by the team and, "Suddenly, the Browns' dressing room is ten times brighter," it was reported in the Lake County *News Herald*.

And Davis said, "I'm happy to be back. I want to make the first tackle, the second tackle, the third tackle and the fourth tackle when we kick off. I want to knock somebody out. I want to make every block."

He didn't, of course, but nobody tried harder - again, typically Davis.

In addition to being a very good football player and an excellent human being, Davis also played the piano well and often did so in churches and in other community activities.

Davis was primarily an insurance policy – and a special teams player - for the Browns for six games that season, then was cut loose again, only to return for one final fling in 1987.

That's when the NFL Players Association went on strike for four games and replacement players were signed to play three of them. Davis was among them, but carried the ball only once, for a seven yard gain in a 34-0 victory over Cincinnati on October 18.

It proved to be his NFL finale, but nobody ever left with a better reputation.

A vocation or avocation?

It was always difficult to determine whether football was a vocation or an avocation for Marshall Harris, who was the Browns starter at defensive left end from 1980-82, after his acquisition in a trade with the New York Jets.

Harris had been the Jets' eighth round draft choice out of Texas Christian University in 1979, but walked out of training camp and was dealt to the Browns for their eighth round pick in 1981.

Not only was the 6-6, 265-pound Harris a tough and aggressive pass rusher and tackler, he also was an accomplished commercial artist.

"I enjoy both ... if somebody forced me to make a choice, one over the other, I don't know what I'd pick," Harris was quoted in a newspaper article in 1980.

As it turned out, somebody else made the choice for Harris.

After the Browns' record fell to 4-5 in the strike-shortened 1982 season, Harris was waived, apparently ending his professional football career.

But not for long.

With the 1984 formation of the United States Football League, which was determined to compete with the NFL, Harris received another opportunity to go back to the game he'd played most of his life.

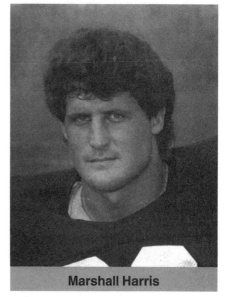

Marshall Harris

He was offered, and quickly accepted a three-year, $550,000 contract to play for the New Jersey Generals, who were owned by multi-millionaire Donald Trump.

"I went from having a shattered ego, because the Browns waived me, to being ecstatic," Harris said of his new job with the Generals. "It seemed that everything had worked out for the best, and that I could continue to combine my two favorite interests, playing football and being an artist."

Much of his ecstasy was based on the fact that his contract with the Generals was guaranteed through the 1986 season.

However, the Generals reneged and Harris's salary, which averaged $183,333 a year, abruptly ended when he was released after playing one season in the ill-fated USFL.

Harris promptly initiated a $3.65 million lawsuit against, not only the Generals, but also the USFL and the USFL Players Association. His attorney, Martin S. List of the Cleveland firm of Duvin, Flinker & Cahn, called it a "unique" case.

"I don't know of any other case like this," List was quoted in the Cleveland *Plain Dealer*. "The union and the league are included because they are in collusion with the Generals in not pursuing Harris's grievance.

"What the Generals are doing is outright immoral. The contract stipulates that, not only is the money guaranteed, it's due and payable immediately."

Harris was embittered. "They've all stonewalled us ... they make their own rules," he said. "It makes me realize that pro football is a business, not a sport, so I'm battling this like a business, too." He did, and won, though he was awarded much less - a total of $320,000 - than the amount of his suit.

And so ended Harris's football career and officially began his career as a full-time commercial artist.

'Born to play pro football'

It can be said that, where defensive end Jack Gregory was concerned, it was a matter of "shoulda," "woulda," and "coulda" for the Browns.

That is, they should have kept Gregory instead of letting him play out his option and get away to the New York Giants in 1972; and if they had, they undoubtedly would have done much better during the lean years of 1972-78, when their cumulative won-lost record was 47-51-2; and perhaps could have won a couple of AFC Central Division championships, instead of finishing second, third, fourth, fourth, third, fourth and third during those seven unproductive seasons.

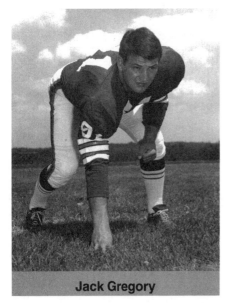

Jack Gregory

As he was described in the Browns' 1971 guide: "This raw-boned Southerner was born to play professional football … there is no doubt that Jack and pro ball were made for each other. As he says, 'I don't like to lose, that's what drives me.'"

All of which motivated the Browns to re-acquire Gregory in 1979, although, by then, the 6-5, 255-pound domineering pass rusher was 35 and well past his prime.

And, when the season ended, so did Gregory's career. He went home to tend his cattle ranch, and cotton and soybean farm in Okolona, Mississippi.

Gregory had been drafted in the ninth round as a "future" (as NFL teams were allowed to do then) out of Delta (Mississippi) State University in 1965, and broke in with the Browns in 1967. He played behind Paul Wiggin and Bill Glass at either left or right defensive end as a rookie, and continued as a back-up in 1968, until Glass was injured at mid-season and retired.

Gregory took over as the starter at right defensive end the next three seasons, and made the Pro Bowl in 1970, but the next year got into a salary squabble with Art Modell.

It led to Gregory playing out his option, but before he could become a free agent he was traded to the Giants for a first round draft choice in 1973.

Despite some difficult personal problems, including the birth of a premature baby son, Gregory in 1972 was a star for the Giants. His 21 quarterback sacks were the most in the NFL, and he was picked on every all-Pro team that year.

But the Giants were even worse than the Browns during Gregory's seven years in New York, and in 1979 he returned to Cleveland for one last season in the NFL.

"I've been in this league long enough to know there aren't too many stories with happy endings," Gregory was quoted in the Philadelphia *Bulletin* prior to his leaving the Giants. You can't beat this game. Sooner or later the game beats all of us.

"If you're a player, you're gonna get cut. If you're a coach, you're gonna get fired. You can't sit back and cry about it, you just have to keep on going. In football, you live a lifetime in one week."

And, upon joining the Browns, Gregory was quoted in the Cleveland *Plain Dealer*: "After what I've been through there's absolutely nothing in this world that can rattle me. People tell me, 'Take it easy, Jack.'

"But, shucks. I don't even know how to spell 'easy' anymore."

Which would have made him ideal for the Browns – if they'd brought him back sooner.

So much for shoulda, woulda, and coulda.

He chose to stay in Cleveland

As a center and linebacker in the days of leather helmets and high top shoes, Mike "Moe" Scarry labored in relative anonymity most of the time on the football field, though he deserves mention for two distinctions:

First, he was one of six members of the NFL champion Cleveland Rams who defected and joined the new Cleveland Browns in 1946, when the All-America Football Conference was formed.

And, second, Scarry was one of the few professional football players – perhaps the *only* one - who also was, simultaneously, a coach of what was then a major college basketball team, Western Reserve University.

It all happened in the mid-1940s.

After the 6-0, 214-pound Scarry played two seasons for the Rams, 1944 and 1945, serving as their captain when they won the NFL championship the latter season, he jumped to the Browns and played for them in 1946 and 1947, making it three years in a row that he played for championship teams.

A former high school star in Pittsburgh and then at Waynesburg (Pennsylvania) University where he'd been awarded a basketball and football scholarship, Scarry went into the Army upon his graduation from college in 1942.

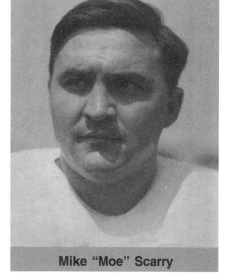

Mike "Moe" Scarry

He saw duty as a second lieutenant with the infantry in Africa during World War II, and was medically discharged in time to join the Rams in 1944. That was the season they compiled a 4-6 record under then-coach Aldo "Buff" Donelli, who formerly coached the Pittsburgh Steelers and knew Scarry well.

Scarry was named captain of the Rams in 1945 by then-new coach Adam Walsh and the team, quarterbacked by Bob Waterfield, went 9-1 and beat Washington, 15-14, for the NFL championship, the only one won by the Rams until then.

Shortly thereafter Rams owner Daniel F. Reeves got permission from the NFL to move the franchise to Los Angeles.

His reason was two-fold: because of failing attendance in Cleveland, and the presence of the AAFC, which included the Browns as one of its eight teams.

But Scarry and five other members of the Rams – halfbacks Don Greenwood and Tommy Colella, fullback-linebacker Gaylon Smith, and two way tackle Chet Adams, as well as assistant coach Red Conkright - refused to leave Cleveland and jumped at contract offers by Paul Brown to join the Browns.

According to a story in the Cleveland *Press* on June 26, 1946:

"Coach Brown said he was impressed by Scarry's leadership, that he seemed to have the knack of pulling the club together the few times (the 1945 Rams) experienced rough sailing."

It proved to be a good move for Scarry, who was named captain of the Browns and helped them win the AAFC championship in 1946 and 1947.

It was during Scarry's second season with the Browns that he took over as coach of Western Reserve's basketball team. When he retired from the Browns at the age of 27 after the 1947 season, he also became WRU's head football coach.

Scarry went on to a long and successful college coaching career, and from 1966-68 served as an assistant to former teammate Otto Graham with the Washington Redskins in the NFL.

When Turkey 'spiked' Bradshaw

Joe Jones – a.k.a. "Turkey" Jones – is best remembered for a "play" he made against the Pittsburgh Steelers on October 10, 1976, in the Browns' 18-16 victory in front of 76,411 fans at the old Stadium.

As recalled by Bill Scholl in a story in the Cleveland *Press* a year later: "A handful of football plays stand out vividly in the memory, and one of the most recallable is Joe Jones holding Terry Bradshaw upside down, shaking him like a piggy bank.

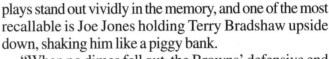

"When no dimes fell out, the Browns' defensive end slammed the oversized piggy bank to the end zone turf in front of the bleachers and the Pittsburgh Steelers' quarterback retired for the day with a sore head and neck."

It was the one most definable moment in the career of the 6-6, 250-pound Jones, who'd been a second round draft choice of the Browns out of Tennessee State in 1970.

Jones played for the Browns in 1970 and 1971, missed all of 1972 with a knee injury, and returned as a starter at left defensive end in 1973.

At the end of the season, however, Jones was traded to the Philadelphia Eagles for receiver Ben Hawkins, in what turned out to be one of the team's worst-ever deals Hawkins played in only two games for the Browns, without a reception, and was waived.

Joe "Turkey" Jones

Jones started for the Eagles in 1974, but early in 1975 lost his job and also was waived. The Browns quickly claimed him on the advice of defensive line coach Dick Modzelewski, who was quoted as saying, "Joe has all the potential in the world to be the best defensive end in football."

Jones was close to being one of the best, especially as a pass rusher, in 1976 and 1977, but lost his starting job in 1978 and was cut loose again. This time he was picked up by the Washington Redskins, for whom he played in 1979 and 1980.

"It was God's will I was traded to the Eagles," Jones said after returning to the Browns. "It was like God put his hand on my head and said, 'This is the way it will be.' I didn't learn much as a player in Philadelphia, but something happened inside me to make me a better player when I returned (to Cleveland)."

Perhaps even more significant in the revitalization of Jones was that, "It shook me up when the Eagles put me on waivers, and the Browns were the last team I expected to show any interest.

"There was nothing wrong with the Philadelphia organization. They treated me fine. It was just a disagreement between the coach and me."

The Eagles coach that year was former Browns captain and future Hall of Famer Mike McCormack.

When pressed for elaboration, Jones admitted, "Yes, I guess it's right to say I was released for disciplinary reasons."

Of the aforementioned play in which he spiked Bradshaw in 1976, Jones said, "It was the biggest play of my career. There wasn't anything dirty about it, because I don't want to hurt people. But there was no way I could have heard a whistle with 80,000 fans yelling."

Whatever, it is a play for which Turkey Jones always will be remembered by longtime Browns' fans – and, certainly, also by Bradshaw

Quarterback to cornerback

He was the star quarterback at the University of Mississippi, won the "Most Valuable Player" award in the Gator Bowl in 1958 and the Sugar Bowl in 1960, and it was taken for granted that he would soon be winning more honors in the National Football League.

But Bobby Franklin wasn't picked in the 1960 college draft until the Browns selected him in the 11th round, and his future in the NFL was doubtful because Milt Plum was then the team's quarterback.

Obviously, however, Paul Brown, then general manager and coach of the Browns, saw something in the scouting reports on the 5-11, 185 pound Franklin that was overlooked by his contemporaries - speed, agility and athleticism, all the attributes needed to be an outstanding NFL defensive back.

And so, while his position was announced as "quarterback" upon his being drafted by the Browns, Franklin was immediately assigned to the defensive backfield where he was a major contributor for the next six seasons, though he also saw limited duty as a punt and kickoff returner. He was the starter at right safety when the Browns beat Baltimore, 27-0, in 1964, the last time they won the NFL championship.

As a rookie, Franklin picked off eight passes, returning two of them for touchdowns, and in his seven seasons

Bobby Franklin

with the Browns was credited with 13 interceptions for 187 yards, and five fumble recoveries.

Because of his "good hands" and ability to throw a pass, Franklin also was the holder for field goal and extra point attempts, and served as back-up kicker, if one became necessary (though it never did as the Browns had Sam Baker in 1960 and 1961, and Lou Groza came out of retirement and played from 1961-67).

The Browns temporarily lost the services of Franklin after the first three games in 1962 when he was ordered to report for service with the Mississippi National Guard at Oxford, Mississippi.

The Guard was federalized by President Kennedy for riot control as a result of racial integration trouble at Franklin's alma mater.

As Private First Class Robert Franklin he served on active duty only three days, primarily, he said, "checking cars at road blocks," and returned to the Browns for their next game, which they won, 19-10, over Dallas.

Franklin's service with the Browns also was interrupted in 1966, when he was waived in training camp and picked up by Atlanta. But the Falcons also waived Franklin after three preseason games and, thinking his playing career was over, he took a job as an assistant coach at Georgia Tech.

However, when the Browns were left with only five defensive backs because of an injury to Walter Beach and the departure of Bernie Parrish in the first couple of weeks of the regular season, they put out an S.O.S. to Franklin.

He answered the call and returned, though only as a fill-in that season, after which he retired again and went back to his job at Georgia Tech in 1967.

The following year Franklin was back in the NFL, this time as defensive backfield coach of the Dallas Cowboys, his playing career finished.

His toughness was legendary

If Len Ford were playing in the National Football League today, there's almost no doubt he'd be one of the few two-way performers - as a tight end in addition to being a great defensive end, which he was for the Browns from 1950 through 1957.

Enshrined posthumously in the Hall of Fame in 1976, Ford was a two way star before he

Len Ford

came to Cleveland in the dispersal draft of players from the All America Football Conference.

Something else that establishes the greatness of Ford as a defensive end is the fact that, because of his exceptional ability at rushing a passer, the Browns switched from the then conventional six man defensive line to a four man front.

It was done by Paul Brown to better utilize Ford's skills, and from that innovation the 4-3 defensive alignment became the conventional one in the NFL.

Before the Browns got Ford, he was an offensive and defensive end for the Los Angeles Dons of the AAFC in 1948 and 1949, after an equally splendid career - also as a two way performer - at the University of Michigan.

In his two seasons with the Dons, Ford caught 67 passes for 1,175 yards and eight touchdowns.

At the same time, he terrorized quarterbacks as the AAFC's best pass rusher.

Brown knew of Ford's pass-catching ability, but the Browns already had some excellent receivers. Thus, Ford concentrated on playing defensive end, and became one of the all-time greats at that position.

Ford's toughness was legendary as was best illustrated by his recovery from an injury in 1950 that nearly ended his career.

In the eighth game of the season, against the then-Chicago Cardinals, Ford constantly beat Pat Harder, a halfback who was supposed to be protecting the quarterback.

Finally Harder, in his frustration, threw an elbow at Ford's face, knocking the defensive end unconscious - and more.

In addition to a severe concussion, Ford suffered fractured facial bones, a broken nose and several shattered teeth.

In those days players did not wear facemasks.

Ford's jaws were wired together and nobody doubted the doctors when they said he'd be out for the rest of the season.

But to Ford's way of thinking, "the rest of the season" did not include the postseason.

Miraculously, Ford, though still weakened and underweight because of the liquid diet he'd endured for two months, played against the Los Angeles Rams in the NFL championship game.

What's more, Ford gave one of his all-time best performances, according to eyewitness reports of the game, won by the Browns, 30-28, on Lou Groza's last minute field goal.

All of which had special significance 26 years later when Ford's daughter Deborah made the Hall of Fame acceptance speech for her dad, who died of a heart attack in 1972.

She said, "My father always taught us that a winner never quits, and a quitter never wins. He was committed to excellence."

And excellent is what Ford probably would have been as a two-way performer.

'The best guard in football'

He was short, squat - OK, even *fat*! - and some of his critics called Abe Gibron a "clown."

But not Paul Brown. Definitely not Paul Brown.

In 1953, Brown, then general manager and coach of the Browns, called Gibron, "The best guard in football. Everytime we need yardage, we ride his shirttails."

Brown further praised Gibron, saying, "Not only is he a fine blocker with great offensive charge and the speed to pull out on running plays, I believe he could be the middle man on the defensive line and do that job as well as anybody."

Enough said? If not, here's more.

In 1955, after the Browns had beaten Green Bay, 41-10, en route to their third NFL championship (in only their sixth year in the league), Packers coach Lisle Blackbourn put his feelings on record in no uncertain terms.

Blackbourn didn't talk about the Browns' great passing attack that featured Otto Graham and Dante Lavelli, or even their stable of runners, which included Maurice Bassett, Fred Morrison, Dub Jones and Ed Modzelewski.

Instead, when asked to appraise the Browns' strength, Blackbourne answered forthwith, "It's those tackles and Gibron. That's the difference between our teams."

Abe Gibron

For the record, the Browns offensive tackles that year were Lou Groza and Mike McCormack, both future Hall of Famers.

But the only player mentioned by name by Blackbourn was Gibron, who played in the Pro Bowl every year from 1953-56, and was selected on the All-NFL team in 1955.

Not only was Gibron one of the best offensive linemen in the Browns first 50 years, he was one of the least expensive. He was picked up from the Buffalo Bills when the All-America Football Conference was disbanded after the 1949 season, and the Browns and San Francisco 49ers joined the NFL.

Gibron captained the Valparaiso College team as a freshman, prior to seeing service in the Marine Corps during World War II. After the war he transferred to Purdue University where he played from 1946-48.

With the Browns, the 5-10, 245-pound Gibron was the starter at left guard each of his seven seasons, through 1956, during which he was flanked by another future Hall of Famer, center Frank Gatski, as well as Groza.

After his retirement Gibron was an assistant coach for the Washington Redskins from 1960-64, an assistant for the Chicago Bears from 1965-71, and head coach of he Bears from 1972-74. His three season record as a coach of the Bears was 11-30-1.

When asked why the Browns were so successful during his playing career, Gibron said, "We had a nucleus of players that kept us going. We built up pride in winning, which is what made us fight so hard when we were behind. We were guys who had come out of the service and hadn't been handed anything.

"The new players you get now aren't as hungry as we were. They're good players, and all that. But they have more money than we did. And between the player who has desire and the one who has ability, well, you always have to take the one who has desire."

There was never any doubt that Gibron had both - ability and desire.

'Not a personality conflict'

His brother got most of the publicity because of his nickname, "The Refrigerator."

But it was Michael Dean Perry who did more for his team, the Browns - on the field and in the locker room - at least until then-coach Bill Belichick decided the 6-1, 285-pound defensive tackle was expendable.

Michael Dean Perry

Perry was made available in the 1995 expansion draft, but when neither Jacksonville nor Carolina claimed him, Perry was released and signed with Denver..

From 1988, when he was drafted in the second round out of Clemson University, Perry, four times an All-Pro selection and a five time Pro Bowler, was the single most dominating interior lineman the Browns ever had since Jerry Sherk.

Art Modell, then-owner of the Browns, denied speculation that the decision to unload Perry was because of a personality conflict between the two men. Modell claimed it was based on Belichick's defensive system that did not permit Perry to free lance as he'd done previously.

It also was Michael Dean's contract – he was to be paid $3.2 million in 1995 - that was a major factor in the decision to let him go, though the money the Browns saved wasn't put to good use. Much of it went to sign receiver Andre Rison, who was a bust for the Browns in his only season in Cleveland.

Modell also defended the decision to cut Perry by pointing out that he went through the expansion draft unclaimed. "This thing (the draft) has been going on for about three hours now," Modell was quoted in the Akron *Beacon Journal*. "(Perry) hasn't been taken by anyone, and you're talking about public reaction? Here you have two teams starting from scratch, with no players and he hasn't been taken by anyone. What further vindication do I need?"

But if Modell felt that the Browns were "vindicated" when neither Jacksonville nor Carolina grabbed Perry, it was a different story a month later.

Then, on February 24, 1995, Perry agreed to a three-year contract worth $7.2 million that included a $3 million signing bonus, with Denver. The deal came a few days after the Broncos also signed James Jones, another starting defensive tackle discarded by the Browns in 1994.

And to increase the discomfort that Modell and Belichick probably felt, Broncos General Manager John Beake told the *Associated Press* that the acquisition of Jones and Perry represented "a cornerstone of our defense," and that, "It's not a step, it's a giant step. We bulked up in one day."

After signing with Denver, Perry diplomatically said he was relieved to be joining the Broncos because, "Now I won't have to chase John Elway around anymore."

Earlier, however, near the end of the 1994 season with the Browns headed for the playoffs, Perry wasn't diplomatic in an article in *USA Today* in which he was quoted:

"Deep down guys are no happier with (Belichick). It's just a smoke screen because we're winning. It's the atmosphere, your working environment. You just don't feel comfortable with him."

The story obviously fueled the personality conflict between Perry and Belichick, and which led to – actually *resulted* in – Michael Dean's demise, Modell's explanation notwithstanding.

Saved by the 'Inner Circle'

It must be concluded that, as a No. 1 draft choice, Charles White was a bust. Especially one who, according to his agent, Michael Trope, signed a contract with the Browns that was worth "in excess of one million dollars, and has the potential for exceeding two million dollars."

White played well enough on occasion during his five years with the Browns from 1980-84, but so much more had been – and, justifiably so – expected of the 5-10, 190-pound running back from the University of Southern California, the 1979 Heisman Trophy winner.

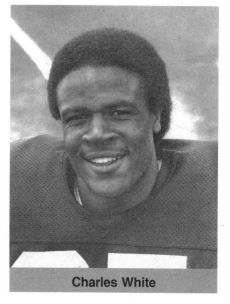

However, White, despite his perceived shortcomings on the field for the Browns, must be given credit for having the guts to go public with his drug addiction which, undoubtedly helped others, including some of his teammates who had similar problems.

White's admission prior to the start of the 1982 season that he had spent about a month that summer in a drug rehabilitation hospital in Orange County, California led to the creation by the Browns of the "Inner Circle."

It was a program administered by the Cleveland Clinic that initially included eight similarly addicted members of the team (whose identities were never made public).

As White said then, "I feel it is important that I can reach out through my experiences to elaborate to some

Charles White

of the young people not to go down the same road I went down. I don't want them to make the same big mistake I made."

His addiction to cocaine began, White said, when he was in college because of what he called "peer pressure" and the pressures involved in playing football.

While he was the biggest star in college football in 1979, White played behind Greg Pruitt his first three seasons (1980-82) with the Browns, was out all of 1983 with a broken ankle, and missed part of 1984 with a knee injury.

His four season statistics with the Browns are hardly worthy of a Heisman winner or first round draft choice: 942 yards gained in 276 attempts, and 83 pass receptions for 684 yards, and a total of ten touchdowns.

In 1985, after being waived by the Browns, White went back "home" – to the Los Angeles Rams – and, at least in 1987, the third of his four seasons there, lived up to all that had been expected of him previously.

White rushed for an NFL-best 1,374 yards and 11 touchdowns in 324 carries, though he was less than spectacular again in 1988 (323 yards gained in 88 carries) and was out of pro football in 1989.

Despite his shortcomings on the field, and whatever regret he might have felt toward the Browns for not sticking with him longer, White was gracious in what became his farewell speech prior to his return to Los Angeles.

"My life turned around here," he said. "If I hadn't come to Cleveland, I wouldn't be on the right track that I am. Playing for a coach like Sam Rutigliano, who cares about people, kept my life straight.

"The Inner Circle has been a great backbone for me, along with God. I fell by the wayside and He forgave me."

A big, tough ... sensitive man

Nobody really considered him a "throw in," but the fact is, Bill Glass wasn't the key player when he was traded to the Browns in 1962.

Jim Ninowski, a strong-armed quarterback, was the main man Paul Brown wanted from Detroit when he swapped Milt Plum to the Lions on March 28, 1962.

Bill Glass

But to "even up" the deal, the Lions included Glass, a 6-5, 265 pound defensive end from Baylor University, and Howard (Hopalong) Cassady, the 1955 Heisman Trophy winner from Ohio State.

As it turned out, Cassady played little and was waived to Philadelphia at the end of 1962, and Ninowski suffered a broken collarbone in the eighth game of the season, was replaced by Frank Ryan and never started again for the Browns.

Glass had been Detroit's first round draft choice in 1957, but he opted initially to play in Canada, which might have helped make him expendable.

He joined the Lions in 1958 and played for them without distinction through 1961, but was a star for the Browns the next six years.

Glass retired after spending most of the 1968 season on the sideline with an assortment of injuries, including broken ribs.

Paul Brown had been after Glass - quietly, of course - since they were together in the Senior Bowl in 1957.

When Jim Houston was called into the service in 1962, Brown was determined to get Glass - again, quietly, of course.

Which might explain why Glass was a "throw-in" in the Ninowski-Plum deal, though not in the estimation of Brown.

A lay minister since 1963, Glass gained renown as an Evangelist, and still is as dedicated and intense a preacher as he was a football player.

But he also was then, as he certainly is now, a caring and sensitive man.

A story that surfaced in 1966 tells it best,

The husband of a nurse at Fairview Park Hospital passed a note via a waitress to Glass one night when they were eating at the same restaurant after a Browns game.

The man wrote about one of his wife's patients, a 16-year old youth, a devoted Browns fan who was facing his third and very serious operation the next morning.

The man left the boy's name and room number with the waitress and probably figured that would be the end of it, though he hoped that Glass might respond.

Glass did. The very next morning. He spent a long time with the boy before his surgery, and visited him afterwards.

Later, a sequel to the story also surfaced.

The boy's father said Glass and his son talked for a long time that night, and prayed together. Then, the boy who had been failing told his father, " I'm not afraid anymore. 1'm not going to die." And he didn't.

That was Bill Glass. A big, strong, tough defensive end.

Also a dedicated, sensitive, caring man.

'No player loved the Browns more'

When Paul Wiggin retired from the Browns in 1968 after 11 seasons as one of the NFL's best defensive ends – and one of the team's all-time most popular players – he made a heartfelt valedictorian speech.

"No player loved the Browns more than I did," said Wiggin, who left to become an assistant coach with the San Francisco 49ers. "It was the hardest thing I ever did to put down that Browns' uniform. I talked over the plusses and minuses of the job with the 49ers and decided I just couldn't turn it down."

Blanton Collier, then coach of the Browns, was as sorry to see Wiggin go as Wiggin was to leave. "Players with the qualities of leadership and character such as Paul has, just don't come along every day," said Collier.

"As his coach, I must say we'll miss him. And as a friend of Paul and his family, I certainly appreciate the reasons which prompted him to retire now."

A sixth round pick in the 1956 draft out of Stanford University where he won All-America honors, Wiggin played for the Browns from 1957-67 and never missed a game.

A key member of the defensive team that shutout the highly-favored Baltimore Colts, 27-0, in the 1964 championship game, the last time a Browns team won the NFL

Paul Wiggin

title, Wiggin played in the Pro Bowl in 1966, and was captain of the Browns in 1967.

Unfortunately, his coaching career was not nearly as successful after he served as an assistant and defensive coordinator (in 1974) for the 49ers for seven seasons, from 1968-75; was head coach of the Kansas City Chiefs for 2 ½ seasons, from 1975-77; and head coach at his alma mater, Stanford, from 1980-83, compiling a 16-28 record. Most recently Wiggin has been pro personnel director of the Minnesota Vikings.

When he took over as coach of the Chiefs, Wiggin was faced with a massive rebuilding job and led them to 5-9 records in each 1975 and 1976, after which he was given a three-year contract extension.

Despite those two losing seasons, everything was great, or so Wiggin thought.

But when the Chiefs lost six of their first seven games in 1977, Wiggin was fired on October 31. The decision by owner Lamar Hunt surprised many observers, and was a distinct disappointment to Wiggin, who said in his farewell remarks to the Kansas City media and fans:

"The Chiefs are on the right track. The whole system is right. I just wish I could be here when the dream comes true instead of being the guy who kept everybody smiling for two years. I know I did a damn good job, and that I'm a damn good man.

"When I'm handing out Halloween candy to the kids tonight, and cleaning out my desk tomorrow, I'm going to hold my head up. I'm not embarrassed about what happened here."

Later Wiggin was quoted in the Kansas City *Star*, "When I was fired, I was bitter and depressed. I think anybody would be. My problem was that, in football, like any kind of athletics, you're asked to fall in love. They say, 'This is your team. Make it a winner.' It becomes your obsession, then your love.

"On the day before I was fired I would have given $1,000 for a day off. The day after I was fired, I would have given $5,000 to be back."

The Browns' first 'Top Dawg'

When he joined the Browns as their first draft choice (22nd overall) out of the University of Southern Mississippi in 1981, Hanford Dixon quickly endeared himself to Cleveland fans with his enthusiasm and hard-hitting play.

The affection was mutual, as Dixon vowed, "My heart is here and always will be in this city, and with the people of Cleveland," as reported in *Browns News/Illustrated.*

But when he left the Browns, after nine mostly productive seasons as one of the best cornerbacks in the NFL, Dixon was disillusioned and disappointed.

His departure came in the wake of criticism by then-coach Bud Carson, and the signing of veteran cornerback Raymond Clayborn, who was slated to replace Dixon.

It also followed the Browns' 37-21 loss to Denver in the 1989 AFC championship game, the third time in four years they'd been beaten by the Broncos for a berth in the Super Bowl.

"I felt I wasn't needed or wanted here," Dixon was quoted in the Lake County *News Herald* when he announced his intention to sign a contract to play for San Francisco. "Believe it or not, there's still a few people who think I can play corner."

Hanford Dixon

Dixon had been left unprotected by the Browns under what was then "Plan B free agency," and had the right to sign with another team.

There certainly were many who, not only thought Dixon could play corner, but – at least prior to the arrival of then-coach Bud Carson in 1989 - considered him to be "quite possibly the best cornerback to ever play for the Browns," according to the *News Herald.*

In his nine seasons in Cleveland, Dixon was credited with 26 pass interceptions, ninth on the team's all-time list, picking off five in each 1984 and 1986

In the *News Herald* story he also was called "perhaps the most criticized" cornerback to ever play for the Browns, an apparent reference to a remark by Carson that Dixon's ability had "slipped," and that he might be better off playing free safety.

It also was reported that Dixon "went so far (in the afore-mentioned press conference) as to suggest he was driven out of town by (the) Cleveland *Plain Dealer.*"

"A lot of the criticism was unjust," Dixon said. "Frank (Minnifield) and I caught the heat for it. We were the scapegoats." Minnifield was Dixon's cornerback partner. "The secondary played well," he insisted. "You have to look at all the aspects of a football game. The secondary always gets blamed. We just didn't win (against Denver in the AFC championship game)."

Whatever, Dixon, a three-time All-Pro (1986-88) who also was chosen to play in the Pro Bowl three times (1987-89), went to the 49ers, but didn't make the team and retired in 1990.

Clayborn, the former New England cornerback who also was a Plan B free agent, didn't fare much better with the Browns. He played in 16 games in 1990 without being credited with an interception, and appeared in one game in 1991 before he retired.

And, while Dixon is gone from the Browns, he'll be remembered as the originator of the "Dawgs" nickname for the team's defensive unit, and subsequently was called "Top Dawg" by his teammates.

Which Dixon was, until – in Carson's opinion – he slipped.

The biggest 'little' man

It is unfortunate that Greg Pruitt's splendid career with the Browns ended in resentment and bitterness when the 5-10, 185-pound running back was traded to the then-Los Angeles Raiders in 1982.

"It was the biggest tragedy in my career," he said of the deal that netted the Browns an 11th round draft choice (that was used to pick linebacker Howard McAdoo, who never made it in the NFL).

"My attitude had always been one of confidence, even when I hurt my knee (in 1979), I still had my confidence. But the trade took my confidence away," Pruitt said in a 1983 story that appeared in the Cleveland *Plain Dealer*.

Greg Pruitt

Particularly distressing to Pruitt was, as he said then: "To this day I have not been given a reason by the Browns why I was traded." He could only surmise that his outspokenness was a factor.

"After all I gave them, I thought I rated better. I wish they had given me the option to retire. I probably would have, as a Brown."

Instead, he went to Super Bowl XVIII with the Raiders and helped them win the 1983 NFL championship with a 38-9 victory over Washington.

Pruitt, used primarily as a kickoff and punt returner for three years by the Raiders, retired after the 1984 season, and later became a player agent.

In four of his nine seasons with the Browns, after being their second round draft choice out of Oklahoma University in 1973, Pruitt – despite his size - was their primary offensive threat as a runner and pass receiver.

Pruitt rushed for 1,000 yards three years in a row (1975-77, and narrowly missed with 960 in 1978), and also was one of the team's leading receivers from 1975-81. He ran for 100-plus yards 17 times, including a career high of 214 against Kansas City in 1975, and his career rushing total for the Browns – 1,158 yards – is fourth best behind Jim Brown (2,359), Leroy Kelly (1,727), and Mike Pruitt (1,593).

Greg Pruitt played in the Pro Bowl four times (1974, 1975, 1977, 1978), and was the Cleveland Touchdown Club's "Offensive Player of the Year" in 1975 and 1978.

Of Pruitt's pass catching ability, backfield coach Jim Garrett said, "He has the most remarkable hands of anybody I've ever seen. He has fantastic hands, like he's catching a tennis ball."

It was Pruitt's physical stature – actually, comments *about* his physical stature – that, Pruitt said, made him so good. "It motivated me. I resented hearing all the time that I was too small."

It also was Pruitt's speed – 4.4 seconds in the 40 yard dash – and agility that made him such a great runner and receiver. He was the Browns' kickoff and punt returner in his first three seasons with the Browns and scored 19 touchdowns as a return specialist.

When asked how he would like to be remembered by Browns fans, Pruitt replied, "As an exciting runner … and I don't think anyone ever saw me loaf."

Both of which would be accurate assessments.

Then he added, "Outspoken, too. If I had it to do all over, I'd have used two words to save my career."

They were, Pruitt said, "No comment."

Not older, just better

When "Big Daddy" – Carl Hairston, that is – came to the Browns in 1984 in a trade for a ninth round draft pick, he arrived, he said, "with something to prove."

Which he did, and did very well for the better part of the next six seasons.

"I wanted to prove that I wasn't over the hill, that I still had some good years left," the 6-3,

Carl "Big Daddy" Hairston

260-pound defensive end was quoted in the Philadelphia *Daily News* in a 1987 story. At the time the Browns were practicing at Vero Beach, Florida, getting ready for another shot at the Super Bowl.

As the AFC Central Division champions, they had just beaten the New York Jets, 23-20, in two overtime sessions, a victory in which Hairston played a major role, credited with three quarterback sacks and nine tackles.

Beating the Jets advanced the Browns to the AFC championship game against Denver (which they would lose, 23-20, in what would forever be lamented, and known as "The Drive").

On this day and in this interview with the *Daily News*, Big Daddy was confident that he'd get back to the Super Bowl, which he'd helped the Philadelphia Eagles reach in 1980, though they lost to Oakland, 27-10.

Time supposedly heals all wounds, but in the case of Hairston, it didn't. He was still resentful that the Eagles had given up on him. Sometimes a player can see the end coming and prepare for it. Hairston never did, which is the reason he had much to prove.

"When it happened, when the Eagles let me go (after eight years in Philadelphia, and serving as their defensive captain his last five seasons) it really shook me up," he said. "I always thought I would end my career in the same place I had started it," after being a seventh round pick of the Eagles out of Maryland-Eastern Shore College in 1976.

"They said I was getting old, but I say I was getting better, not old."

The Browns obviously thought so, too.

Big Daddy was their defensive captain in 1988 and 1989, and was named their "Defensive MVP" by the Cleveland Touchdown Club in 1987. He racked up 37 ½ quarterback sacks in his six seasons with the Browns.

Marty Schottenheimer, then coach of the Browns, called the acquisition of Hairston a "steal." As he said, "To get (Hairston) for a ninth round draft pick was incredible. He has always been a player I've held in very high esteem."

When the Browns traded for Hairston, they planned on using him mainly as a pass rushing specialist. But Big Daddy ended up winning a starting job which he held until 1989, when, at the age of 36, he was replaced – except in certain situations – by a younger player.

But still, Hairston refused to give in to his advanced years.

When the Browns waived him in 1990, Hairston signed on with the Arizona Cardinals and played another season, appearing in all 16 games, after which Al "Bubba" Baker, another elderly – but still effective – pass rusher commented: "Big Daddy will be the first player to earn a Pro Bowl check and social security check in the same year."

It turned out to be a slight exaggeration as Hairston finally hung up his cleats in 1991, after 15 NFL seasons and 224 games, most of them good.

The Browns' 'other Pruitt'

He was called "that other Pruitt," not because Mike Pruitt wasn't as good as Greg Pruitt, but because he came to the Browns three years later.

And, as Art Modell liked to say in the late-1970s and early-1980s when Mike was the fullback and Greg the running back, "What one Pruitt can't do, the other can," which was close to being 100% accurate.

Of all the running backs who have played for the Browns in the team's 50 years, only two - Hall of Famers Jim Brown and Leroy Kelly - rushed for more yardage than Mike Pruitt's 1,593 (with Greg Pruitt right behind in fourth place on the all-time list).

However, it didn't start so promisingly for Mike Pruitt, the Browns' No. 1 draft choice out of Purdue University in 1976. In fact, it wasn't until Sam Rutigliano took over as coach of the Browns in 1978 that the "other Pruitt" began to live up to expectations.

"I can't put my finger on it," Pruitt said in a 1980 newspaper article, "but I could relate to Sam, maybe because right at the very beginning he showed confidence in me.

"I don't want to be critical of Forrest Gregg (the Browns coach from 1975-77), but if he had stayed here, I probably would have asked to be traded. I was dying on the vine. Instead, I feel like an important part of this

Mike Pruitt

team now." Which he most definitely was. Pruitt rushed for 1,000-plus yards three straight seasons (1979-81) and again in 1983, and was a Pro Bowler in 1980 and 1981.

Not surprisingly, Pruitt's favorite season was 1980 when the Browns, then a.k.a. the "Kardiac Kids" because they came from behind so often to win, and captured the AFC Central Division with an 11-5 record.

"We felt invincible," he said in an article in a recent edition of *Browns News/Illustrated*. "Behind by ten points with five minutes to go? No problem. Hit Ozzie Newsome over the middle for 10 yards. Hit Reggie Rucker on a 22-yard run. A draw to me for 10 more. Pitch to Greg Pruitt for 9. Fake a draw, bootleg to the right and back to Ozzie on a screen pass for 15 yards – touchdown! Man, we had weapons. We thought we could beat anyone, anywhere. This was our year to go to the Super Bowl."

But it wasn't. The Browns lost their first playoff game to the eventual Super Bowl XV champion Oakland Raiders, 14-12, on a frigid day at the Stadium.

"It's 10 below zero. The wind chill factor is 50 below. It's the coldest day of my life," continued Pruitt. "The game, like normal, came down to the last 15 seconds. I had just gained 10 yards to the Raiders' 15. There was enough time to kick a field goal and win. Then it was off to sunny California to play the (San Diego) Chargers.

"A play comes from the sideline. Instead of kicking a field goal, it's Red Right 88. I said to myself, 'Oh, no. Not a pass.'"

But it was, and it was intercepted by the Raiders' Mike Davis. End of game.

Fortunately, not all of Pruitt's memories of his career with the Browns are unpleasant. He played for them through 1984, spent 1985 with Buffalo and Kansas City, and after one final season with the Chiefs in 1986, retired with the reputation for having been "that other Pruitt" – as well as being one very good running back for the Browns.

Jim Brown's constant escort

Think about it for a minute.

In virtually every photograph of the great Jim Brown running a sweep around end, there's a stubby, fireplug-type guy wearing No. 66 escorting him, leading the blocking.

Which is one of the best recommendations that can be advanced for electing Gene Hickerson to the Pro Football Hall of Fame.

Gene Hickerson

But don't bother to ask Hickerson if he belongs. He'll shrug and say it doesn't matter one way or another.

Typical of Hickerson's low-key attitude was the way he informed Browns owner Art Modell of his decision to retire after a 15-year career as one of the National Football League's best offensive linemen, though he played only 14 seasons.

After practice one day late in 1973, Hickerson tapped Modell on the shoulder and said, "This will be my last year."

That was all. No elaboration. Nothing. Period.

And three games later, Hickerson retired.

Only two players, Lou Groza, who played 17 seasons, and Clay Matthews, 16, surpassed Hickerson's longevity with the Browns, and only Mattews (232), Groza (216) and Doug Dieken (203) played more games than Hickerson's 202.

Hickerson was named to the Pro Bowl six straight years, from 1965 through 1970, and was voted the National Football League's outstanding blocker in 1969.

It all began for the 6-2, 250-pound linemen in 1957 when he was a seventh round pick in the college draft out of Mississippi, tabbed as a "future."

When he joined the Browns in 1958, then-coach Paul Brown appointed Hickerson a "messenger," one of two guards who alternated carrying plays into the quarterback.

It was a job Hickerson held for four seasons, though he missed all of 1961 after suffering a broken leg in the opening preseason game. Hickerson was a starter at either left or right guard until the day he retired.

Hickerson's former offensive line-mate, Dick Schafrath, always considered his longtime friend a "put-on-artist."

"All the time I played with Gene, he tried to act as though there was nothng to the game (of football)," said Schafrath.

"When it came to lifting weights, he acted like a weakling if the coaches were around, but when he thought nobody was looking, I saw him press 250 pounds with ease."

Schafrath said it was the same during training camp when linemen were required to run a mile in seven minutes by a certain specified date.

"I always thought Gene could do it the first day we were in camp, but he always waited until the deadline day," said Schafrath.

"I think he considered himself something of a rebel."

Which might be the reason Hickerson never lamented being bypassed by the Hall of Fame electors.

But those who saw him lead Jim Brown's sweeps and pass block for Milt Plum, Frank Ryan, Bill Nelsen and Mike Phipps, can't understand why he hasn't made it.

Unsung, but not unappreciated

Others received greater publicity and recognition, but Ray Renfro is more conspicuous among the Browns' all-time pass receivers, and was, as then-coach Paul Brown called him in a 1961 article in the Cleveland *Press*, "the real artist of all the flankers I know."

Brown also said that Renfro was "a great competitor and an inspiration to his teammates" because he often played with injuries that would have side-lined others.

Renfro, who was unmarried early in his career with the Browns, often baby-sat for the children of his team-mates, and among his many admirers was longtime equipment manager Morrie Kono. "He's a guy who would do anything to help," Kono said about Renfro in a Cleveland *News* story. "I'm sure he'd sweep the floor if I asked him."

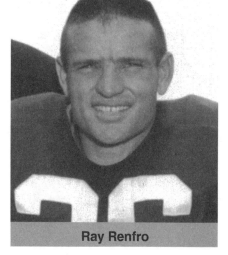
Ray Renfro

Nicknamed "Rabbit" because of his speed and elusiveness, Renfro was a fourth round draft choice of the Browns in 1952 out of North Texas State College where he won Little All-America honors in 1951.

Renfro also was a basketball and track star in college and ran the 100-yard dash in 9.5 seconds - but wasn't allowed to play football until he was a junior in high school.

As a flanker (as wide receivers then were called), Renfro also ran with the ball, and returned punts and kick-offs his first four seasons with the Browns, though he was best known as a receiver, and played with distinction for the Browns through 1963.

"When I was starting high school my folks wouldn't let me play football because they were afraid I'd get hurt. Besides, we lived in the country (deep in the heart of Texas) about five miles from the school, and if I played, I'd have to walk home very late," Renfro said in a Cleveland *Plain Dealer* story in 1960.

"Finally, our school had Parents Night at a game and I talked my folks into going. It was the first football game they'd ever seen, and sat right behind the players' bench. That sold them. They always thought football was two men fighting over a ball. After that game they said it was OK for me to play – and they never missed another high school or college game I played in."

Renfro, who appeared in five NFL championship games, two of which the Browns won (in 1954 and 1955), is still the franchise leader with an average of 19.6 yards per reception, and is second only to new Hall of Famer Ozzie Newsome among the leaders in receiving yardage with 5,508 (to Newsome's 7,980). In his 12 seasons and 142 games for the Browns, Renfro scored 55 touchdowns.

A member of the Pro Bowl in 1954, 1958 and 1961, Renfro played in 14 games in which he gained 100-plus yards receiving, which also is a franchise-best, and was named the Browns' "Man of the Year" by the Cleveland Touchdown Club in 1961, and "Pro of the Year" by the American Legion Post 738 in 1964.

After his retirement as a player, Renfro served as an assistant coach in the NFL for Detroit, Washington and Dallas through 1972. He died of cancer at the age of 67 in 1997.

Renfro's oldest son Mike, a wide receiver at Texas Christian University, also played in the NFL for Houston and Dallas (1978-87) after being a fourth round pick of the Oilers in the 1978 draft.

Born to play for the Browns

It could be said that Jim Houston was born to play for the Browns, which he did - very well - from 1960 through 1972.

The 6-3, 236 pound defensive end/linebacker grew up in Massillon, Ohio, played for Massillon Washington High School, and earned All-America honors at Ohio State University in 1958 and 1959.

Then Houston was drafted No.1 by Paul Brown, who also previously served at Massillon and Ohio State before becoming the first coach of the Browns in 1946.

Jim Houston's bloodlines also enhanced his credentials, as two older brothers preceded him into the National Football League - Lin, an offensive lineman and charter member of the Browns through 1954, and Walt, also an offensive lineman who played for Washington in 1955.

It was Lin who inspired Jim to become a professional football player, but it was a loss by the Browns that brought him to Cleveland.

"I stood in great admiration of my brother and all the other great athletes that the Browns had," Jim had said.

"Lin would take me to the games and I'd see Otto Graham, Mac Speedie, John Yonakor, Horace Gillom and all of the great players the Browns had in those years."

Jim Houston

But it wasn't until much later, as a sophomore at Ohio State, that Jim Houston allowed himself to dream of possibly following his older brothers into the NFL.

"I considered it an impossible goal ... although, I also felt, if everything went right, maybe someday it would happen," he said.

"Then, all of a sudden I was playing for the Browns."

Ironically, Houston wound up with the Browns because they lost a late-season game, 21-20, to San Francisco in 1959.

It dropped the Browns behind the 49ers in the final standings - and also boosted them one place ahead of San Francisco in the 1960 college draft.

Which resulted in what Houston called his "total surprise" when the Browns picked him.

The 49ers had told Houston that they planned to draft him No. 1.

"I just about had my bags packed to go to San Francisco ... and it was a total surprise when Cleveland picked me," he said.

Houston was a starter for eight seasons, served as the Browns' defensive captain and made the Pro Bowl four times.

As one of the high profile members of the team who played under Brown from 1960-1962, Blanton Collier from 1963-1970, and Nick Skorich in 1971-72, Houston's comparison of the three was interesting.

It was "more enjoyable" under Collier, he said, citing a "more relaxed atmosphere," and suggesting, "maybe we had more success because of that."

But then, Houston himself also was a major factor in the Browns' success in those days.

And his contributions to the team also contradict one of the most popular cliches in the coaching profession, the one that claims nothing good does come out of a loss.

In this case, a loss enabled the Browns to draft Houston.

The 'thinking man's quarterback'

He was described early on by super agent Leigh Steinberg as "the epitome of the thinking man's quarterback," and nobody who saw Bernie Kosar lead the University of Miami to the national championship in 1983, and the Fiesta Bowl in 1984 would disagree.

"Give him a defense and he'll find a hole. Give him a game plan and he'll improve it. Give him a wrinkle and he'll smooth it out. He knows where to throw it, when to throw it, and how to throw it. Sidearm? No problem," added Steinberg. And finally, "It's hard to imagine a more intelligent quarterback."

It also was hard to imagine anyone who wanted more desperately to play for the Browns, which Kosar did while growing up in Boardman, Ohio.

However, it was Kosar's great ability that almost cost him the chance to play for his favorite team. Because of his success as a collegian, it was a given that he would be the first pick of somebody in the National Football League - though almost certainly not the Browns - when Kosar would become eligible for the college draft in 1986.

Bernie Kosar

But then, with the help of another agent, A.J. Faigin of Akron, Ohio, and Ernie Accorsi, then general manager of the Browns, Kosar found a way to circumvent the obvious. Despite having another season at Miami, Kosar declared himself eligible for the Supplemental Draft in 1985 - though that didn't immediately solve the problem.

The Browns had to trade four draft choices - including two No. 1s in 1985 and 1986 - to the Buffalo Bills for their first pick in the Supplemental Draft in order to pick Kosar, making the quarterback's lifelong dream come true.

For the next 8 1/2 seasons - until a falling out with then-coach Bill Belichick turned Kosar's dream into a nightmare - he starred for the Browns, leading them into the NFL playoffs five times, four as the AFC Central Division champion.

Little did he realize at the time - the eighth game of the 1993 season - that his final pass for the Browns would come on November 7, in the waning seconds of a 29-14 loss to Denver at the Cleveland Stadium. It was a 38-yard touchdown to Michael Jackson on a play he'd drawn up in the dirt. After the game Belichick berated Kosar for not running the play that had been sent in by the coach. A couple of days later, when it became obvious that the two men could no longer co-exist on the same team, Kosar was released.

But he wasn't out of a job for long. He was signed by the Dallas Cowboys, helped them win the Super Bowl that season, and in 1994 joined the Miami Dolphins, for whom he served as a back-up to Dan Marino through 1996, then retired.

After 12 seasons in the NFL, Kosar's statistics are glittering: 2,002 completions (in 3,357 attempts) for 23,301 yards and 124 touchdowns with 87 interceptions. His statistics also are prominent among the Browns' individual records: 1,853 completions (in 3,150 attempts) for 21,904 yards, which rank second in franchise history to only Brian Sipe, and Kosar's 116 touchdown passes are third, behind 154 by Sipe, and 134 by Frank Ryan.

Despite the acrimony that caused his 1993 departure from his favorite team, Kosar's affection for Cleveland continued after his retirement three years later, and he joined Al Lerner and Carmen Policy in the formation of the new Browns in 1999.

Not one of Belichick's favorites

Leroy Hoard was not one of Bill Belichick's favorites – though he should have been, as the former University of Michigan running back has proven since the old Browns left Cleveland in 1995.

Oh, Hoard's record doesn't include Hall of Fame numbers, but there's no doubt he deserves more credit than he might be given in a casual glance at the numbers he has posted in the NFL.

Leroy Hoard

The first player (45th overall) selected by the Browns in the 1990 draft – they didn't have a first round pick that year – the 5-11, 225-pound Hoard distinguished himself as a tough, hard-nosed runner though he often played in the shadow of his higher-profile backfield teammates.

His one glaring fault was a penchant for fumbling, which might have been the reason Belichick seemed to have little faith in Hoard's ability. He fumbled 27 times in his six seasons with the Browns, including six as a rookie, and eight in 1994.

In 1990 and 1991, Kevin Mack and Eric Metcalf got the ball most of the time, as did Metcalf and Tommy Vardell in 1992 and 1993.

Hoard came into his own in 1994, when he was given more opportunities and responded by rushing for a career-high 890 yards (in 209 attempts for a 4.3 average), with two 100-yard games (and one of 99 yards).

It earned for Hoard a place on the AFC roster for the Pro Bowl. He also made the Dallas *Morning News* All-Pro team in 1994, and was picked as the co-MVP (with offensive tackle Tony Jones) by the Akron Browns Backers Club

Hoard also was a better-than-average receiver out of the backfield as his record of nine touchdown passes in 1991 would indicate. They are the second most in a season by a running back in NFL history, and the most by a member of the Browns.

In 1995, Belichick's final season as the Browns' head coach, and the team's last year in Cleveland, Hoard played in only 12 games because of injuries, though he still gained 547 yards in 136 carries (a 4.0 average).

"I don't know the reason," Hoard was quoted in the Cleveland *Plain Dealer* when asked why he wasn't utilized more. "There always seemed to be somebody else (who was featured in the Browns' running game)."

Whatever, when the Browns moved to Baltimore and became the "Ravens," Hoard started the season with them, but lasted only two games and was cut – but wasn't out of work for long, just three games.

He was signed by Carolina on October 1, though he played only three games for the Panthers and was released again on October 22 – but again, wasn't out of work for long.

After sitting at home for two weeks, Hoard received an offer from the Minnesota Vikings. "I jumped at it," he said. "I wanted to play, but especially I wanted to prove that the others (Baltimore and Charlotte) were wrong."

Which he has done, especially in the opinion of the Vikings.

In the final six games of the 1996 season Hoard rushed for 420 yards, and was Robert Smith's running mate in 1997 and 1998 - which should have sent a message to Belichick.

A very expensive controversy

John Wooten was not only a very good offensive lineman for the Browns; he also was a very outspoken guy.

Unfortunately – for Wooten as well as the Browns – he came to be better known for the latter than the former, and it turned out to be a factor in cutting short his professional football playing career.

As Wooten was quoted in a 1968 article on the Cleveland *Plain Dealer*: "I've worked hard every day of my life to make things better. I'll holler from the highest mountain … I'll hang on to what is right."

A fifth round draft choice in 1959 out of Colorado University, Wooten became involved in a racial controversy with Ross Fichtner in the summer of 1968.

It began when Wooten, a Pro Bowler in 1966 and 1967, accused Fichtner of discrimination against the team's black players by not inviting them to a golf outing.

Fichtner denied the charge, but the damage was done as the story exploded in the newspapers and fans of the Browns were taking sides in the ongoing dispute.

Subsequently, both Fichtner and Wooten were waived by the Browns, which resulted in a charge against Modell by Harry Edwards, a black sociology professor at San Jose (California) State College.

John Wooten

Edwards, commenting on Wooten's complaint of discrimination, and Art Modell's action in cutting both Wooten and Fichtner, accused the Browns owner of "white-listing" Wooten. Edwards said, "This should not be permitted to happen without our taking action."

Modell responded angrily, saying, "I won't dignify (Edwards') statement with a comment."

Then-NFL commissioner Pete Rozelle also became involved after a meeting with Wooten.

Rozelle would not comment on the situation, but admitted he encouraged Modell to resolve the controversy between, not only the two men, but also the two sides – black and white players.

The bottom line was that, not only were the Browns embarrassed as an organization, the ugly feud cost the team both players.

Modell said he tried to trade them, but could find no team willing to give up a draft choice or a player for either Fichtner, a defensive back, or Wooten.

The loss of Wooten was particularly distressing to Blanton Collier, then coach of the Browns. Wooten was an integral part of the offensive line that was regarded by many as the best in the NFL. Alongside Wooten at left guard was left tackle Dick Schafrath, with Fred Hoaglin at center, Gene Hickerson at right guard, and Monte Clark at right tackle.

The following season Fichtner wound up with the New Orleans Saints, though he appeared in only four games and was released at the end of the year.

Wooten was signed by the Washington Redskins, though he, too, saw little action, and neither played in the NFL after 1968.

Wooten also had been involved as one of five Browns players who held out as a group for better contracts in 1967, and after his retirement from the Redskins, became a player agent, and at one time reportedly represented "about 200 players."

Later, he returned to the NFL with the Dallas Cowboys as a scout.

'He had the best pair of hands'

They called him "Gluefingers," for obvious reasons.

"He had the best pair of hands for catching a football I've ever seen," Paul Brown once said about Dante Lavelli.

But Brown had another nickname for Lavelli, one that he said was more appropriate, which it might have been.

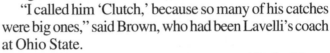

Dante Lavelli

"I called him 'Clutch,' because so many of his catches were big ones," said Brown, who had been Lavelli's coach at Ohio State.

It was Brown who switched the eventual Hall of Fame receiver from right halfback to end.

But it also is true that Lavelli came close to choosing a professional baseball career after high school in Hudson, Ohio before he ever went to Ohio State.

Lavelli was offered a minor league contract by the Detroit Tigers, and if he had signed it, instead of enrolling in college, the Browns - and professional football - probably would not have known one of the game's most gifted receivers.

It was Brown who hired Lavelli as one of the original Browns in 1946, after Lavelli came home from the Army and World War II, during which he saw combat duty in the "Battle of the Bulge."

There were about a dozen ends trying out for the team that first year, and Lavelli was among the least known. A couple of candidates named Alton Coppage, who had played with the Chicago Cardinals in the National Football League, and John Rokiskey, an All-American from Duquesne University, were the first starters. But not for long.

Each dropped passes early in the Browns first game and it wasn't long before Brown sent Lavelli in at right end.

Another unheralded candidate named Mac Speedie was inserted at left end, and just like that a legend was born.

Lavelli led the AAFC that first year with 40 receptions for 843 yards, a 21-yard average. He capped the season by hauling in the winning touchdown pass in the championship game as the Browns beat the New York Yankees, 14-9.

Lavelli was an AAFC all-star in each of the league's four seasons, and he continued his pass catching mastery after the Browns joined the NFL in 1950.

Lavelli caught 37 passes for 585 yards that first season and electrified the "old guard" by grabbing 11 passes and scoring two touchdowns in the Browns' 30-28 victory over the Los Angeles Rams in the championship game.

In his 11-year career that ended in 1956, Lavelli caught 386 passes for 6,488 yards, though only the NFL figures count in the record book: 244 receptions for 3,908 yards in seven years.

Lavelli made the All-NFL team in 1951 and 1953, started three of the first five Pro Bowl games, and was elected to the Hall of Fame in 1975.

At the induction ceremonies, Lin Houston, another original member of the Browns, had this to say about his ex-teammate: "Dante was the greatest guy at catching a ball in a crowd that I have ever seen. You never had to worry about him. He wanted to win in the worst way.

"And the tougher it got, the tougher he got."

'He belongs in the Hall of Fame'

When the Browns came into being in 1946 with the incomparable Otto Graham their quarterback in the All-America Football Conference, he – and coach Paul Brown – were blessed with two of the greatest receivers that ever played professional football.

One was Dante Lavelli, who was elected to the Hall of Fame in 1975.

The other, who was - his peers insist - as good as Lavelli, though their styles differed, was Mac Speedie, a 6-3, 205-pound receiver who'd been a 15th round draft choice of the Detroit Lions out of the University of Utah in 1942, though Uncle Sam beckoned first.

Speedie wasn't drafted higher because of a physical handicap he suffered as a youngster; a bone deficiency left him at the age of eight with a left leg that was two inches shorter than the right. It required him to wear a steel brace from ankle to hip and, each week for four years, an orthopedist would adjust a screw that stretched the leg.

But the handicap didn't prevent Speedie from participating in track, basketball and football in high school in Salt Lake City, Utah. According to reports, he ran the 100-yard dash in less than 10 seconds, and also was proficient as a hurdler.

Mac Speedie

As Brown said in the 1973 book, *The Cleveland Browns*, "(Speedie's) track experience taught him a wonderful sense of how to run, how to change speed and no one quite knew how to play against him because of this."

Speedie played for an Army team against Brown's Great Lakes Naval Training Station during the war and when the coach formed the Browns, Speedie was one of the first players he contacted. Speedie quickly signed and, paired with Lavelli, gave the Browns a passing attack unmatched in the AAFC, and later, if only briefly, in the NFL.

"Lavelli had one of the strongest pairs of hands I've ever seen," Brown said. "When he went up for a pass with a defender you could almost always count on him coming back down with the ball. Nobody could take it away from him once he had it.

"Speedie was perhaps a more instinctive receiver and more deceptive. He was so tall that when running at top speed, he seemed to be gliding easily. That's why so many defensive backs were fooled. If I played against him, I might have considered guarding him with three men in some combination. Everything he did was instinctive."

Speedie scored 25 touchdowns on 211 receptions for 2,554 yards in his four years in the AAFC, and was equally proficient in the NFL from 1950-52 (with 138 receptions for 2,048 yards and nine touchdowns). He was the NFL's leading receiver in 1952 with 62 catches for 911 yards and five touchdowns, including a club record 11 for 157 yards in a 28-13 victory over the Chicago Cardinals on November 9.

Speedie was a Pro Bowler in 1951, and won All-Pro honors in 1952, then left the Browns – some said because of a disagreement with Paul Brown - and resumed his career in the Canadian Football League for the next several years. He died at 73 in 1993.

A final tribute was paid to the talented receiver by former teammate, defensive back Tommy James, who said, "Mac Speedie should be in the Hall of Fame with Lavelli. I covered the guy every day in practice (and) I never saw a better receiver than Mac Speedie."

55

Well deserved and long overdue

When Ozzie Newsome was finally elected to the Pro Football Hall of Fame in 1999 it was, in the opinion of most observers - and certainly Browns' fans who reveled in his contributions from 1978-90 - an honor well-deserved and long overdue.

Three times previously the gifted and popular tight end was bypassed by the Hall of Fame electorate, which was difficult to understand in view of his outstanding statistics.

Newsome's 662 receptions for 7,980 yards and 47 touchdowns established him as the NFL's all-time leading pass-catching tight end, placed him fourth among all of the NFL's all-time receivers, and he also is the No. 1 receiver in the history of the Browns.

Ozzie Newsome

What's more, Newsome holds the Browns' top three single season reception marks with 89 in both 1983 and 1984, and 69 in 1981; his 150 consecutive games with at least one reception is the second longest in NFL history; remarkably, he caught 557 consecutive passes without a fumble; was voted All-Pro in 1979 and 1984, and played in the Pro Bowl in 1981, 1984, and 1985; and was the first rookie ever selected by the Cleveland Touchdown Club as the Browns' "Offensive Player of the Year (1978)."

Now vice president of player personnel for the Baltimore Ravens, the franchise that was the Browns in Cleveland from 1946-95, Newsome's presenter at his induction into the Hall of Fame was former teammate Calvin Hill.

"There might be some people disenchanted that I'm with Baltimore, but I only played football for two teams – the University of Alabama and the Cleveland Browns," Newsome said at the time of his election to the Hall of Fame. "I am a Cleveland Brown. I wore that orange helmet."

Newsome shrugged off having to wait four years to be elected, saying, "The longer it takes, the more you appreciate it." And, as Hill said, "The Hall of Fame has definitely made itself a better place because of Ozzie."

Newsome's value to the Browns was well expressed by Sam Rutigliano, who was coach of the team when Newsome was drafted, and the man who recommended that he switch positions, from wide receiver, which he was in college, to tight end.

"Every game plan we put together (during Rutigliano's tenure from 1978-84), we said, 'What are they (the opposing team) going to do to take away Ozzie?' that's how much he meant to us.

"His election to the Hall of Fame is well deserved, and long overdue."

Newsome was the Browns' second No. 1 draft choice (and 23rd overall) out of the University of Alabama where legendary then-coach Paul "Bear" Bryant called him "the best end I ever coached." It also was Bryant who nicknamed Newsome the "Wizard of Oz," and his acquisition has to be one of the best moves ever made by the Browns.

To obtain the draft right to pick Newsome the Browns in 1977 traded quarterback Mike Phipps to the Chicago Bears.

When he first joined the Browns, Newsome was quoted in the Cleveland *Plain Dealer*: "A preacher once told me, 'Whatever you do, be the best at it.'

And now there can be no doubt Newsome was just that. The best.

The man who knew them all

Nobody knew the Browns better - more intimately, nor could relate to their physical well-being better - than Dr. Vic Ippolito, who was the team physician from its beginning in 1946 until he semi-retired in 1978.

"Dr. Vic," as everyone knows him, continued on the job through the 1980s as "consulting physician" with Dr. John Bergfeld.

He probably saw more Browns games than anybody - "every game until I missed one on the West Coast in 1989," he said. And each one is still a special thrill.

The reason Dr. Vic could relate to the players so well is because he undoubtedly would have been one of them if the Browns had been organized, say, 10 or 12 years earlier.

Ippolito was one of the greatest athletes in the history of Western Reserve University and the old "Big Four," the unofficial but highly competitive conference in Cleveland at the time.

It included Baldwin-Wallace College, John Carroll University and Case Tech, in addition to Western Reserve.

Dr. Vic Ippolito

As Ippolito recalled, "There were some great teams , some great games and some great athletes."

Ippolito was one of the latter after starring in football, basketball and baseball at Cleveland Heights High School.

He was a fleet and shifty running back - they were called "halfbacks" then - and also played quarterback while setting a flock of records at WRU. He was All-Ohio three years, and also played basketball and ran track before graduating in 1933.

Ippolito graduated from Western Reserve medical school in 1936 and entered private practice. When Mickey McBride formed the Browns, Dr. Vic was one of the first men he appointed as a club official, after Paul Brown was hired.

"Jim Brown was the greatest player I ever saw, and probably the strongest, too," Ippolito once said. "Brown missed one quarter in nine years of play, and even then he didn't want to stay out. He had a cerebral concussion and was dazed. I wouldn't let him go back in the game. To top it all, I never heard him complain (about pain)."

Dr. Vic called Otto Graham, the Browns' first and greatest quarterback, "one of my all time favorites," and also praised former stars Mike McCormack, Gene Hickerson and Doug Dieken. "McCormack amazed me by playing a game three weeks after undergoing (major) surgery on his knee for a torn cartilage.

"I'm also positive that Hickerson played the last four years of his career with a torn cartilage in his knee that he refused to have x-rayed.

"And Dieken could have played in any era. He'd constantly tell me this hurts, or that hurts, but he always played."

Of Paul Brown, Ippolito said, "He was a great innovator. He started all the things that are now common practice in coaching. He made football the sport that it is today.

"Whether you liked him personally or not, you had to put Paul Brown right up at the top of the list of all-time great football coaches."

Take it from the man who knew them all better than anyone.

A very special 'unsung hero'

Sam Rutigliano, when he was coaching the Browns in 1983, once remarked after studying films of a 30 - 7 victory over Pittsburgh: "You should see the job Robert (E.) Jackson did on Jack Lambert. It was the best anybody in the league ever did.

"If I were a sportswriter, I'd write about Jackson, the unsung hero, after the game."

Robert E. Jackson

Jackson really was an unsung hero almost constantly during - but even before - his career as an offensive lineman for the Browns from 1975 through 1985.

Robert (he doesn't like to be called "Bob") was a high school quarterback in Charlotte, North Carolina where his twin brother Kenny was a wide receiver.

Jackson never made an all-conference team in his life, not in high school or at Duke University, nor with the Browns.

But his Browns' head coaches - Forrest Gregg, Rutigliano and Marty Schottenheimer - all considered the 6-5, 250-pound Jackson something special.

"Robert is really a Roger Dangerfield ... nobody, but nobody recognizes him," Doug Dieken once said about Jackson. They played alongside each other for 10 years and, as Dieken also said of Jackson, "He was like my third arm."

Jackson was recruited by Duke as a quarterback, but was switched to tight end as a sophomore, then to center and played offensive tackle as a senior.

When the National Football League held its 1975 college draft, Jackson expected to be picked in the ninth or tenth round.

But he wasn't. Not in any of the 17 rounds as 442 other players were selected.

In fact, Jackson wasn't drafted at all.

"I kind of lost myself for a few days," he said. "It was embarrassing to get built up like that and not get drafted."

By the time Jackson's wounded pride was soothed, a Browns scout was knocking on his door, offering a contract - though it was really only a tryout.

Jackson jumped at the opportunity and, in his first scrimmage in minicamp, he was matched against Mack Mitchell, a defensive end who'd been the Browns' No. 1 draft choice.

"I was scared to death, but I did pretty well against him and I felt confident I could play in the NFL," said Jackson.

Gregg and his assistants were confident too.

"(Jackson) was overlooked in the draft because he'd lost some weight and scouts thought he was too small at 220 pounds," said Gregg.

It didn't help Robert E.'s image when the Browns drafted another Robert Jackson, this one Robert L., No. 1 in 1978.

Thereafter, Robert L., a hard-hitting linebacker, was the Jackson who got most of the publicity, though he was forced into retirement prematurely after suffering a severe knee injury.

But Robert E. went on and on, though mostly anonymously because, as the old saying goes, offensive linemen go unnoticed until they make a mistake, and Jackson didn't make many.

He played 160 games - 126 as a starter - in 11 seasons, which makes you wonder why Jackson was so often an 'unsung hero."

A very fortunate broken arm

Warren Lahr suffered a broken arm in an automobile accident during his first training camp with the Browns in 1948, and it might have been the best thing that happened for his career.

Then a rookie who had been signed as a free agent out of Western Reserve University, Lahr was trying to make the team as a T-formation quarterback.

It was a position held quite securely by Otto Graham, and the backup job belonged to another veteran, Cliff Lewis.

The broken arm eliminated Lahr, but he came back the following year as a defensive back and won a job.

Lahr became a starter by the middle of that 1949 season, and was a regular until his retirement 11 years later, in 1960.

Lahr held the Browns record for career interceptions - 40 for 530 yards and five touchdowns in 10 seasons (only National Football League games counted) - until Thom Darden came along and, also in 10 years, picked off 45 passes for 820 yards and two touchdowns.

As a college quarterback, Lahr was called a "passing sensation" by Tom Davies, his coach at Western Reserve. Lahr played at WRU in 1942, and resumed his collegiate career in 1946 and 1947 after serving in the Navy during World War II.

Warren Lahr

In the spring of 1948, when Lahr was thinking about what he might do after graduation, something else happened that had a profound effect on his future. Lahr was offered a contract by the Pittsburgh Steelers.

Lahr was eligible to sign with a professional team because he had not been drafted, and his college class graduated while he was serving in the Navy.

The $3,000 offer from the Steelers looked good to Lahr, one of nine children in a family from the coal mining community of West Wyoming, Pennsylvania, and he was leaning toward accepting it when the father of a WRU teammate interceded.

The man told Lahr he could get him a tryout with the Browns, who were then dominating the All-America Football Conference. They'd already won the chamionship in 1946 and 1947, and would win it again in 1948 and 1949, as well as the NFL title in 1950.

Lahr thought about it and realized he'd have a better chance with the Browns, and rejected the Steelers' contract.

"I shudder to think how different things might have been if my friend's father had not come along and changed my mind," Lahr said later.

It proved to be a wise decision as Lahr became one of the great defensive backs in the NFL - thanks, of course, to that auto accident that broke his arm and eliminated him as a quarterback candidate.

After his retirement, Lahr became a television analyst on Browns' games in 1963, a job he held through the 1967 season.

Two years later, at the age of 45, Lahr suffered a heart attack and died.

One of his former coaches, Blanton Collier, paid Lahr this tribute in his eulogy: "He was a great athlete, a great competitor and a gentleman. He's the kind of fellow you'd like to have for a son."

Like an invisible albatross

It was during the college draft of 1973 and the Browns, who would pick eighth, one notch behind the Cincinnati Bengals, were holding their collective breath, hoping the wide receiver they desperately wanted would still be there.

At least, that's what owner Art Modell and then-coach Nick Skorich insisted when Cincinnati took Isaac Curtis, leaving Steve Holden for the Browns, thinking – or at least *claiming* - they had "stolen" Holden from Paul Brown, then coach of the Bengals.

Steve Holden

When their cheering subsided, Modell all but predicted Holden, who'd played his college football at Arizona State University, was surely headed for the Hall of Fame.

In fact, as reported in the Cleveland *Press* under Bill Scholl's byline four years later: "The Browns ... put Holden in a rating category comparable to O.J. Simpson in 1969, and ahead of Terry Bradshaw in 1970. He was classified as a 'can't miss' athlete, and one member of the (organization) classified him as a super star.

"So what happened? Well, nothing much. Holden is in the hospital and may never return. The Browns aren't saying it, but placing Holden on a reserve list with a non-football illness ... could be the first step in his departure.

"Waivers must be asked before Holden can rejoin the Browns and it seems unlikely every one of the 27 other NFL teams will pass him up. One claim and he's gone after recovering from emergency appendectomy surgery."

The story proved to be accurate. Holden was claimed – ironically by the Bengals – though he played only six games for them, without catching even one pass, and was let go.

In his four seasons with the Browns, from 1973-76, Holden caught a total of 62 balls for 927 yards and four touchdowns. He was used almost exclusively as a kick returner in 1976 when, also ironically, he set a then-club record by taking 31 punts and also led the team with 19 kickoffs.

On the other hand, Curtis, the wide receiver from San Diego State, the one the Browns said they didn't want, went on to play with distinction for Cincinnati for 12 seasons, through 1984, catching a total of 416 passes for 7,101 yards and 53 touchdowns.

What's more, Curtis made the All-NFL team as a rookie, and again each year through 1976, for four in a row, and was a major contributor to the Bengals in their drive to Super Bowl XVI, after the 1981 season. It always was the inevitable comparison with Curtis, like an invisible albatross around his neck, that bothered Holden the most.

After his career ended, though Curtis was still going strong, Holden was quoted on the subject in the Akron *Beacon Journal*.

"You can't compare people unless you put them in the same situation," Holden was quoted as saying. "What would Isaac Curtis have done if he had been drafted by the Browns; what would I have done if I had been drafted by the Bengals?"

There is some logic, of course, to what Holden said.

But, in retrospect, with the complete records of both players under scrutiny, there is no doubt that the Browns were terribly wrong – or guilty of some very misleading cheerleading – when they insisted that Steve Holden was the player they wanted, not Isaac Curtis.

Bernie's personal coach-caddy

In the vernacular of professional football, Gary Danielson didn't throw passes, they were "ducks" and "wobblers," and nobody ever referred to him as a "classic" quarterback.

But neither did Browns fans criticize Danielson for lacking guts or leadership or any of the intangibles that constitute - again in the vernacular of pro football - a "winner."

Indeed, Danielson was a winner during his all too brief career with the Browns after he was saved from NFL limbo where he was rusting out with the Detroit Lions.

The Browns got him in 1985, upon the arrival of Bernie Kosar out of college, and with the realization that Paul McDonald, their quarterback in 1984, was not the answer, either as a starter or backup.

Gary Danielson

Danielson, envisioned by then-coach Marty Schottenheimer as Kosar's personal coach and confidante, was pressed into full-time duty on several occasions in 1985 and responded remarkably well. He shares credit with Kosar for leading the Browns to the AFC Central Division championship and into the playoffs, though they lost in the first round to Miami, 24-21.

Danielson is best remembered for his fourth quarter performance in a 35-33 victory over the New York Giants after replacing Kosar and the Browns losing, 33-21. Danielson ralled the Browns to two touchdowns for the victory that sealed the Browns first trip to the playoffs in three years.

As then-general manager Ernie Accorsi commented, "I don't think there was any question we were not even close to a playoff team (in 1985) without Danielson. And, in my experience in this league, I've never been around an athlete or professional at any higher level than Gary."

Danielson's performance, and the maturing of Kosar, considerably brightened the Browns' hopes for 1986. But that was before disaster struck Danielson.

Apparently fully recovered from shoulder surgery he underwent seven months earlier, Danielson sustained a fracture and dislocation of his left ankle in the third quarter of a hollow, 25-22, victory over the Los Angeles Raiders in the final pre-season game.

Kosar, by his own admission, was "devastated" after Danielson's injury. "He has had such an impact on my life ... hopefully, he'll be back to lead me and to coach me."

Danielson was, though not until 1987, but then suffered another broken ankle in the second game of the 1988 season. It proved to be the end of his playing career and the following spring Danielson, then 37, was waived by the Browns.

It all began for the gutsy quarterback on a low note in 1974 when he graduated from Purdue University but wasn't drafted by an NFL team. Danielson joined the World Football League and played three seasons for two franchises before that league folded.

Left without a team, Danielson took a job in a sheet metal plant, then was invited for a tryout with his hometown Detroit Lions in 1977. He made the team and the next eight seasons was in and out of the lineup, alternating with Eric Hipple.

When the Lions traded with Buffalo for Joe Ferguson in 1985, the Browns jumped at the chance to get Danielson as a caddy for Kosar.

And though, in his four years with the Browns, Danielson played in only 16 games because of injuries, his impact was great due to his field leadership and close relationship with Kosar.

'The best ... prospect in 15 years'

The date was July 28, 1977, and the Browns were in the process of winding up a routine, training camp practice session.

Then-coach Forrest Gregg was smiling as he observed Robert L. Jackson, a.k.a. "Stonewall," the middle linebacker out of Texas A&M University who'd been their first round draft choice and 17th overall that spring.

Robert L. Jackson

As Gregg reached for his whistle to end the session, the offense ran one more play. Quarterback Brian Sipe handed off to a running back who hit the middle of the line. Almost simultaneously Jackson slammed in to the point of attack.

There was a scream of pain and, when the players unpiled, Stonewall was writhing on the ground, his left knee bent grotesquely, his face twisted in agony.

Trainer Leo Murphy hustled on to the field and needed only a cursory examination to know that Jackson was seriously injured.

Jackson was carted off the field and his leg packed in ice. Later, at the Cleveland Clinic, Dr. John Bergfeld issued the bad news. It was, he said, the worst knee injury to a football player he'd ever seen.

Owner Art Modell, who was there when Jackson went down, said in a Cleveland *Plain Dealer* story, "It's a terrible blow to the entire Browns' organization. Jackson is the best defensive prospect I've seen here in 15 years."

And so, instead of bolstering the Browns' defense as expected when he was drafted, Jackson spent the season in rehabilitation.

Greg Pruitt, who knew Jackson because they came from the same neighborhood in Houston, Texas, said of his injured teammate: "I thought he had the ability to dominate an entire offense. He was strong enough to take on the offensive line, and fast enough to catch the running backs. Now ... well, who knows?" he was quoted in a story in the Cleveland *Press*.

"I thought my career might be over," Jackson said. "I thought about it everyday. I had a long talk with my parents and they asked me whether I wanted to play anymore. I decided I did, if I could. It was a disgusting year, watching road games on television and going to the Stadium on crutches. Until then I'd had nothing worse than a pulled hamstring, and that kept me out only one week."

When he finally was able to return, in July 1978, then-coach Sam Rutigliano redesigned the entire defensive concept to better utilize Jackson.

Rutigliano switched from the traditional four down linemen-three linebackers alignment, to three down linemen-four linebackers in order to keep Jackson and veteran Dick "Bam-Bam" Ambrose on the field at the same time.

But then, almost a year later, again in training camp, Jackson re-injured his left knee. This time, although painful, it was diagnosed as only a matter of "breaking adhesions" that had formed from the original injury. Jackson missed only the first two games of 1978.

But when he returned for the next 14 games – and through the next four seasons, three with the Browns and part of 1982 with Atlanta – Jackson never again played as had been expected, and "the finest defensive prospect" retired, his football career prematurely ended.

The 'Special Deliverer'

He was the original "Special Delivery" Jones, and the nickname was perfect.

Edgar Jones realty "carried the mail" for the Browns in the early days of the franchise, as the sportswriters used to chronicle the deeds of Paul Brown's and Mickey McBride's team.

From their inception in 1946 through 1949, the Browns dominated the All America Football Conference, and Special Delivery Jones was one of the reasons they were good.

Jones was joined in the Browns' first string backfield that first season in the AAFC by, of course, quarterback Otto Graham, fullback Marion Motley, and halfback Don Greenwood, who had jumped to the new team from the Rams when they moved out of Cleveland to Los Angeles.

The Browns' four year record in the AAFC was 52-4-3, including victories in all four championship games, before they were invited to join the National Football League in 1950.

Unfortunately for Jones and the Browns, he suffered a severely dislocated shoulder on October 14, 1949, as they were beating the Los Angeles Dons, 61-14. He was advised to retire to avoid further, possibly permanent physical damage.

Edgar "Special Delivery" Jones

Jones, 5-10 and 195-pounds, played his collegiate football at the University of Pittsburgh, and served four years in the Navy during World War II.

He ran from what was then called the left halfback position in the conventional T formation backfield, and also played defensive back in those days of single platoon football.

Jones usually got the ball when the Browns were in third and short yardage situations, and usually the hard-nosed running back got what was needed for a first down.

In his four seasons with the Browns, Special Delivery gained 1,509 yards in 289 carries for a 5.22 average, and scored 18 touchdowns.

Jones also was an accomplished pitcher and often expressed regret that he couldn't combine a professional baseball career with football.

In a 1947 story in the Cleveland *News*, Jones is quoted as saying, "I am convinced I can pitch in the big leagues ... I can outpitch about five guys on the Indians' staff."

(That was the season Bob Feller won 20 games for the Indians, but nobody else won more than 11.)

When Jones was 17, he was on an all-star team picked to face the then-famous "Gashouse Gang" St. Louis Cardinals in an exhibition game in Scranton, Pennsylvania.

"We lost," Jones said. "But they only got four hits off me in three innings."

The next year, 1939, Jones was given a spring training tryout with the Cincinnati Reds.

They offered him a minor league contract, but Jones' parents encouraged him to accept a football scholarship to Pitt instead.

He did, and became one of the Panthers' greatest stars, before going into the Navy.

Jones was going on 26 when the war ended, hardly an age to begin a minor league baseball career, and he jumped at the chance to join the fledgling Browns.

And thus began the legend of the original Special Delivery Jones - the only regret being the shoulder injury that prevented him from graduating with the Browns into the NFL.

The 'mad dog' was a bust

When Mike Junkin was drafted No. 1, fifth overall, out of Duke University in 1987, the Browns said he played "like a mad dog in a meat market."

It is a statement that will live in infamy, and probably hound Junkin forever because, as it turned out, he was a bust and his selection will be long remembered as one of the worst in Browns history.

Mike Junkin

In fairness to the 6-3, 238-pound linebacker it must be pointed out that he was hampered by a severe injury to his wrist that cut short his rookie season, and then hurt his knee in 1988.

Junkin, who was extensively scouted during his outstanding career at Duke by Dom Anile, played only fifteen games for the Browns - four in 1987 and eleven in 1988. He was traded in 1989 to the Kansas City Chiefs and appeared in only five games for them that season, then was cut loose and never played again in the NFL.

While it was Anile who was credited – or, perhaps, should be *blamed* – for rating Junkin so highly, Marty Schottenheimer, then coach of the Browns, also endorsed the rookie when he joined the team.

"I have no doubt that Mike Junkin will be an excellent player in this league," Schottenheimer was quoted in the Browns' media guide.

Ernie Accorsi, then general manager of the Browns, also predicted a bright future for Junkin, saying, "Wait until this kid buckles his chinstrap. He plays like a crazy man. (The fans) are going to love him."

But they didn't – and to make the selection of Junkin even costlier, the Browns paid a very dear price for him.

They packaged All-Pro (1983, 1986) and four time Pro Bowl linebacker Chip Banks (who'd been a first round pick himself in 1982), along with their first and second round choices in 1987, in a trade with San Diego to move up high enough to get the player Anile called a "mad dog."

What's more, in a 1989 story that appeared in the Cleveland *Plain Dealer*, it was reported that the Browns picked Junkin "with full knowledge he had tested positive for steroids," which caused other NFL teams to exclude him from their plans.

And when the Browns finally decided they'd made a mistake, they traded Junkin to the Chiefs, then coached by Schottenheimer, for a fifth round draft pick. It was used to select receiver Vernon Joines whose NFL career consisted of 20 games in 1989 and 1990.

Before joining the Browns in 1987, Junkin was a holdout for nearly four months, finally signing on August 10 for a reported $1.8 million over four seasons.

Junkin's wrist injury, a chip fracture, was suffered on November 1, in the Browns' seventh game, a 27-24 loss in San Diego, when he was blocked by the Chargers' Pete Holohan.

He underwent an eight hour operation, during which steel pins were inserted to repair the wrist on November 13, and didn't play again until the following season when he went down again, this time with a knee injury in the 12th game.

It ended Junkin's disappointing career with the Browns and, obviously, he didn't fare much better for the Chiefs, appearing in only five games for them in 1989, and never played in the NFL again.

Tougher than pulling teeth

The date was October 10, 1976, the Browns were playing Pittsburgh and losing, 10-6, in the second quarter of a game at the Stadium, when Brian Sipe got hurt.

Earlier that season Mike Phipps, who'd been the starter, had gone down so there was nobody else but Dave Mays.

He was a rookie, and one of the first black quarterbacks in the National Football League.

After Sipe got hurt, Mays said, "I was sorry for him, but glad for myself to get the opportunity, I hope it can be the start of something good for me."

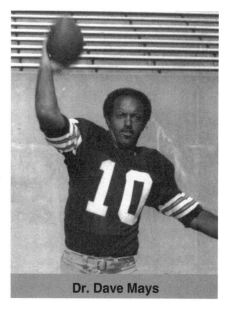

Dr. Dave Mays

It almost was. After replacing Sipe, Mays engineered a comeback that won the game, 18-16.

It was the last defeat the two-time Super Bowl champion Steelers would suffer that season.

A week later, however, Sipe started against Atlanta, and Mays played only a couple more times the rest of that season.

When 1977 rolled around, Mays was still on the roster in a backup role, though his position was a little better because Phipps had been traded to Chicago for a first round draft choice in 1978.

With Phipps gone, Sipe was the starter, but again was injured in the ninth game of the season.

So Mays again came off the bench and again played well, completing 17 of 32 passes for 296 yards and three touchdowns, although, this time, Pittsburgh prevailed, 35-31.

A week later, with Sipe still hurting, Mays opened at quarterback and the Browns beat the New York Giants, 21-7.

That game, however, was to be the only one Mays ever started in the NFL.

When Sipe was sound, Coach Forrest Gregg put him back in the lineup and, once again, Mays took a seat on the bench.

When the 1977 season ended, Mays' statistics showed 67 completions and six touchdowns in 121 attempts, though he also was intercepted 10 times.

The following year, with Sipe now blossoming into one of the NFL's premier quarterbacks, Mays was confronted with even more competition.

The Browns had picked quarterback-punter Johnny Evans in the second round of the college draft, and Mays also had to beat out veteran Terry Luck and rookie Mark Miller to preserve his spot on the roster.

He couldn't, and was waived in training camp.

It was a great disappointment for Mays, who had broken all the passing records at Texas Southern. He also had played two years for Shreveport in the World Football League before joining the Browns as a free agent punter-placekicker-quarterback.

Upon leaving the Browns, Mays signed with Buffalo and served as the Bills' backup quarterback in 1978 and 1979, then retired from football to become Dr. David W. Mays, a dentist, with offices in Cleveland.

As for the trade that sent Phipps to Chicago, the Browns used the first round draft choice in 1978 to select a wide receiver from Alabama who was switched to tight end, by the name of Ozzie Newsome.

To Cleveland with misgivings

Mike McCormack's first professional football game was against the Browns in 1951. Afterwards he told reporters, "I hope I never see that team again."

The disheartened rookie was then a linebacker and offensive lineman for the New York Yankees, a team that didn't last long in the National Football League, though McCormack did.

Mike McCormack

And McCormack, who played his college football at the University of Kansas, also saw a lot of the team he hoped to never see again.

McCormack saw so much of the Browns - though his perspective was quite different - he was elected to the Hall of Fame in 1984.

The Yankees franchise, which was turned back to the NFL and moved to Dallas in 1952, merged with Baltimore in 1953.

McCormack, at that time, was spending two years (1952, 1953) in the Army, and while he was serving Uncle Sam, he was traded to the Browns in one of the NFL's biggest ever deals, and joined his new team in 1954.

Fifteen players were involved in the trade, 10 sent by the Browns to Baltimore for five, including, primarily, McCormack and defensive tackle Don Colo. The Browns also received linebacker Tom Catlin, defensive back John Petibon and offensive lineman Herschel Forester in the deal.

Defensive backs Don Shula, who became one of the NFL's most successful coaches, and Carl Tasseff, both former John Carroll stars, were among the players traded to Baltimore.

When McCormack joined the Browns the plan was for him to replace the retired Bill Willis at middle guard/linebacker, which he did, but only for that one season.

Then McCormack was switched to offensive right tackle, a position he played spectacularly well for the next eight years.

And during McCormack's career with the Browns, they reached the NFL championship game four times, winning the title twice.

"I went (to Cleveland) with some misgivings because I didn't know what to expect," McCormack was quoted in a book about the Browns. "I heard that (Coach Paul Brown) was a real taskmaster ... but my admiration for him grew every year."

McCormack, who became an NFL head coach himself after serving as an assistant to Vince Lombardi and George Allen, compared them with Brown.

"(Each) had such great belief in what he was trying to do and his method of doing it.

"There's Paul (Brown), his organization and great belief in basic fundamentals. If you're well prepared fundamentally and do the things the right way, you're going to win.

"Lombardi's method was motivation and condition. He believed that if he drove you to the brink and had you in such great physical condition, you're going to win.

"Allen believed in experience, that if you get the experienced player who has made the mistakes elsewhere, he is not going to make them now, because he has learned from them.

"All three systems ... were very different, but they're all the same in a way," said McCormack.

All were winners - as was McCormack for the Browns, even though he once hoped he'd never see them again.

When perseverance prevailed

When the Browns won the AFC Central Division in 1980 and were headed - as the so-called "experts" predicted - to their first Super Bowl, a key contributor to the team's success, though often unnoticed, was Tom DeLeone, then one of the NFL's premier centers.

That's because centers, like baseball umpires, usually are inconspicuous until they make a mistake. Then everybody pays attention.

The usually-anonymous DeLeone was picked by his peers on the All-Pro team in 1979 and 1980, which in itself was a remarkable achievement considering the adversity he had to surmount en route to becoming a star for the Browns.

By his own admission, the only reason he made the football team at his junior high school in Kent, Ohio "was because the coach didn't believe in cutting anybody," DeLeone was quoted. "About 90 guys came out for practice ... football was big stuff. (But) I didn't make the traveling squad. I never even got a game jersey."

Tom DeLeone

But perseverance paid off for DeLeone and, by the time he reached Roosevelt High School in Kent he took over as the starting center after five games in 1966. That was his junior year and the regular center had been kicked off the team. DeLeone kept the job as a senior and - again, by his own admission - was "shocked" to receive several offers of scholarships, including one from Ohio State.

Woody Hayes, then coach of the Buckeyes, sold Tom on going to Ohio State.

"(Hayes) told my mom he guaranteed I would get an education and graduate. He told me I'd be playing regular in my sophomore year, and everything happened the way he said. He never lied to me," said DeLeone, outspoken in his respect for the late coach.

DeLeone won All-America honors and captained the Buckeyes in his senior year, during which he suffered a knee injury that required surgery, and missed the final game.

But it didn't deter the Cincinnati Bengals from picking DeLeone in the fifth round of the 1972 draft.

DeLeone didn't play much for the Bengals in 1972 and 1973, only as a snapper for punts and field goals, and in 1974 when he was too active - in coach Paul Brown's opinion - in the NFL strike during training camp, DeLeone was traded to Atlanta.

Upon joining the Falcons, DeLeone sustained several physical problems and, discouraged, left the team. When he returned later that season, he was waived and claimed by Houston. But, after only four days with the Oilers, he was waived again.

That's when the Browns offered DeLeone a job. He jumped at the chance and, midway through the 1974 season - which had begun with so much frustration - DeLeone took over as the starting center, replacing John Demarie, who was switched to guard..

But again, DeLeone was stricken with more adversity. His wife Susie, whom Tom married earlier that year, was found to have cancer. She died two years later, in 1976.

DeLeone continued as the Browns regular center for the next 10 years, retiring at age 34 after the 1984 season.

He was voted the "George Halas Award" as the NFL's most courageous player in 1976, an honor that was well deserved, for more reasons than one.

The Browns' first quarterback

Cliff Lewis always will be the answer to two of the Browns' most fascinating trivia questions.

Question No. 1: Who was the starting quarterback in the Browns' first game, a 44-0 victory over the Miami Seahawks in 1946?

Question No. 2: Who threw the first touchdown pass in the Browns' history?

Cliff Lewis

The logical response to both would be Otto Graham, who starred for the Browns from their inception through 1955, was elected to the Hall of Fame in 1965, and is regarded by many as the best quarterback to ever play football.

However, Lewis, a charter member of the team that dominated the All-America Football Conference and then the National Football League, was much more than the key to a couple of trivia questions.

It was Lewis, a former Lakewood (Ohio) High School, Duke University and Fleet City (U.S. Navy) quarterback who took the first snap from center Moe Scarry in that first game in the AAFC, September 6, 1946, in front of 60,135 fans in the Stadium.

In fact, Lewis was the starting quarterback in the first three games the Browns played, all of them victories - over Chicago, 20-6, and Buffalo, 28-0, in addition to beating Miami.

Graham took over as the starting quarterback in the fourth game, a 24-7 triumph over New York, and was the Browns regular quarterback in every game thereafter for 10 years.

For the record, it also was Lewis, nicknamed "The Rivet" because of his stature (5-11, 165 pounds) and toughness, who passed - 19 yards to Mac Speedie - for the first touchdown in Browns history.

Of course, there's more to those stories than meets the eye.

Graham, an outstanding single wing tailback at Northwestern University, missed the first few weeks of training camp because he was playing for the College All-Stars in their annual exhibition game against the 1945 NFL champion Los Angeles Rams.

Lewis, also a defensive back, started those first three games because Graham wasn't familiar enough with the T-formation offense installed by Paul Brown.

But Graham quickly learned all there was to know and took over at quarterback.

Lewis became the Browns' regular safety, though he occasionally spelled Graham at quarterback, and returned punts and kickoffs until his retirement in 1952.

Lewis' statistics are interesting, if unspectacular. In six seasons with the Browns, he completed 30 of 71 passes for 524 yards and seven touchdowns, with five interceptions. He was 11-for-30 for 125 yards and one TD in 1946.

Lewis also returned 76 punts for 548 yards, 14 kickoffs for 288 yards and intercepted 30 passes, including a high of nine in 1948.

Trivia buffs also will find it interesting that Graham was the starting safety in the Browns' first game, again because of his unfamiliarity with the offense.

And for the clincher, which should stump even the most rabid Browns' fan, Graham also intercepted five passes in 1946, and seven in his career as a part-time safety that ended in 1950, when he concentrated solely on playing quarterback.

The audacious quarterback

Milt Plum's legacy - more so than his passing - always will be that he had the audacity to criticize Paul Brown.

In a Cleveland *Plain Dealer* article on February 18, 1962, Plum said that, because of Brown's iron-fisted hold on the reins of the team:

• The Browns were in a rut and would never win another championship;

• Team spirit and morale were at an all time low; and

• The quarterback, Plum himself, was no more than a "mechanical man" because he did not have the authority to change plays at the line of scrimmage.

What Plum's criticism did, however, was get him traded.

Exactly 40 days later Brown dealt Plum and two other players (running back Tom Watkins and linebacker Dave Lloyd) to Detroit to re-acquire quarterback Jim Ninowski, defensive end Bill Glass and running back Howard (Hopalong) Cassady.

It also helped develop another significant episode in the history of the Browns - the firing of Paul Brown as coach nine months later, after the team failed to win the National Football League championship for the seventh year in a row.

Milt Plum

That also was the major complaint about Plum's leadership. In his four seasons as the Browns' quarterback the team made it to the playoffs only once, and never to a championship game, even though he was the NFL's top-ranked passer in 1960 and 1961.

In fact, Plum's 110.4 statistical rating was the highest in the history of the NFL at that time.

Plum, who played his collegiate football at Penn State, was a second round draft choice (behind only Jim Brown) in the 1957 lottery, and backed up Tommy O'Connell that season.

Plum took over as the Browns starting quarterback in 1958 and was No. 1 through 1961.

And while his four-year statistics were impressive - 586 completions in 1,007 attempts for 8,324 yards and 64 touchdowns with only 34 interceptions - the Browns weren't terribly successful.

They went 9-3 and were one-and-out in the playoffs in 1958, and were 7-5 in 1959, 8-3-1 in 1960, and 8-5-1 in 1961.

Ironically, the deal that brought Ninowski as Plum's projected replacement, resulted in the installation of Frank Ryan as the starting quarterback, a job he held through 1967.

Ninowski, originally the Browns' backup in 1958 and 1959, was traded to the Lions in 1960. After returning to Cleveland to replace Plum, Ninowski broke his collarbone in the eighth game in 1962 and never started again for the Browns.

Ryan, who had been acquired from the Los Angeles Rams as Ninowski's caddy, then took over the team and quarterbacked the Browns through 1967, during which they played in the NFL championship game twice (1964 and 1965).

Plum spent the next six years in Detroit, alternating with Earl Morrall, then played one season with the Rams, and another with the New York Giants before retiring in 1970.

But his legacy always will be that he's the guy - perhaps the *only* one - who had the audacity to criticize the great Paul Brown.

He might have been the greatest

The way Paul Brown envisioned it, the Browns would be unstoppable with Ernie Davis teaming up with Jim Brown in the backfield, and the coach went out on a limb to try to make it happen.

It never did, however, not because Brown failed in his quest to acquire Davis, but because the 1961 Heisman Trophy winner contracted leukemia and died before he played a professional game.

It was a devastating loss, personally and professionally, as Davis was as likable off the field as he was good on it.

Not only did the Browns lose Davis, they also lost Bobby Mitchell, who went on to make it into the Hall of Fame.

Practically a carbon copy of Brown, Davis also was a star at Syracuse University. The Browns obtained him in a trade with Washington for Mitchell, a veteran running back, and a No. 2 draft choice.

The Browns got into a bidding war with Buffalo of the American Football League, but signed Davis for $80,000, which was less than the Bills were offering.

"I didn't sign with the Browns to break Jim Brown's records, nor because I could play with him," Davis said then. "I signed because I think the Browns are a wonderful organization."

Ernie Davis

But Davis got sick during workouts with the College All-Stars in July and his illness was diagnosed as leukemia.

Though Jim Brown reportedly wanted the coaching staff to let Davis play in a pre-season game, Paul Brown refused.

It was a decision most of the players endorsed, as expressed by Mike McCormack, then the Browns' offensive right tackle and one of the team's leaders.

"I know I would have hated to have been a lineman in front of Ernie ... miss a block, have him get hit hard and a week later find out that he lost his state (of remission), whether it was from the tackle or what," McCormack was quoted as saying.

"Everybody admired (Davis) ... he was a great athlete who possibly could have given us the (Paul) Hornung-Jim Taylor duo that Paul (Brown) wanted."

Davis was introduced to a thunderous standing ovation prior to the Browns first exhibition game in 1962, but didn't play and spent the season undergoing treatment while the Browns were struggling again, compiling a 7-6-1 record.

For awhile Davis's illness was in remission, raising a glimmer of hope that perhaps the vibrant young man of 23 might beat the dread disease and win the biggest battle of his life.

But it was false hope.

On May 16, 1963, Davis paid a visit to Art Modell at the Cleveland Stadium. "It was good, though I later realized he'd only come to say goodbye," said Modell.

After Davis left the Stadium, he checked into the hospital. "It's nothing serious," Modell said he'd been told by Davis. But it was serious.

And two days later Davis died.

As a final tribute the Browns retired Davis's uniform No. 45 - even though it was never worn in a game.

Dave Logan's difficult decision

Dave Logan, one of the Browns' all-time best receivers, was almost "lost" to the team before he ever arrived in Cleveland in 1976.

And, for awhile back there, the 6-4, 216-pound former three-sport star at the University of Colorado admitted to having some misgivings about the choice he made.

Logan was drafted by teams in three professional sports leagues - football, baseball and basketball.

He was a third round selection of the Browns a year after he'd been tabbed in the fourth round by the Kansas City Kings of the National Basketball Association, and in 1973, fresh out of high school where he was a pitcher-shortstop in baseball, had been picked in the 20th round by the Cincinnati Reds.

Dave Logan

"There were times I'd look at the phenomenal salaries that even some of the mediocre baseball and basketball players were being paid and second guess myself," he was quoted in 1979, when the Browns were beginning to hit their stride as the "Kardiac Kids."

But Logan, a key member of that team quarterbacked by the then-incomparable Brian Sipe, didn't lament that decision for long.

"The way things turned out for me, I don't have any regrets, none whatsoever," said Logan, who played for the Browns for eight seasons, through 1983, catching a total of 262 passes for 4,247 yards and 24 touchdowns. He was traded to Denver in 1984 for a fourth round draft choice that the Browns used to pick offensive lineman Rickey Bolden.

Injuries kept Logan out of all but four games with the Broncos in 1984, and he retired after the season and subsequently became a broadcaster of Denver games.

Further testimony as to Logan's versatility and ability is that, in 1977 under then-coach Forrest Gregg, he served as the Browns' back-up quarterback, to be used in an emergency, or for a trick play. He also played tight end as well as wide receiver.

In 1979, when the "Kardiac Kids" went 9-7, and in 1980, when they won the AFC Central Division with an 11-5 record, Logan teamed with Reggie Rucker and Ozzie Newsome to give the Browns the most prolific trio of receivers in the NFL.

As then-coach Sam Rutigliano said, "There's not another team that gets the production and balance that we do from Logan, Rucker and Newsome. For sure, nobody has three receivers who have made such dramatic contributions as our people, in terms of clutch and game-winning catches. I've never seen anything like it."

In 1979, Logan caught 59 balls for 982 yards and seven touchdowns, Newsome's totals were 55 for 781 yards and nine touchdowns, and Rucker's were 43 for 749 yards and six touchdowns.

In 1980, Logan was on the receiving end of 51 passes for 822 yards and four touchdowns, Newsome 51 for 594 yards and three touchdowns, and Rucker 52 for 768 yards and four touchdowns.

Perhaps, because of his size and athletic ability, Logan would have been successful in Major League Baseball with Cincinnati and/or the NBA with Kansas City.

But there's no doubt he made the right decision by joining the Browns in the NFL.

What more could he prove?

Even as a young player with the Browns, Chuck Noll gave every indication he'd be the successful football coach he later became.

Listen to longtime trainer Leo Murphy talk about Noll, who grew up in Cleveland and graduated from Benedictine High School and the University of Dayton.

Chuck Noll

"Charlie," as Murphy called the man who went on to coach the Pittsburgh Steelers, "always was a football intellectual. He always knew what he was supposed to do on every play, and he knew the assignments of the other players."

A guard and linebacker for the Browns from 1953 through 1959, Noll was one of the "messengers" who alternated carrying plays to the quarterback.

He was a fullback and guard at Benedictine, which went undefeated and won the city championship in Cleveland in 1948,

Noll played offensive tackle and linebacker at the University of Dayton where Joe Gavin called him "the best pro prospect I ever coached."

Noll was a 20th round draft choice of the Browns, and the hard-nosed, blond haired kid from the tough East Side neighborhood quickly became a favorite of Coach Paul Brown.

In his seven seasons with the Browns, Noll played in four National Football League championship games - the forerunner of the Super Bowl - two of which they won, in 1954 and 1955.

And, after taking over as head coach of the Steelers in 1969, Noll's teams went on to play and win four Super Bowls.

Though his coaching career in Pittsburgh didn't start on a positive note, the Steelers under Noll put together 13 consecutive winning seasons from 1972 through 1984.

Noll retired from the Browns at the age of 27, and immediately joined the San Diego Chargers as an assistant in 1960, remaining through 1965. He went to work for former teammate Don Shula with Baltimore in 1966.

Four years later Noll was hired by the Steelers, who were then doormats in the NFL, having won only 11 games in the previous three seasons.

Noll wasn't an immediate improvement as the Steelers went 1-13 his first season and followed with a 5-9 record in 1970, and 6-8 in 1971.

But three years later Noll led them to their first of four Super Bowls - after the 1974, 1975, 1978 and 1979 seasons.

While coaching was Noll's vocation, it certainly wasn't his whole life. He flies his own plane, is an accomplished scuba diver and raises orchids, is a devotee of classical music and strums a guitar for relaxation.

As the fifth winningest NFL coach of all time with a 194-140-1 record (behind George Halas, Shula, Tom Landry and Curly Lambeau), it would seem that Noll should have been honored somewhere along the line as Coach of the Year by the Professional Football Writers Association of America.

But, inexplicably, it didn't happen, which leads one wonder what more Noll could have done to win the award.

The mistake that cost Sam's job

He was supposed to be the next Brian Sipe, a strong-armed, resourceful and intelligent field general who would take the Browns to the next higher level.

The very presence of Paul McDonald, in fact, was a major reason the Browns didn't try to out-bid Donald Trump and the New Jersey Generals of the fledgling United States Football League for Sipe's services in 1984.

It was the opinion of both owner Art Modell and coach Sam Rutigliano that McDonald, a 1980 fourth round draft choice out of USC, was ready to replace Sipe, then 34, a veteran of 10 NFL seasons.

Paul McDonald

And to show their faith in McDonald, who'd led USC to two Rose Bowl victories and a national championship, the Browns gave the 6-2, 185 pound quarterback a new, three year contract worth a reported $1.775 million, including $500,000 the first season.

At the time, the Los Angeles Express of the USFL reportedly was offering McDonald $1.3 million over three years.

As Rutigliano said in expressing confidence in McDonald, "I have no questions about whether we can succeed with him. McDonald is a proven winner and we're excited about what he can do for us. He's a special player and will help put us in the playoffs."

But his dedication to McDonald was a mistake that cost Rutigliano his job.

The coach was fired midway through the 1984 season as the Browns lost seven of their first eight games and finished with a 5-11 record under Marty Schottenheimer.

Much of McDonald's problems in 1984 could have been blamed on inadequate protection by his offensive line. He was sacked 53 times, including 11 in a 10-6 loss to Kansas City in the fourth game, although, to his credit, he never publicly complained.

McDonald also was charged with 16 fumbles and was intercepted a league-leading 23 times while completing 271 of 493 passes for 3,472 yards and 14 touchdowns. It was in the wake of that dismal season that the Browns felt compelled to make the deal with Buffalo that cost them four draft choices, including two No. 1s, to acquire Bernie Kosar in the 1985 Supplemental Draft. Shortly thereafter they also traded for veteran quarterback Gary Danielson which effectively, though not immediately, ended McDonald's career with the Browns.

With Kosar and Danielson aboard in 1985, McDonald reported to training camp and said, "If the Browns don't want me, if I don't figure in their plans, I would be very confused because they went through a great deal to get me signed a year ago. Obviously, they wanted me then. As far as I'm concerned, it (quarterback) is still my job until somebody takes it away.

"And, whatever happens, there will be many more adventures for me after football, which is only one stopping point for me."

What happened was that Kosar took over as the No. 1 quarterback and was backed up by Danielson. McDonald remained with the Browns in 1985, though he was third on the depth chart and didn't take one snap from center or throw even one pass.

When the season ended, so did the brief and unspectacular McDonald era.

He was let go by the Browns and went to the Dallas Cowboys in 1986, but appeared in only one game and retired from football when that season ended.

A career nearly frozen away

It was during the NFC championship game on December 21, 1969 that Walter Johnson, at that time considered by some in the Browns hierarchy to be the best defensive tackle in the team's history, almost lost three fingers on his right hand - and his football career.

Walter Johnson

Playing on an icy, freezing afternoon in Minnesota where the chill factor was 20 degrees below zero, the Browns were beaten by the Vikings, 27-7, and Johnson suffered a frost-bitten right hand.

"I had jammed three fingers (in practice) so I got a shot of Novocain before the game," the 6-4, 274-pound lineman testified then. "Near the end of the first quarter my hand started aching. As the game went on, it became worse and worse."

What Johnson didn't realize was that his hand was freezing. Because they were losing, the Browns defense was on the field for long periods of time and, in his defensive stance, Johnson planted his right hand on the frozen turf. By the end of the game his hand was, literally, a chunk of ice.

The effects of the Novocain wore off completely on the team bus after the game and by the time the Browns reached the airport, Johnson was in agony.

Upon arrival in Cleveland, he was rushed to a hospital and for almost 24 hours it was uncertain whether three fingers would have to be amputated.

"If they would have amputated the fingers, I would not have been able to continue playing," said Johnson. "You have to do too much grabbing with your hands, and your fingers are very important."

Had the doctors amputated the three fingers, Johnson probably also would have had to give up a professional wrestling career that he started during the football off-season and continued after his retirement at the end of the 1976 season.

Nicknamed "Zoom," because of his speed - 5.0 seconds in the 40 yard dash - and quickness for his size, Johnson was selected by NFL players and coaches for the Pro Bowl three times, (1968-70). But he was never picked on the All-Pro team, and made no secret of the fact that he resented being snubbed by the sportswriters who do the voting.

Picked as a "future choice" by the Browns with their third selection in the second round of the 1965 draft, Johnson quit Los Angeles State, where he'd played fullback and offensive lineman, with a year's eligibility remaining to turn pro. It angered his college coach who claimed the Browns had "influenced" Johnson to quit school.

In those days a player could not come out of college and become eligible for professional football by "declaring" his intention to do so, as is the case now.

"(The Browns) don't have any business signing a boy when he has a year to play, charged Homer Beatty, coach of the Los Angeles State team. "They waved so much money in (Johnson's) face, he couldn't turn it down."

But Beatty's protest to the NFL fell on deaf ears as Browns owner Art Modell testified, "We knew (Johnson) wasn't going back to school under any circumstances."

Whatever, it launched an excellent 12-year professional football career for Johnson - though it almost ended much sooner.

The 'hot dog' receiver

He liked to paint his shoes orange, called himself "Web-Star," and had a penchant for spinning the football at the feet of a beaten cornerback, or slamming it to the ground in front of a fallen safety, all of which identified Webster Slaughter as a "hot dog" receiver.

But the man could play, which he did – very well – for the Browns from 1986, when he was their first draft choice (second round) out of San Diego State, through1991.

As was written in the Boston *Globe* prior to the AFC championship game on January 17, 1988, "(Slaughter) has, in a sense, made his reputation like Guy Lombardo. He has made it celebrating." And because of it, the article continued, "Not everyone was happy to see Slaughter catch 47 passes for 806 yards (17.1 per catch) and seven touchdowns this (1987) season. Not everyone was elated by the fact he has caught at least one pass in each of his 28 games as a Brown. Not everyone appreciates celebrations.

Webster Slaughter

"But, as Slaughter says, 'It's exciting to run out and break free for a touchdown or a long catch. So I spin the ball a couple of times. I'm not trying to insult the defensive back. All I'm doing is celebrating my catch. Defensive backs should worry more about what I do before the catch.

"'I'm not cocky. I just play aggressively. I weigh 165 pounds. I'm not going to intimidate anybody. But sometimes defensive backs don't like you doing your job. They expect you to back down so they can do their job.

"'I just can't see somebody just coming up to you and saying, 'Get the hell out of the way.' If you back down one time, the whole league will try to do it. So I want to show them I can be just as physical as they can.'"

Slaughter, a Pro Bowler in 1990 and All-Pro in 1989, still holds the Browns single season reception yardage mark – 1,236 – set in 1989. The 65 passes he caught that year are tied (with Greg Pruitt) for fourth most in franchise history (behind Ozzie Newsome, who holds the top three places). Unfortunately, when Slaughter's contract expired after the 1991 season, negotiations with the Browns dragged into 1992 and wound up in court.

Ultimately, Judge David Doty declared Slaughter a free agent before the owners and NFL Players Association reached an agreement, and he signed with the Oilers.

"If I could have gotten what the Browns paid (free agent receiver) Mark Carrier ($1.2 million a year for three years), I'd still be in Cleveland. I wasn't asking for that much money," Slaughter was quoted in the Lake County *News Herald*.

"What made me leave is they wouldn't budge from their offer, but when I finally got free agency, they were willing to budge. Why couldn't they take that stance before free agency?"

Reportedly, Slaughter signed with Houston for $2 million over two years, while the best the Browns offered was a two-year pact for about $1.8 million. And what did Carrier do for the $1.2 million a year the Browns paid him? He caught 72 passes for 1,189 yards in 1993 and 1994, and went to the Carolina in the expansion draft in 1995.

Slaughter played for the Oilers from 1992-94, signed as a free agent with Kansas City in 1995, and ended his NFL career with the New York Jets in 1996.

Confessions of a 'Gypsy'

George Ratterman used to joke that sometimes his five children were confused about their dad's first name.

"For awhile they thought it was 'Wewant,' as in 'We-want-Ratterman,'" the former Notre Dame quarterback would tell banquet audiences.

George Ratterman

When the laughter subsided, Ratterman would say that he had "the best job in the world," as the Browns' second string quarterback.

Which he did, but only from 1952 through 1955, when he served as Otto Graham's understudy.

Then Graham retired and Ratterman, an excellent college quarterback and veteran pro, took over as the starter, only to break an ankle midway through the 1956 season. He was replaced by Tommy O'Connell and soon thereafter retired.

Anytime Graham had a bad game - though it wasn't very often - the chant would begin: "We-want-Ratterman, We-want-Ratterman."

And there were times the fans got Ratterman.

In those four seasons as Graham's understudy Ratterman completed 89 (of 147) passes for 1,290 yards and 14 touchdowns.

He enjoyed himself immensely most of the time, even if his humor wasn't always appreciated by Coach Paul Brown.

Once Ratterman posted a notice on the locker room bulletin board informing players of a meeting of the "fake field goal holders." Reportedly, several members of the team tried to attend, much to the delight of Ratterman - if not Brown.

Another time, when Ratterman was in the game, Brown, as he always did, sent in a play with one of the "messenger" guards.

Ratterman snapped to the messenger, "I don't like that play ... go get another one." The guard started to return to the bench until Ratterman caught him.

When he graduated from college in 1947, Ratterman was called "the greatest all-around athlete in the history of Notre Dame," by then-Coach Frank Leahy.

Ratterman went on to play in the All America Football Conference for three seasons, then with the New York Yankees of the National Football League in 1951 after a brief stint in Canada.

He was acquired by the Browns in a trade for two long-forgotten guys named Stan Williams and Bill Forester.

After retiring in 1957, Ratterman wrote a book that was appropriately titled, "Confessions of a Gypsy Quarterback."

It was a series of anecdotes, among them the revelation that, "In 10 seasons of playing not much football, I collected a whopping total of $172,969.91 in salary and playoff money."

The "confessions" also told of the time prior to the 1955 season when it appeared Graham was going to retire. Brown offered Ratterman a $5,000 raise to $19,000, which would make him the fourth highest paid player in the NFL.

Ratterman didn't agree immediately, saying he wanted to discuss it with his wife.

When he did, Mrs. Ratterman said, "Are you some kind of a nut? Sign the contract before (Brown) comes to his senses."

Now he's called 'Senator'

He was renowned as one of football's all-time great characters - and eaters - but Dick Schafrath also was one of the Browns' best players from 1959 through 1971.

Once, Schafrath ran, jogged, walked and finally limped 61 miles from the Cleveland Stadium to his old high school football field in Wooster, Ohio to win a bet.

Another time he and a companion paddled a canoe the 55 miles across Lake Erie from Canada to Cleveland.

Schafrath often was thrown out of all-you-can-eat restaurants because he "abused" the privilege. His appetite - or stomach capacity - seemed to hold no bounds.

As a high school kid, his mother reportedly sent Schafrath to his summertime construction job with a bushel basket of sandwiches for his - nobody else's - lunch.

And when he retired, Schafrath revealed that he'd received regular "treatments" from a hypnotist during his 13 year playing career. They gave him the "edge" he needed to totally concentrate on playing to the best of his ability, he said.

Dick Schafrath

The Browns drafted Schafrath in the second round out of Ohio State in 1959 with the intention of playing him as a defensive end. But Schafrath was switched to offense and, in his second season, replaced Lou Groza as the starting left tackle. He was a regular until he retired and was replaced by Doug Dieken.

Not long afterwards, as Richard P. Schafrath, he embarked upon a second career, this one in politics. In 1985 he was appointed an Ohio state senator for the 19th District (Loudonville), a position he still holds after being elected in 1986 and re-elected in subsequent campaigns.

It was Schafrath's dogged determination, and his outstanding (some would call it "outrageous") capacity for food that made him one of the best pass protectors in the National Football League. He was picked for the Pro Bowl six times.

When Schafrath first reported to the Browns out of college he was 6-3 and weighed about 215, hardly the dimensions needed to play either defensive or offensive tackle.

Paul Brown told Schafrath to add some bulk - at least, 30 pounds - by the time training camp opened three months later.

And so, when Schafrath stepped on the scale the first day of camp, the needle swung around to 248 Brown was delighted. Until, that is, it was discovered that Schafrath had a chunk of iron inside his athletic supporter that weighted some 20 pounds.

The attempted deception didn't anger Brown, who was quoted as saying, "Anybody who will go to this extreme to make my team, deserves a chance - but you'd better get your weight up."

Schafrath did both. At one point in his career, he weighed 270.

When Schafrath revealed he'd been helped by a hypnotist, he said, "I wasn't a natural athlete. I wasn't big and I wasn't fast. I had to make up for it with hustle and desire.

"Hypnotism gave me the edge I needed. If you want to be the best, imagine how much better you can be if you have total concentration."

Whatever the reason, Schafrath definitely was one of the best - as well as one of the great characters and eaters.

Minni and the 'scoundrels'

Together with Hanford Dixon, Frank Minnifield helped comprise the best cornerback duo in the NFL even before they were voted the starters in the 1988 Pro Bowl, the first time in history two players from the same team were voted No. 1 at those positions.

It all began when Minnifield – a.k.a. "Mighty Minni" – joined the Browns in 1984 from the Chicago Blitz of the defunct United States Football League, and was paired with Dixon, who was the team's No. 1 draft choice in 1981.

Frank Minnifield

They were arguably the best cover tandem in the NFL through 1989, when Dixon was replaced on the right corner by Raymond Clayborn, while Minnifield continued as the starter on the left side through 1992.

Minnifield's attitude was best expressed in a statement he made in 1988, to wit: "Wide receivers are the scoundrels of the earth. Throughout the game they try to be your friend. Then they catch a pass and they want to go through this Indian war dance and spike the ball on you. You're nothing but a scoundrel when you do something like that."

Minnifield's career with the Browns, however, was not as rewarding – for him or the Browns - as it probably should have been, ending as it did after he'd filed suit against the NFL claiming owners had colluded against him and others to hold down salaries.

Testifying on June 24, 1992, Minnifield said the NFL's free agency system then in effect unfairly restricted players from choosing where they want to work.

"I believe pro football players should have rights like everyone else in this room," he said. "I don't believe a man should be able to stop another man from working."

One of eight NFL players participating in the suit, Minnifield testified that, although all were free agents in 1990, they were restricted under the NFL's then-Plan B, which allowed teams to protect 37 players, with the rest of the players on the roster becoming unrestricted free agents.

A protected player could accept offers from other teams, but the player's current team had the right to match any offer. If it declined to match, it got compensation from the team that signed the player. Minnifield said he solicited offers when his 1989 contract expired and negotiations with the Browns bogged down. But he received no offers despite having been selected to play in the Pro Bowl four times (1987-90), and also was a consensus All-Pro four times (1986-89).

Minnifield finally re-signed with the Browns three games into 1990 for $700,000, and $800,000 in 1991, though both were below the $1 million a year he'd been seeking.

"I agreed to it because I really didn't have any choice," Minnifield claimed.

Though Minnifield and his seven partners in the lawsuit did not win, their efforts led to changes in the NFL's policy regarding free agency. Unfortunately, the chances didn't come soon enough to help Minnifield. Despite being rated as one of the best cornerbacks in the NFL, Minnifield was not offered a contract by the Browns in 1993, and his football career ended.

"It's not a matter of economics," then-owner Art Modell argued when asked why the Browns were no longer interested in retaining Minnifield. "It's a matter of competitive needs and the direction we want this organization to head. He could come in at the minimum salary of $100,000 and it doesn't alter our position."

Blame it on the coach

The pro scouts didn't think Reggie Langhorne, who ran the 40 yard dash in 4.56 seconds, was fast enough to play in the NFL. They also questioned his pass-catching techniques, and weren't sure that he was a good enough blocker.

What's more, Langhorne played his collegiate football at a Division II school, little Elizabeth City State University in North Carolina.

Reggie Langhorne

But there wasn't any doubt about Langhorne's toughness, and early on with the Browns he quickly proved that the negative reports on his abilities were wrong - though not to the satisfaction of then-coach Bill Belichick.

The Browns selected Langhorne in the seventh round of the 1985 draft, six years before the arrival of Belichick, and he turned out to be one of Bernie Kosar's favorite targets. Langhorne was the team's leading receiver three straight seasons (1988-90) with 162 catches for 2,114 yards, and several times played with injuries that would have sidelined players with less determination.

Once he played – and played well – despite having two broken ribs. Another time he played less than three weeks after undergoing an emergency appendectomy.

Unfortunately, Langhorne was allowed to get away because of differences with Belichick, and he played with – and starred for – the Indianapolis Colts in 1992 and 1993, after signing with them as an unprotected free agent.

As reported in the Medina *Gazette* early in the 1991 season: "Langhorne's problem with Belichick … quickly escalated into a public event, primarily because of Belichick's pointless secrecy and deception. The Langhorne scenario lacked only a tent, a parade of elephants and a dozen clowns crammed into a Volkswagen."

According to the story, "Langhorne began the three-ring circus when he walked off the practice field (after the Browns' third game of the 1991 season) to protest his demotion on the depth chart," and was fined $45,000 and suspended for one game

When Langhorne said he wanted to be traded, Belichick's response was called "stunning." He ordered Langhorne to go home and stay there until they could resolve the dispute.

Somewhere along the way, there supposedly was a heated argument between the two, and the result was that Langhorne was placed on the inactive list prior to the fourth game of the season, a 13-10 loss to the New York Giants. Belichick would not say why Langhorne was not available to play, though the reason seemed obvious to all.

General Manager Ernie Accorsi was evasive when asked. "I'm not going to talk about it," he said. "It's a private matter between Bill and I and the organization and Reggie, and that's where it's going to stay with me."

Langhorne, however, left no doubt about the situation. "I love it here, and I would stay here, except for Belichick," he said. "I respect him as a coach, but as a person he's (expletive deleted)." He called his last season with the Browns "the worst year of my life" because of Belichick.

When the season ended, Langhorne was left unprotected by the Browns. He signed with the Colts for $650,000 over two years, and became one of the best receivers in the NFL. He caught 65 passes for 811 yards in 1992, and had 85 catches for 1,038 yards (both career highs) in 1993.

The leader of the 'Kardiac Kids'

The unfortunate and unfair legacy of Brian Sipe revolves around two separate incidents during his otherwise splendid career with the Browns from the time he was a 13th round draft choice in 1972, until he left in 1984.

First was the January 4, 1981 playoff game against eventual Super Bowl XV champion

Brian Sipe

Oakland, in which Sipe's pass was intercepted in the Raiders' end zone with 49 seconds remaining, finalizing an excruciating, 14-12 loss for the Browns.

It has been called "the play that won't die," and probably will continue so until the Browns wipe away the memory with another NFL championship.

The other was Sipe's decision to accept a $2 million, three year contract to play for the New Jersey Generals in the new and, as it turned out, short-lived United States Football League.

Otherwise, Sipe should be remembered as an outstanding and resourceful quarterback from the time he became a starter in the second game of 1976, through 1983 - and especially in 1980 when he was the acknowledged best in the NFL.

But success didn't come quickly or easily for Sipe. He spent his first two years with the Browns on what was then the "taxi squad." He became the No. I quarterback by default, taking over when Mike Phipps suffered a shoulder injury.

Two weeks later, on Sept. 26, 1976, in the wake of an embarrassing, 44-13, loss to Denver, Peter Hadhazy, then the general manager of the Browns, publicly criticized Sipe.

Hadhazy complained that the Browns would never win until they got a better quarterback, which, apparently, provided all the inspiration Sipe needed.

He engineered one comeback victory after another in 1979 and 1980, including 18 in the final two minutes when the Browns were called the "Kardiac Kids," with good reason.

Sipe was named "Player of the Year" in the National Football League in 1980, and his staunchest supporter was then-coach Sam Rutigliano.

Sipe passed for a team record 4,132 yards in 1980, and nobody in the history of the Browns - not Otto Graham, Frank Ryan, Bill Nelsen nor Bernie Kosar - is close to Sipe's career marks: most yards passing, 23,713; most yards passing in one season, 4,132; most yards passing in one game, 444; most touchdown passes in a career, 154; most touchdown passes in one season, 30; most passes completed, 1,944; most consecutive completions, 14; most games touchdown passes, 23; and most passing attempts, 3,439.

"If you put Brian next to a guy like Terry Bradshaw or Bert Jones, he suffers in comparison," Rutigliano said at the time. "But Sipe is extremely bright and has great mental toughness. It's the same kind of toughness the Johnny Unitases and Bart Starrs and Otto Grahams had.

"And Brian proves his leadership every week. He might be the best ever at standing in there and concentrating in the face of a rush. He just doesn't feel the pressure."

All of which made Sipe perhaps the greatest fan favorite in the history of sports in Cleveland - at least until the "play that won't die," and his defection to the USFL.

Which is a shame, considering the great memories created by the quarterback who wasn't supposed to be good enough-but was.

The coach who 'made' Sipe

Jim Shofner was a first round draft choice of the Browns in 1958, and for seven seasons was an outstanding cornerback, one of the best in the National Football League.

But Shofner's greatest contributions to the Browns might have come 14 years after he retired as a player in 1964.

The soft-spoken Texan, a former star running back at Texas Christian University, returned to the Browns in 1978 as their quarterbacks coach.

Jim Shofner

That was the season, not at all coincidentally, that Brian Sipe began to blossom into stardom.

By 1980, with Shofner still at his side, Sipe became the best quarterback in the National Football League.

He passed for 4,132 yards and 30 touchdowns as the Browns won the American Football Conference Central Division championship and came close to reaching the Super Bowl for the first and only time.

Shofner shrugged off credit for Sipe's development, saying, "Brian and I had a great relationship, personally and professionally, but he was coming fast before I got there … he didn't need me to do what he did."

Which might be true.

But the fact is, Shofner left the Browns after the 1980 season, accepting a better job as offensive coordinator of the Houston Oilers.

Again coincidentally or not, Sipe's effectiveness took a severe nosedive.

So did the Browns. Their record fell from 11-5 in 1980, to 5-11 in 1981.

Shofner returned to the Browns as their offensive coordinator in 1990, after nine years with Houston, Dallas and St.Louis/Phoenix, but left again after a year to take a better job with the Buffalo Bills.

Shofner came to Cleveland in 1958 with glittering credentials as a running back at TCU. It didn't take Paul Brown long, however, to convert Shofner to a defensive back.

Many longtime Ohio State fans remember Shofner without great affection - for a 90-yard punt return for a touchdown that gave TCU an 18-14 victory over the Buckeyes in a 1957 game.

The Detroit Tigers probably remember Shofner, too. A third baseman then, Shofner signed a minor league contract with the Tigers, but he opted for a professional football career instead, which he never regretted.

Neither did the Browns.

Shofner doubled as a backup flanker to Ray Renfro in 1958, then replaced veteran Don Paul as the Browns starting right cornerback in 1959, a position he held for five seasons, until he retired.

Shofner returned to his alma mater as an assistant coach in 1964, and later worked for San Francisco until he took over as head coach at TCU from 1974 through 1976, before returning to professional football as an assistant coach.

And while he was successful as a defensive back for the Browns, Shofner will – and should be – longer remembered as the man who helped Brian Sipe become the most productive quarterback in the NFL in 1980 as leader of the "Kardiac Kids."

Brown's best high school player

Considering the many great players Paul Brown coached in high school and college before organizing the Browns in 1946, it's fascinating to recall the one he designated best of them all.

It was Horace Gillom, who's noted primarily as a punter for the Browns from 1947 through 1956, though he did so much more.

Horace Gillom

In a Cleveland *Plain Dealer* story on September 30, 1947, shortly after Gillom had joined the Browns out of the University of Nevada where he'd been a teammate of Marion Motley, Brown said:

"Horace Gillom was the best all around athlete I coached at Massillon (Ohio)Washington High School. He was successful in everything he did."

When Gillom was in college, he scored six touchdowns in one game as an offensive end, which receivers then were called. He also played linebacker for Brown at Massillon and in college.

With the Browns during their domination of the All-America Conference, Gillom backed up both Dante Lavelli and Mac Speedie, and was a starting defensive end as well as the team's punter.

When Lavelli, who's in the Hall of Fame, broke a leg in a pre-season game in 1948, Gillom replaced him and the Browns never missed a beat, going 8-0 before Lavelli returned to the lineup.

After the Browns were admitted to the National Football League, Gillom's service as a receiver was limited, although Brown was quoted in the Cleveland *News*, August 18, 1950:

"(Gillom) may not be a regular (receiver) for us, but all the other (NFL) clubs, they'll take him as an offensive end."

In that same story assistant coach Dick Gallagher said, "When you think it over, Gillom might have been the most valuable man on our club the past two years."

The article also reported: "Horace never has been a sensational pass catcher ... he is not as fast and shifty as Speedie and Lavelli, nor as sure a catch.

"But he is a tough man in scrambling for a pass and the Browns still talk about the catch he made against Buffalo (in 1949) that netted the Browns their comeback, 28-28, tie."

Despite his versatility, it was Gillom's punting that gained him the fame he enjoyed for 10 seasons with the Browns.

Gillom led all NFL punters in 1951 with a 45.5 average, and again in 1952 with 45.7.

He was noted for high, booming punts that his teammates called "rainmakers," giving them plenty of time to get downfield after the return men.

Gillom finished with a lifetime NFL average of 43.8, and to put that in perspective, only Gary Collins in 1965 had a better season punting mark (46.7) than Gillom did in his career.

And only Don Cockroft, who kicked for the Browns from 1968 through 1980, launched more punts than Gillom's 385 in seven NFI. seasons.

Not bad for a guy who played offensive end, defensive end and linebacker, in addition to being one of football's all-time best punters.

But then, maybe that's what Paul Brown saw in Horace Gillom when they were together at Washington High School in 1940.

A protege of two old masters

Even when he was an 11 year old halfback in the CYO League in Painesville, Ohio, Don Shula made clear his competitive spirit and fierce determination to excel.

"I remember one time in particular," Shula's mother said a few years ago, "when Don's team lost a game and he went under the grandstands and cried his eyes out.

"He was always that way. He always wanted to win, and if he didn't, he was a hard loser. Not a bad loser, but a hard one."

Shula never changed, though the occasions that he lost were few since playing for the Browns in 1951 and 1952.

The winningest coach in NFL history, Shula's 33 year record - six seasons at the helm of the Baltimore Colts 27 as coach of the Miami Dolphins - is 328 - 156 - 6 for a winning percentage of .678.

His teams also played in six Super Bowl games, winning two of them, and his overall playoff record in 19 years was 19 - 17.

Another who recognized Shula's potential was the late Herb Eisele, then football coach at John Carroll University.

Shula was a defensive back and running back at John Carroll from 1947-1950, and set a career rushing record, averaging 6.8 yards per carry. The Browns made him a ninth round draft choice in 1951.

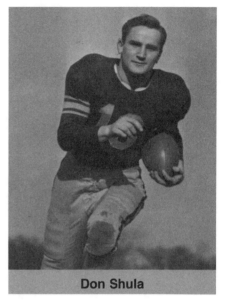

Don Shula

"(Shula) always was inquisitive, he was always asking me why this and why that," Eisele said before his death in 1985.

"When we practiced, he always wanted to know what everybody else was supposed to do on every play, and why. He said it gave him a good feeling to know all the assignments."

Shula's work ethic - and determination to excel - never changed, though he was only an average defensive back for the Browns, and was traded to Baltimore, in one of the NFL's biggest deals, on March 26. 1953.

Fifteen players were involved, Shula and nine others, including his former John Carroll teammate, Carl Taseff. They went to Baltimore in exchange for five Colts - Mike McCormack, Don Colo, Tom Catlin, John Petibon and Herschel Forester.

Shula played for Baltimore from 1953-56, for Washington in 1957, and went into coaching in 1958.

Carroll Rosenbloom, who owned the Colts, hired Shula as head coach in 1963, and in 1968 he took them to Super Bowl III (a 16-7 loss to the New York Jets).

Shula took over the Dolphins in 1970 and led them to the NFL's only undefeated (17-0) season in history in 1972, and into the Super Bowl five times, winning twice, in the 1972 and 1973 seasons.

His six trips to the Super Bowl are the most by any coach, he was the youngest coach to win 100 and 200 games, was voted the NFL's Coach of the Decade (the 1970s) by the Hall of Fame, and was named NFL "Coach of the Year" three times.

Shula played for Paul Brown and was an assistant to Blanton Collier, and later said, "I tried to learn from both and copy neither."

Obviously, he did spectacularly well.

The 'adoption' of Galen Fiss

One of the most heart-warming stories ever told about the Browns focused on captain and linebacker Galen Fiss, who played for the team with distinction from 1956-66.

It took place in September 1965, when Fiss was recovering from an operation on his left knee, and the story was related in a letter to the Cleveland *Plain Dealer* by Rev. Thomas Cullen, chaplain at Shaker Medical Center.

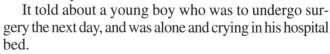

Galen Fiss

It told about a young boy who was to undergo surgery the next day, and was alone and crying in his hospital bed.

"Then a rather husky man, slowly moving with the aid of crutches, entered the boy's room," Father Cullen wrote. "The conversation went something like this:

"'Hello, Brian. How are you doing tonight? I know you miss your mom and dad, but you sure are a brave boy to be here. Suppose you and I make an agreement.

"'I have a son about your age. I miss being with him, just as you miss your mom and dad. Suppose, while you're in the hospital, I take the place of your dad, and you take the place of my son. That way we can both help each other.'

"Tears changed to a smile and the answer came quickly. 'That would be swell,' the young man exclaimed. And soon he was sleeping peacefully.

"The boy didn't know that his 'adopted dad' was Galen Fiss, captain and linebacker of the Browns, but that's who it was," concluded the priest.

To those who knew Fiss, his attention to the lonely boy awaiting surgery was typical of the man who had been a fullback at the University of Kansas. He was acquired by the Browns in 1956 and played for them through 1966.

It is significant that during his 11 year playing career in Cleveland, the Browns suffered only one losing season, his first, 1956, when the team's record was 5-7.

Fiss became a starter at outside linebacker after five games of his rookie year and, except for a couple of injuries that temporarily sidelined him, including 1965, was a regular every season thereafter until his final year with the Browns.

The high point, of course, was 1964 when Fiss was named to the Pro Bowl and played a major role in the Browns' 27-0 victory over Baltimore, giving them their first NFL championship in eight years, since 1955 - and also their last.

Early in that title game at the Stadium, Colts quarterback Johnny Unitas flipped a screen pass to Lenny Moore and the halfback raced toward the goal line with two teammates in front of him.

But Fiss, the right linebacker, knifed through the two Baltimore blockers and brought Moore down with a crunching, touchdown-saving tackle. Several members of the media who covered the Browns that season called it the top defensive play of the year.

When Fiss retired and returned to his home and insurance business in Kansas City, he was quoted as saying, "Joining the Browns was the greatest thing that ever happened to me and my family."

And just as he was happy to play for the Browns, there's no doubt the organization was every bit as pleased to have him on the team.

Football's 'Jackie Robinson'

The headline in the Cleveland *Press* that day - August 6, 1946 - undoubtedly shocked many people.

It still would today, but now for a different reason.

"Willis Tries Out With Browns, May Open Way for Negro Players," the headline blared over a story by veteran sportswriter Bob Yonkers.

Then, a few months after Branch Rickey had broken baseball's so-called "color barrier" by signing Jackie Robinson - but eight months before Robinson played his first major league game for the Brooklyn Dodgers - black players were tacitly barred from professional football.

And while it was Rickey who opened the door for Robinson, it was Paul Brown who granted Willis a chance to continue his football career as a professional with the Browns.

As Yonkers wrote: "Big Bill Willis, All-Big Ten tackle at Ohio State in 1943 and 1944, has been granted permission to try out with the Browns and is accorded a brilliant chance to become the first Negro player signed by an All-America Conference team."

Brown said of the 6-2, 210-pound Willis, "He will do us a lot of good if he still has it. He was like a black panther when he played for me at Ohio State."

Bill Willis

The story continued, "Brown added that there is nothing in the league constitution to prevent All-America Football Conference elevens from hiring colored players.

"National Football League teams have used them off and on for many years and at least one of them, Duke Slater, became one of the greatest performers in the league's history."

Willis was a member of Ohio State's championship teams in 1942 under Brown and in 1944 under Carroll Widdoes. Aware that blacks were unwelcome in professional sports, he took a job at Eastern Kentucky State College in 1945.

When the AAFC was founded in 1946 by Chicago *Tribune* sportswriter Arch Ward, and Cleveland taxicab magnate Arthur B. (Mickey) McBride purchased a franchise and hired Brown to coach the team, Willis asked for a tryout.

Soon after signing with the Browns, Willis was joined by another black player - and also a future Hall of Famer - Marion Motley.

Of course, both made the team and became stars.

For most of his career Willis was a two-way performer. In addition to guard on offense, he was a middle guard/linebacker on defense. As such he was credited by Brown for revolutionizing that aspect of defensive play.

"(Willis) became the real pioneer of what is now the middle linebacker," Brown said in a published history of the Browns.

"Sometimes we'd put him up as the center of a five-man line, but quite often, to take advantage of his speed and agility, we'd drop him back and allow him to go to the play.

"(Willis) had no peer through much of his professional career," added the coach.

Willis played for the Browns through 1953, and his 1977 election to the Hall of Fame culminated a long and often arduous journey - in many ways paralleling the journey taken by Jackie Robinson.

'A remarkable player and person'

After it was over, after he was spared the embarrassment of nearly causing the Browns to lose the AFC Central Division championship in the final game of the 1989 season, Clay Matthews could smile and joke about his career-long ambition to make a "creative" play.

In this case, in the division-deciding game against Houston in the Astrodome on December

Clay Matthews

23, Matthews recovered an Oilers' fumble on the Cleveland 30 yard line as the Browns were clinging to a 17-13 lead with less than five minutes remaining.

If Matthews, a veteran linebacker who was the first of the Browns' two first round draft choices in 1978, had simply fallen on the fumble, the victory probably would have been locked up. But no. Matthews did not do things like that. That would be too conventional. And Matthews was not your conventional NFL player.

As he once said in a story in the Cleveland *Plain Dealer*, "I'll just sit and think of ways to make unusual plays. I think about lateralling the ball. I envision these unusual scenarios. I've envisioned somehow getting the ball on an interception or fumble and running for the end zone with time expiring ... then realizing there's no way I can make it to the end zone and drop-kicking the ball to win the game."

In the afore-mentioned scenario, Matthews scooped up the errant Houston snap as it rolled away from quarterback Warren Moon, apparently securing the victory that would give the Browns a 9-6-1 record and the AFC title. However, in a misguided burst of creativity, Matthews leaped to his feet, wheeled around and lobbed a lateral to Chris Pike, his shocked defensive tackle teammate. But Pike couldn't hold the ball, it was recovered at the Cleveland 27 by the Oilers Earnest Givins, and on the next play Moon lofted a touchdown pass to Drew Hill, giving Houston a 20-17 lead.

Whatever prayer Matthews said to himself as he returned to the bench was answered. The Browns pulled out the victory with 39 seconds left, 24-20, on a four yard touchdown by Kevin Mack, absolving Matthews of mortification.

He left the Browns after the 1993 season, and somewhat reluctantly closed out his excellent 19-year professional career with the Atlanta Falcons (1994-96), saying, "If I can't play in the NFL, there's always the park leagues and the semi-pros."

Unfortunately, Matthews long will be remembered by fans for his "creative," albeit ill-advised lateral that almost cost the Browns their place in the 1989 playoffs.

Instead, the Hollywood-handsome, 6-2, 245-pound Matthews, who played his college football at the University of Southern California, should be cited for playing in five Pro Bowl games and being voted All-Pro three times, as well as for holding Browns' records for playing the most games, 232 (217 of which he was a starter), and for playing the most consecutive seasons, 16 (more than any linebacker in the history of the NFL and one less than Lou Groza's franchise longevity mark of 17, 1950-59 and 1961-67).

As then-coach Bill Belichick said of Matthews in 1993: "He's the ultimate team player in all respects, from preparation, practice and meetings to leadership and performance. Clay is as consistent and dependable as any player I've seen ... he is a remarkable player and a remarkable person."

A long time coming

It took awhile – the better part of eleven years, in fact – for Vinny Testaverde to live up to the lavish expectations predicted of him when he was the first player selected in the 1987 NFL draft by the Tampa Bay Bucaneers.

Then the reigning Heisman Trophy winner for his play at the University of Miami where he had succeeded Bernie Kosar in 1985, Testaverde had all the physical attributes required of an NFL quarterback – especially a strong arm on a 6-5, 227-pound body.

But something always seemed to be lacking during his time with the Bucs, though the team itself, born of expansion in 1976, didn't do much to complement the handsome quarterback who, early-on, had been compared to Hall of Famer "Broadway Joe" Namath.

After six undistinguished seasons in Tampa Bay, in which he was the starter for all but the first half of 1987 – and during which the Bucs' won-lost record also was an undistinguished 28-67 – Testaverde was allowed to go away. He was signed by the Browns as an unrestricted free agent on March 3, 1993, ostensibly to back-up Kosar.

But when Kosar was fired by then-coach Bill Belichick after eight games in 1993, with the Browns' record 5-3, Testaverde took over and – unfairly - became the target

Vinny Testaverde

of abuse by the fans, most of whom idolized Kosar and hated Belichick.

After Kosar's dismissal the Browns won only two of their remaining eight games and finished the season with a 7-9 record, third in the AFC Central Division.

With Testaverde at quarterback in 1994 the Browns rebounded to 11-5, and qualified as a wild card in the playoffs, beating New England, 20-13, but losing to Pittsburgh, 29-9. It was Testaverde's best season in his eight years in the NFL.

The Browns regressed to 5-11 in 1995 – after which the franchise moved to Baltimore - though Testaverde's statistics again were impressive. He completed a career high 61.5% of his passes, 241 of 392 for 2,883 yards and 17 touchdowns, with 10 interceptions.

He was even better in 1996, though the team, now called the "Ravens," compiled a worse record, winning only four games while losing twelve. Testaverde passed for a career high 4,177 yards and 33 touchdowns with 19 interceptions.

However, the inconsistency for which Testaverde had been known throughout his career, surfaced again in 1997. He threw for 2,971 yards and 19 touchdowns, but was intercepted 15 times as the Ravens went 6-9-1, and Testaverde changed teams again. He went to the New York Jets in 1998, rejoining Belichick, an assistant coach on that team, and hit his peak. Testaverde accomplished virtually everything that had been expected of him twelve years earlier.

Testaverde took the Jets to the AFC Eastern Division championship, leading them to a 12-4 record, again completing better than 61% of his passes – 259-of-421 - for 3,256 yards and 29 touchdowns, with a career low (as a starter) seven interceptions. Testaverde went on to lead the Jets to the brink of Super Bowl XXXIII, beating Jacksonville, 34-24, in a divisional playoff game, before losing the AFC championship game to Denver, 23-10.

Testaverde's emergence was a very long time coming but, at least for the Jets, was well worth the wait.

A mistake that lasted too long

It was one of the most controversial trades in National Football League history and - in retrospect – probably the one that Art Modell and the Browns regretted more than any other.

Paul Warfield, who became one of football's greatest receivers, was sent to the Miami Dolphins on January 26, 1970 in a deal designed to solve what Modell and Coach Blanton Collier perceived was the Browns' major need: A quarterback to replace aging and injury-prone Bill Nelsen.

Paul Warfield

"We felt we had to do it." Modell said then, and repeated often. "It was the overwhelming consensus ... that we had a pressing need for backup protection behind Bill Nelsen.

"We were worried about Nelsen holding up. We didn't think he could continue to be the top flight quarterback we felt we needed to win in the NFL."

But Mike Phipps, the quarterback that Modell and Collier thought the Browns needed, never lived up to expectations after he was picked with the No. 1 (third overall) draft choice they got from Miami for Warfield.

And so, trading Warfield, the 6-1, 190 pound prototype receiver, always will invoke "what if" speculation about-and-by the Browns, despite the re-acquisition of Warfield in 1976.

By then Warfield was 34 and his skills eroded, especially his blazing speed, which was one of his greatest attributes.

Warfield played two more seasons with the Browns, through 1977, and his 14-year NFL statistics provide eloquent testimony to his ability: 427 receptions for 8,565 yards and 85 touchdowns, an average of 20 yards per catch, a touchdown every five receptions, and a touchdown every 1.8 games.

He played on three NFL championship teams - the Browns in 1964, and the Dolphins in 1972 and 1973 when they won Super Bowls VII and VIII.

Six years after his retirement Warfield was accorded football's ultimate honor by being elected to the Hall of Fame.

"Now that it's happened to me, it's mind blowing, awesome, hard to believe ... I have to pinch myself, " Warfield said on the steps of the hallowed Hall of Fame in Canton, Ohio the day he was inducted.

"The only thing I ever thought about was to be a better player every day I played."

Which Warfield was, from the time he played at Warren (Ohio) Harding High School, won All-America honors as a receiver and defensive back at Ohio State, during his six seasons with the Browns after they drafted him No. 1 in 1964, and especially through his five years with the Dolphins.

Warfield jumped to the ill-fated World Football League in 1975, and returned "home" a year later.

When Warfield was drafted, Collier's plan was to play him at cornerback because, "We need more speed back there," he said.

Fortunately, that near-mistake was quickly rectified.

Unfortunately, the Browns couldn't rectify the other mistake, trading Warfield to the Dolphins, until it was too late.

A 'steal of the century'

When the Browns acquired Joe DeLamielleure in a trade with Buffalo on September 1, 1980, a source in the NFL was quoted as calling it "a steal of the century."

To get the then-29 year old, 6-3, 245 pound guard, the Browns sent two second round draft choices in 1981 and 1982 to the Bills. DeLamielleure, who'd been a member of the Bills' famed "Electric Company" line that blocked for Hall of Famer O.J. Simpson, and a Pro Bowler for Buffalo for five consecutive seasons (1975-79), was surprised by the trade, but also "pleased" beyond words.

"Pleased isn't the word to use to describe how I feel," he said. "I didn't know the Browns were interested, although Tom DeLeone told me at the Pro Bowl last year how great it is with the Browns because of Sam Rutigliano. It's almost too good to be true."

DeLamielleure was available because of a contract dispute with Bills coach Chuck Knox. It kept him out of training camp until the final week, two days before he was traded to the Browns.

A first round draft choice of the Bills in 1973 after he'd won All-America honors at Michigan State, DeLamielleure left Buffalo with a 103 consecutive games-played streak that he extended with the Browns to 175, second longest in the NFL at that time.

Joe DeLamielleure

He played with distinction for the Browns through 1984, again winning Pro Bowl honors in 1980, and was a key factor in the success of the "Kardiac Kids." He was the offensive team captain in 1983, but was waived on August 12, 1985 by then-coach Marty Schottenheimer, who cited DeLamielleure's "deteriorating pass-blocking skills."

DeLamielleure returned to Buffalo and played one more season for the Bills, then retired to a business career and high school coaching job in Charlotte, North Carolina.

It was after DeLamielleure retired from football that he revealed to a Rochester, New York sports writer that the use of steroids was rampant in the NFL.

"Not in 1980 or '81, but from 1982 on I saw a lot of changes in people's size, and a it was happening all around the league," DeLamielleure was quoted in the Rochester *Times-Union* on August 14, 1991. In the story, DeLamielleure named his Browns' teammate, Lyle Alzado, and former Pittsburgh Steelers lineman Steve Coursen - who was, at that time, awaiting a heart transplant - as "the first casualties of the 'steroid generation,' ex-NFL players turning 40 and turning up with a myriad of unexplainable health problems." Both subsequently died at relatively early ages. "It's the tip of the iceberg," DeLamielleure said. "Around the NFL, steroid use was like drinking water, that's how common it was and everyone knew."

To make matters worse, "Steroid use wasn't limited to marginal players trying to win a spot on the roster. It was Pro Bowl players, too. A lot of star players in the mid-1980s used," DeLamielleure said, declining to name any other than Alzado and Coursen. He was angry that the NFL didn't begin until two years after he retired.

But DeLamielleure wasn't bitter, just happy, he said.

Happy that he was able to put together a splendid 13 year career in the NFL - and that, when he left the game, his acquisition by the Browns did indeed prove to be, as had been predicted, "One of the steals of the century."

The player called 'Dopey'

With a nickname like "Dopey," it would seem that Don Phelps would have to be very good to play in the NFL.

Which he was, though not for long.

And though his professional football career was brief, lasting less than three full seasons from 1950 through the first game in 1952, Phelps came to the Browns with impressive credentials and a solid recommendation from his University of Kentucky coach, the legendary Paul "Bear" Bryant.

Dopey Phelps

The 5-11, 185-pound halfback was a four-year star at Kentucky after returning from Army duty during World War II.

"Dopey" – or Phelps – was said to "run like a jet-propelled rabbit" in a story that appeared in the Cleveland *Press* after he made a 69-yard touchdown run as a rookie in the Browns first NFL game against Philadelphia in 1950.

It was the Browns' first exposure to the NFL after dominating the All-America Football Conference for four seasons, from 1946-49.

Phelps also returned a kickoff 85 yards for a touchdown in another exhibition game against Green Bay in that pre-season and, as the story also reported:

"Non-stop flights to touchdown land became a habit with Phelps at Kentucky, so it should surprise nobody that he was an aerial gunner during the last mess (World War II). He was with an Army bomber squadron in the South Pacific for 2 ½ years.

"'I shot down three Japanese planes and came home with a Silver Star, Air Medal and Purple Heart,' Phelps said, unboastingly."

He also was a track star in high school and college, and in 1947 was clocked at 9.6 seconds in the 100-yard dash, and 21.3 in the 220, both of which were close to what were then world records.

Phelps was a fifth round selection in the 1950 college draft, and was billed as the speedster that Coach Paul Brown felt was needed to team up with fullback Marion Motley and right halfback Dub Jones in the backfield. At that time the Browns employed the-then conventional four-back T-formation.

However, while playing briefly as a spot runner out of the backfield – he ran from scrimmage 55 times for 263 yards and three touchdowns in 17 games – Phelps was used primarily as a kickoff and punt returner, a job he performed very well.

His totals with the Browns: 19 punt returns for 192 yards and one touchdown, and 15 kickoff returns for 391 yards.

Phelps' career ended after the Browns waived him in 1952.

As for that nickname, "Dopey," Phelps explained, "I got it during my freshman year in high school. 'Snow White and the Seven Dwarfs' was a popular movie around that time and a lot of my chums said I reminded them of Dopey.

"I guess it's because I was so bashful and slow. I never did talk to the girls in those days. I was scared to death of them," he was quoted in the *Press* story.

"But I sure got over that in a hurry. I found myself a little honeybunch and married her."

An unfortunate legacy

It is unfortunate and grossly unfair that the lasting memory most fans have of Earnest Byner is that he fumbled to end the Browns' chances of beating Denver in 1987 and going to Super Bowl XXII.

The mere mention of his name recalls Byner, No. 44, starting to his left and high-stepping toward the end zone for what would have been the game-tying touchdown.

Earnest Byner

And then, Broncos cornerback Jeremiah Castille, lurking in the shadows of Mile High Stadium, comes from nowhere to strip the ball loose at the Denver three yard line. The fumble is recovered by Castille at the one, with 1:05 left, and the Browns are dead.

While so many have trouble forgetting what happened that day in Denver, Byner himself put it out of mind a long time ago – except when he's reminded of it.

As he acknowledged in a story in the Cleveland *Plain Dealer* a year later, "It's funny, when I'm out and people talk to me, it's like they're lost for words when it comes to mentioning that game. They're afraid it's going to get on my nerves or something."

For the record, it didn't … it doesn't … it never will.

Not because Byner is insensitive to the significance of what happened, but rather, as he has said, "You've got to have perspective. It was one play in my life. It won't change my life, it won't change me. I felt like I had given it my all (in that game). I played well. I had nothing to be ashamed of."

Byner is right. He did play well, scoring two touchdowns in the Browns' 21 point third quarter. He also had a 53-yard pass reception in the drive that tied the game at 31-31 with 10:48 to play.

But those heroics are overlooked when the game, won by the Broncos, 38-31, is recalled

A tenth round draft choice out East Carolina College in 1984, the 5-10, 215-pound Byner was a bargain, and often was referred to as "the heart and soul of the Browns' offense", playing for them through 1988, and again in 1994 and 1995.

In what certainly was one of the Browns' worst-ever deals, Byner was traded to the Washington Redskins on April 23, 1989, for running back Mike Oliphant. As written by Bob August in the Lake County *News Herald*, "The Browns wanted to get rid of Byner in the worst way – and did."

Oliphant played little and not very well for the Browns in 1989 and 1990, and has been out of pro football since. Byner, on the other hand, rushed for 1,000-plus yards in two of his five seasons with the Redskins in 1990 and 1991 (as he did for the Browns in 1985).

He returned to the Browns as a free agent in 1994 and remained with the organization when it moved to Baltimore in 1996. Byner played for the Ravens through 1997, when he retired and has since been their player development director.

Byner is ranked sixth in Browns history in the seven years he wore a Cleveland uniform with 3,583 yards rushing behind Jim Brown, Leroy Kelly, Mike Pruitt, Greg Pruitt, and Kevin Mack, and his 29 touchdowns rushing are fifth most in team history.

But still – again, unfortunately and unfairly - the mere mention of Byner recalls *The Fumble*, and little else about the hard working and underrated former running back.

'Billy the Kid,' a.k.a. 'The Rock'

When he joined the Browns as their second round draft choice in 1953, Billy Reynolds had two nicknames: "The Rock," and "Billy the Kid."

The latter was understandable. It's what Reynolds had been called during his four year career as a star running back at the University of Pittsburgh when he was, indeed, a kid, and

Billy Reynolds

rejected a professional baseball contract to stay in college and play football. But the former? "The Rock?" Reynolds explained in an article in the Cleveland *News* during his first training camp with the Browns.

"They started calling me 'The Rock' when I was a sophomore at Pitt," said Reynolds. "It happened because me and a kid named Jimmy Danter hit head on in a game. The other guy was a buddy from my hometown (St. Mary's, West Virginia) who was playing for West Virginia University.

"It was on the kickoff. The other guy came at me and I went at him, and because we knew each other so well, we knew we wouldn't sidestep each other. We bumped heads, pretty hard, and knocked ourselves cold.

"I came to the next quarter and played some more. But Jimmy was out all night. After that I was known as 'The Rock,' as well as 'Billy the Kid.'"

Reynolds' three season career with the Browns was interrupted by Uncle Sam after the 5-10, 188-pound halfback won a job and alternated with Dub Jones in 1953 and 1954. He returned from two years in the Air Force and served as the Browns' kickoff and punt return specialist in 1957. Reynolds was traded to the Pittsburgh Steelers in 1958, saw limited duty with them and was out of the NFL in 1959. He tried to make a comeback in 1960 with Oakland, but played only six games for the Raiders and retired as a player, his knees literally worn out from several injuries.

He returned to Cleveland and, for many years thereafter was an amateur football and basketball official.

Though his NFL statistics are meager – he rushed for 585 yards in 176 carries, and returned 40 kicks for 985 yards – Reynolds was outstanding in college, especially as a senior when he led Pitt to a 22-19 upset victory over Notre Dame in 1952.

It was a performance that probably had much to do with his being drafted by the Browns in the second round.

Reynolds ran 80 yards for a touchdown on the first play of the game, and outgained the entire Notre Dame backfield with 169 yards.

Reynolds also had a memorable game as an NFL rookie, when the Browns beat the New York Giants, 7-0, on October 25, 1953 in Yankee Stadium. He carried the ball 18 times for 74 yards. "That game was my biggest thrill in football, even bigger than our upset of Notre Dame when I was in college, because beating the Giants was so important for us," said Reynolds. In those days the Giants were the Browns' biggest rival in what was then the NFL's Eastern Conference.

The Browns finished the 1953 season with an 11-1 record, their only loss coming at the hands of the Philadelphia Eagles, 42-27, in the final game, though they subsequently were beaten by Detroit, 17-16, for the NFL championship.

'In a way, it wasn't fair' to Fair

It was his name, rather than his accomplishments for the Browns, that made Fair Hooker so memorable.

Even the Browns acknowledged in an early news release that the wide receiver's name was "a guaranteed attention getter," after Hooker was picked out of Arizona State University in the fifth round of the 1969 college draft.

Not only was it an attention getter, it often provoked derision, which was reason enough that Hooker steadfastly declined to discuss the subject.

Browns fans also paid close attention - perhaps *unfairly* - to Hooker because he became the designated successor to future Hall of Famer Paul Warfield, who was traded to the Miami Dolphins in 1970 in order to obtain quarterback Mike Phipps.

It would have been a difficult task for any receiver, not just Hooker.

As it was, Hooker's best season was 1971, when he caught 45 passes for 649 yards, fulfilling – if only briefly – an ambition he had nurtured since childhood, growing up in Monrovia, California.

"I wanted to play pro football ever since I began watching the teams on television," Hooker was quoted in a Browns' news release.

Fair Hooker

He went to Arizona State on a football scholarship and, ironically, it was another former Sun Devils' receiver, then highly-touted Steve Holden, who hastened Hooker's departure from the Browns.

They were matched against each other from the time Holden was picked in the first round of the 1973 college draft and, as Chuck Heaton wrote in the Cleveland *Plain Dealer*:

"In a way, it wasn't fair. First, to carry the burden as the replacement for Paul Warfield. And now after getting established as a regular, to be challenged by the Browns' No. 1 draft choice.

"That's the situation with Fair Hooker ... though the veteran isn't complaining. 'Competition is good for anyone,' he said. 'I believe it makes you work harder and makes you better. You concentrate and you learn more. I'm planning to be the starter. (Holden) will have to take the job away from me.'

"Regarding Warfield, Hooker said he hadn't really looked on it as a burden. 'I know some of the fans were bitter and I still hear about it once in awhile. But a burden? No,' he insisted.

"To ward off the challenge (of Holden), Hooker said, 'My aim is to get open more and to be a better target. I dropped some passes, maybe a few too many. You have to avoid the tendency to run before you catch the ball.

"'I'm emphasizing looking the ball right into my hands. With four seasons behind me and three as a regular, I believe that I'm just coming to my peak.'"

As it turned out, Hooker retained his job though his receptions decreased to 18 for 196 yards in 1973, from 32 for 441 yards in 1972 to 18 for 196 in 1973.

But a year later Holden took over as the starter and Hooker, who was hampered by several injuries and appeared in only seven games, catching only four balls for 48 yards.

Then, in 1975, the Browns acquired Reggie Rucker in a trade with New England, and Hooker was waived, his football career ended.

A career tragically cut short

It was said that Don Fleming loved football so much he'd play it on the sandlots if he hadn't made it with the Browns in 1960.

But the defensive back from Shadyside, Ohio did make it with the Browns, spectacularly well, which is why his accidental death on June 4, 1963, was such a devastating loss to the team.

Don Fleming

Fleming and a fellow worker were electrocuted on an off-season construction job in Orlando, Florida.

Adding to the grief and consternation felt by the entire organization was that two other Browns died that off season, one of them Ernie Davis, only 2½ weeks earlier.

Davis died of leukemia, and Tom Bloom, another defensive back the Browns had drafted sixth out of Purdue University, was killed in an automobile accident in March.

The Cardinals, who were then playing in Chicago, had drafted Fleming in 1958, but he chose instead to return to the University of Florida to get his engineering degree.

Browns cornerback Bernie Parrish, a former Florida teammate and close friend, recommended Fleming to Paul Brown, and a trade was made on May 12, 1960.

Fleming started at safety as a rookie, and established himself as one of the best in the National Football League for three years.

Not only was he highly praised by his Browns' coaches and teammates, Fleming also was one of the best athletes, a three sport star, at Shadyside High School.

"We never had a boy who did such a fine job in all three sports," said Larry Falbo, then athletic director at the school. "Don was, above all things, a competitor."

Two-and-a-half years after Fleming's death his widow filed a $700,000 damage suit against the Florida Power Co.

The amount was based partially on what Fleming's earning power with the Browns would have been, including an estimated $250,000 in salaries during his playing career.

Owner Art Modell testified at the trial that Fleming had been signed for a salary of $8,300 and a $500 bonus in 1960.

His pay was raised to $10,000 in 1961, to $12,000 in 1962, and Fleming had agreed to a contract for $13,000 for 1963.

There were many accolades for Fleming at the trial, which provided more insight into the character and ability of the young man, whose 26th birthdate was three days after his death.

"Don was as good a defensive back as the Browns had," said Parrish, an All-Pro defensive back himself in 1961 and 1964.

And Lou Groza testified, "There's no doubt Don would have been one of the great defensive backs in pro football."

As further proof of the high regard the Browns had for their fallen teammate, they renamed their then-practice field at Case Western Reserve University "Fleming Field" in 1964.

Fleming Field is still in use at the university, though the Browns moved their practice facilities to Berea in 1972.

Fleming's No. 46 also is one of the five uniforms retired by the Browns. The others: No. 14, Otto Graham; No. 32, Jim Brown; No. 45, Ernie Davis; and No. 76, Lou Groza.

'This was meant to be'

Officially, Don Cockroft's career with the Browns ended on August 31, 1981, when he was waived and his job handed to Dave Jacobs, a soccer-style place kicker.

However, in actuality, the decision to replace the 13-year veteran whose 1,080 points are still most in franchise history, probably was made by then-coach Sam Rutigliano and his staff seven months earlier, on January 4, to be exact.

That was the date the Browns lost, 14-12, in a division playoff game to the wild card Oakland Raiders who went on to beat Philadelphia in Super Bowl XV.

The record shows that the Raiders prevailed because they intercepted a pass from Brian Sipe in the end zone with 49 seconds remaining. Ever since fans have lamented the failed pass play - "Red Right 88" - that would have given the Browns a victory.

But the fact is, Rutigliano called for a pass in that final minute - the Browns had a second-and-nine at the Raiders 13 yard line - because he'd lost confidence in the kicking ability of Cockroft, who was ailing with a sore back and a torn cartilage in his left knee.

Don Cockroft

Earlier in the game Cockroft missed an extra point and two field goal attempts of 47 and 30 yards, although, in fairness, it should be stated that he was successful in kicking two field goals of 30 and 29 yards, giving him 16 of 28 for the season. Thus, when training camp opened in July, the Browns had Jacobs and three other kickers competing with Cockroft for the job he'd inherited from Lou Groza in 1968. He also served as the Browns punter from 1968-76.

Cockroft, whose field goal accuracy percentage had been the best in the NFL from 1968-79, underwent knee surgery in the off-season and reported to camp ready to meet the new challenge to his jobs. "I'm the first to admit last season was not what I would have liked it to be," he said. "But now that my knee is 100 percent sound, I don't anticipate any of the problems I had. I have as much snap in my leg as I ever did. I don't think I have slowed up a bit."

But he was wrong. Only two days prior to his being waived Cockroft failed on three kicks, one point after touchdown that hit the goal post upright and fell back, another that was blocked, and a 52-yard field goal that fell far short.

When informed of the decision to make Jacobs the extra point and field goal kicker, Cockroft reacted with the same degree of class he had shown throughout his career.

A devout Christian and active member of the Fellowship of Christian Athletes, Cockroft told reporters, "This was meant to be. The Lord has something else in mind for me now," then admitted that which others had suspected. "I also believe the decision was made, to a great extent, a long time ago ... it possibly might even go back to the playoff game (against Oakland) last season."

So ended Cockroft's 13-year career with the Browns that began when he was a third round draft choice out of Adams State in Colorado where he had led the nation with a 48 yard punting average as a freshman in 1964. He finished as the Browns' second most prolific scorer, behind only Groza's 1,349 points. When Groza retired after the 1967 season, Cockroft took over as the Browns place kicker, a job he held with distinction - until January 4, 1981, when the end came, as it eventually does for every player.

The Browns got lucky

In 1979 and 1980 he'd been a nemesis of theirs, a guy who'd helped the hated Pittsburgh Steelers beat the Browns – when they were the "Kardiac Kids" - three times in four games, once with a field goal that almost cost them the AFC Division championship.

And so, when Matt Bahr became available in 1981, when the Browns were struggling with

Matt Bahr

kicker Dave Jacobs, they quickly traded to get him from the San Francisco 49ers, giving up a ninth round pick in the 1983 draft.

It proved to be a good deal as Bahr kicked for the Browns for nine seasons, through 1989 (though he was injured and missed 13 games in 1987). His 677 points – on 143 field goals and 248 kicks after touchdowns – are fourth most in franchise history.

From the time he was waived by the Steelers at the end of 1980, through four games with the 49ers in 1981 (before he came to Cleveland) and the first four with the Browns in 1983, Bahr was successful on 78 consecutive points after touchdowns.

Bahr's streak dated back to October 26, 1980 when one of his kicks was blocked and ultimately allowed the Browns to beat the Steelers, 27-26, at the old Stadium.

A trademark of Bahr's was his constant coolness under fire. If he ever felt pressure, he never let it show, although, as he once explained, fearing that he might be stressing, was a point of concern to his teammates.

After Bahr's 32-yard field goal with eight seconds remaining gave the Browns a 24-24 tie to send the game into overtime – a game they eventually won, 30-24 – against San Diego on September 25, 1983, he related what happened in the huddle moments before his clutch kick.

The Chargers had called time to increase the pressure on Bahr and, as the Browns waited, then-quarterback Paul McDonald tried to keep the kicker loose. "Paul came up to me and said, 'Hey, Matt, that book you're reading, (Devil's Alternative), did you finish it? How was it?'" said Bahr, as he was quoted in a story that appeared in the Cleveland *Plain Dealer*.

"I told him, 'Oh, yeah, the book was fine. You want to borrow it?' Outwardly, I didn't show any emotion, but inwardly, I had to laugh. I knew what Paul was doing, that he was trying to take my mind off the situation. I appreciated his effort, but it wasn't really necessary."

"Actually, I was pleased because it was good for him to have his mind on the book, and trying to help me relax instead of getting all uptight about the kick (because McDonald was the holder)."

Bahr was replaced as the Browns kicker in 1990 by Jerry Kauric, and was waived, though it didn't end his football career. Bahr kicked for the New York Giants through 1992, spent half of the 1993 season with Philadelphia, then joined the New England Patriots and kicked for them through 1995.

His 17-year career totals: 1,422 points on 300 field goals (of 415 attempts for 72.3% accuracy), and 522 kicks after touchdown (of 534 attempts). Only nine players in the history of the NFL have scored more points, led by George Blanda's 2,002.

Matt Bahr's older brother Chris also was an NFL kicker from 1976-89, and scored 1,213 points, for a total of 2,635, believed to be the most ever by a brother combination.

The tough and 'dirty' old man

When he played for the Chicago Bears and New York Giants against the Browns, Erich Barnes was called rough, tough and, yes, "dirty," too,

But after he was acquired by the Browns in 1965 in a three team deal involving Mike Lucci, Barnes' image changed.

At least his new teammates' perception of Barnes changed.

Suddenly Barnes, also known as the "Old Man," was considered affable, friendly, even happy-go-lucky, though his reputation for aggressiveness on the field remained the same. He played left cornerback - and very well - for the Browns through 1971, and was instrumental in their reaching the National Football League title games in 1968 (won by Baltimore, 34-0) and in 1969 (won by Minnesota, 27-7).

Erich Barnes

When Barnes retired, he admitted his greatest disappointment was that he never played on a championship team.

Barnes liked to say that his attitude was "relaxed," as opposed to "happy-go-lucky," as a reporter once called him. "I think that 'happy-go-lucky' might indicate an unstable person, and I'm certainly not that," said the 6-3, 205-pound former Purdue University star and All-Pro cornerback.

" There is such a mental strain in playing professional football, it helps to be relaxed during the week. A smile here and a laugh there make it easier for everybody.

"But the day of the game is something else. Then I get serious. That's no time to be joking around. I don't, and I don't want people around me to do it."

It helps to explain an incident that caused Barnes to be widely criticized by fans who were outraged by what they saw in a game against the Cardinals in St. Louis in 1966, won by the Browns, 38-10.

Browns running back Walter (Flea) Roberts was pushed out of bounds near the Cleveland bench by defensive back Bobby Williams.

Barnes launched a kick at Williams and players from both teams converged on the scene, all with fire in their eyes. A brawl between the two teams almost erupted,

After peace was restored, a St. Louis fan ran onto the field and tried to attack Barnes.

The letters to the editor were filled with complaints about Barnes, who wrote a letter himself, defending his action.

"I swung my foot, but I am not even sure that I touched him," Barnes said in the Cleveland *Plain Dealer* on December 23, 1966.

"It was more a chastising gesture. I had no intention of hurting him. (But) I think the whole thing's been blown out of proportion. There's no problem between Williams and me."

Barnes was critical, however, of the fan who raced onto the field and tried to attack him.

"People made such a fuss about the other incident, but I don't see how they can justify a fan coming out of the stands and hitting me. I had my helmet off and he almost knocked me out."

That was Erich Barnes, a rough, tough, even dirty player if he played against you - but a "relaxed, happy-go-lucky" guy when he was on your side.

An ultimatum that back-fired

It all began so splendidly for Thom Darden, and most of the rest of his nine year career with the Browns was just as great, for him and the team.

But, when the end came it was an acrimonious split for the free safety who still holds the Browns record for most pass interceptions - 45 for 820 yards and two touchdowns - and won All-Pro honors in 1978.

That also was the season Darden was named the Browns' "Defensive Player of the Year" by the Cleveland Touchdown Club, and "Northern Ohio Pro of the Year" by the Sports Media Association of Cleveland and Ohio.

Darden grew up in Sandusky, Ohio and was a star on his high school football team, while dreaming of playing for his favorite NFL team, the Browns, which he and his father often traveled to Cleveland to see play.

He went to the University of Michigan where he won All-America honors in leading the Wolverines to an 11-0 record and into the Rose Bowl in 1971, then was the Browns' first round pick in the 1972 college draft.

Life could not be better for the 6-2, 195 pound defensive back who had been a receiver in high school, and played quarterback for the Wolverines in 1970 before Coach Bo Schembechler switched him back to free safety, a position at which he excelled.

Thom Darden

However, while almost everything was going well for Darden, there were two occurrences that weren't so pleasant.

First, Darden suffered a severe injury to his left knee during a pre-season game against Philadelphia in 1975. He underwent major surgery and was sidelined the entire season, which undoubtedly was a factor in the Browns' 3-11 record that year.

Then, on December 21, 1980, as the Browns - then aptly nicknamed the "Kardiac Kids - were putting the finishing touches on their 11-5 season with a 27-24 victory over Cincinnati, Darden was flagged, and subsequently fined $1,000 for an "unnecessarily rough" hit on Bengals receiver Pat McInally.

"I won't pay it," was Darden's initial response. "By fining me they (the NFL) should fine the institution of football because, ever since I started playing this game in the fourth grade, I was taught to do exactly what I did against McInally."

What he did was to hit McInally as he was leaping to catch a pass. Darden's forearm or elbow hit McInally and knocked him unconscious. McInally had to be carried off the field - although he later returned to play and even caught a long touchdown pass.

"What really bothers me," continued Darden, "is that the whole thing made it look like I took a cheap shot at McInally. It's the stigma of it, that people might interpret this as meaning I am a dirty player, and I'm not. I've been taught to play this way, and I do."

But then, the following season, for whatever reason, Darden didn't play the same way and was replaced as the starting free safety by a younger and faster Clinton Burrell.

By season's end Darden was outspoken in his unwillingness to be, as he said, "a bench warmer," and angrily issued a "start-me-or-trade-me" ultimatum.

Eight weeks later, on February 15, 1982, Darden, whose career with the Browns began so well, was waived, and he never played pro football again.

He said he couldn't stand pressure

Ara Parseghian was called "a blue chip player who's at his best under pressure," when he joined the Browns in 1948, disdaining his senior year of eligibility at Miami University of Ohio.

But it was Parseghian himself who once claimed he couldn't stand pressure.

It happened when someone suggested that he played the piano so well he could be a night-club entertainer. Parseghian replied, "Oh, no. I couldn't stand the pressure."

Ara Parseghian

Oh, no, indeed, though that contention has long since been belied by Parseghian's record as a player and coach. Especially as a coach.

When he signed with the Browns, then the two-time defending champion of the All America Football Conference, Parseghian said he quit college early because "the money is too good to turn down." Then he was a leading candidate to join fullback Marion Motley in the starting backfield of the Browns.

"I've had a lot of experience and I'm thinking about getting married," continued Parseghian, who'd been a star at South High School in Akron, Ohio, before enrolling at Miami, where he established himself as one of the country's outstanding running backs.

Parseghian played briefly for Paul Brown at Great Lakes Naval Training Center during World War II, which was a factor in his decision to leave college early.

While Parseghian didn't disclose the amount of the Browns' offer, he did admit that he turned down a better deal - a $13,000 contract that included a signing bonus - with the Pittsburgh Steelers of the National Football League.

"Ara is a money player all the way," he was described by his college coach, George Blackburn. "He loves to show up someone who has a reputation for being good."

Unfortunately for the Browns, Parseghian didn't get much of an opportunity to "show up" many opposing players. Injuries limited him to action in 12 games in 1948, when the Browns won their third straight AAFC championship, and only two games in 1949, when they won again, then were invited to enter the NFL.

Because of those football injuries, Parseghian now walks with the aid of a cane after undergoing four operations on his hip and is facing a knee replacement surgery.

Parseghian rushed for 135 yards and a touchdown in 32 carries in 1948, and only 31 yards in 12 carries in 1949, after which he retired as a player - though he did not relinquish his involvement with football. Parseghian went on to "show up" many opposing teams as a college coach before retiring in 1975 at the age of 52.

Parseghian's coaching career began in 1949 as an assistant to Woody Hayes at Miami - which has become known as the "cradle of coaches." When Hayes moved up to Ohio State in 1951, Parseghian succeeded him at Miami. After five winning seasons at Miami, Parseghian took over as head coach at Northwestern University from 1956-63, then was hired to rebuild Notre Dame's sagging football fortunes, which he did remarkably well.

Parseghian's 11-year record with the Irish was 95-17-4, and included two national championships. Only Knute Rockne's teams won more games at Notre Dame.

Not bad for a guy who claimed he couldn't stand pressure.

The tackle known as 'Battler'

Lou Rymkus was an original Brown, one of the first players signed by Paul Brown in 1946 when the team made its debut, and went on to dominate the All-America Football Conference.

Rymkus was a tackle – a *two-way* tackle, as football was played in those days – and usually was on the field for an average of 52 minutes a game.

Lou Rymkus

As it turned out, the only problem Rymkus caused for Brown was forcing the coach to make a decision when platoon football came into being in 1948.

Brown kept Rymkus on the offensive line and, as the coach later commented, called the 6-4, 231-pound tackle "the best pass protector I've ever seen."

Of course, that was early in Brown's coaching career and, presumably, others came along who were as good or better, though Rymkus, prior to his death at 78 on October 31, 1998, took pleasure in repeating the praise of his mentor.

And mentor is what Brown was to Rymkus, whose professional football career began in 1943, as a fifth round draft choice of the Washington Redskins when he helped them win the NFL's Eastern Division championship. With the Redskins as a rookie, Rymkus was chosen on the All-National League second team.

While with the Redskins, Rymkus accomplished a feat he believed was a record for a tackle, according to a story that appeared in the Cleveland *Plain Dealer* in 1948. He scored two touchdowns in consecutive games. The first came against the then-Chicago Cardinals when he blocked and recovered a punt in the end zone.

The next week Rymkus, the story said, "really went wild" by intercepting a pass and returning it 30 yards for a touchdown. Earlier in that same game, Rymkus also picked off a pass and returned it 40 yards before being run out of bounds near the goal line.

Rymkus, who'd earned All-America honors at Notre Dame, entered the Navy in 1944, played for Bainbridge (Maryland) Naval Training Station against Brown's Great Lakes Naval Station team, and jumped to the Browns when the AAFC was formed.

It was when he played for Notre Dame that Rymkus was nicknamed "Battler," which stuck with him throughout his active career, with good reason. It started in a game against Georgia Tech, when Rymkus took an elbow to the mouth.

It opened a nine-stitch gash, though Rymkus wouldn't let the doctor make the repairs until the halftime intermission. He was back on the field when the game resumed, and played the rest of the way with his mouth swathed in bandages.

"Battler" was a member of the Browns for seven seasons through 1952, in each of which they played in a league championship game, including their four in the AAFC and three in the NFL. Rymkus retired into a distinguished college coaching career that began as an assistant at Indiana University in 1953.

When the American Football League came into being in 1960, he was hired as the first head coach of the Houston Oilers, and led them to a 10-4 record and the league championship. It earned for Rymkus the AFL's first "Coach of the Year" award.

When the Oilers went 1-3-1 in their first five games in1961, Rymkus was dismissed. He held several front office jobs in the NFL after that, but never was a head coach again.

Was it the Browns' best deal?

The acquisition of Bob Gain ranks as one of the best deals - perhaps *the best* - made by the Browns in their first 50 years in, first, the All-America Football Conference (1946-49), and then the National Football League (1950-95).

A two-time, two-way tackle who won All-America honors at the University of Kentucky under Paul "Bear" Bryant from 1947-50, Gain won the Outland Award as the top lineman in college football, and was the No. 1 choice of the Green Bay Packers in the 1951 draft.

Bob Gain

However, when he was unable to reach agreement on a contract with the Packers, Gain opted to play in 1951 for the Ottawa Rough Riders in the Canadian Football League where he made the All-Canada team.

It caught the eye of Paul Brown, then general manager and coach of the Browns, and he made the Packers an offer they couldn't refuse - fortunately for Gain and the Browns, if not, as it turned out, for Green Bay.

Gain, 6-3 and 250 pounds (which was then large for an NFL lineman), came to Cleveland in exchange for four players who have since been forgotten - wide receiver Dan Orlich, fullback Bill Schroll, and halfbacks Ace Loomis and Dom Moselle.

Gain immediately became a starter on the Browns de-fensive line in 1952, but suffered a broken jaw in the fourth game, not returning until the final two weeks of the season. Then Uncle Sam beckoned in 1953 and Gain spent that year serving with the Army Air Force in Japan and Korea.

He returned in 1954 and was a starter for the next 11 seasons, until he suffered a career-ending broken leg in the fourth game of 1964, a 27-6 victory over Dallas. The injury kept him out of the Browns' 27-0 victory over Baltimore for the NFL championship, the last won by the franchise.

During his career with the Browns they also won the NFL title in 1954 and 1955, and he played in the Pro Bowl five times (1958, 1959, 1960, 1962 and 1963), and has been enshrined in the Cleveland Sports Stars Hall of Fame, as well as the National Football Foundation and Collegiate Football Hall of Fame.

The highlight of his career at Kentucky was the Sugar Bowl game in 1951 when the Wildcats beat Oklahoma, 13-7, ending the Sooners' 31 game winning streak, then the longest in college football history. "The score doesn't reflect how easily we handled (Oklahoma)," he said.

Gain also played in the 1950 Orange Bowl, the 1951 Senior Bowl, and the 1951 College All-Star Game.

Though he had the natural ability to play on both sides of the ball, which he did in college, Gain said he preferred defense.

"I liked to hit people. On defense you could grab people and push them around," he said, also suggesting that it took greater ability to play defense. "Because the offense knew the snap, playing defense you had to be quick enough to play a retaliating game."

As for the four players the Browns traded to acquire Gain, all played briefly for Green Bay - Loomis from 1951-53, Moselle in 1951 and 1952, and Orlich and Schroll in 1951 – but none as well or as long as Gain did with the Browns.

Now it's 'Mr. Ambrose, esquire'

When he played for the Browns they called him "Bam-Bam", with good reason.

"He's a hitter, a real *hard* hitter," was then-coach Sam Rutigliano's succinct appraisal of linebacker Dick Ambrose.

But that was before Ambrose's nine year NFL career was ended by a broken ankle in 1983.

Dick Ambrose

It happened in the sixth game of the season against the New York Jets. An infection developed that required more extensive surgery and Ambrose never played again.

His retirement from football, however, led to a new career. Ambrose went back to college, earned a law degree and is now a practicing attorney in Cleveland.

Ambrose began with the Browns as a 12th round draft choice out of the University of Virginia in 1975. In his rookie season Ambrose beat out veteran Bob Babich as the starting middle linebacker, lost the job in 1976 when he suffered several minor injuries, but won it back in 1977, when he was honored by the Touchdown Club as the Browns "Defensive Player of the Year."

He remained a starter until the broken ankle ended his playing career.

The "Bam-Bam" nickname was coined in Ambrose's first training camp when his tackles impressed the coaches and players, as well as fans who were watching practice.

In a newspaper interview then, Ambrose made his football philosophy seem very simple - and in so doing, established his potential as a future barrister.

"To begin with, who likes to get hit?" he asked rhetorically. "There's got to be something wrong with a guy who likes to get hit.

"The only time the impact of a tackle is shared equally is when a ball carrier gets his shoulder into the tackler. But if the tackler gets his shoulder into the ball carrier from the armpits down - you know, like when you hit somebody with your shoulder pads in the rib area - he, the ball carrier, is taking the worst of the collision.

"That's why I like to hit somebody as hard as I can. I'd rather hurt the ball carrier than be hurt myself - though I'm no sadist," he said. "It's a case of hurt or get hurt."

The aggressive – and articulate - linebacker who grew up in New Rochelle, New York and played high school football at Iona Prep, didn't offer any excuses for losing his starting job in 1976, again establishing his credentials as a future lawyer.

When asked about the so-called "sophomore jinx," Ambrose said, "Getting to start as a rookie was a pleasant surprise. But I never felt I had it made. I knew I had to play well to keep the job, and I guess I didn't," though he certainly did the next seven seasons.

Ambrose's older brother Tom once offered testimony as to Dick's tenacity.

"I would characterize him this way: If he makes up his mind to do something, nothing will stop him," said Tom, who recalled another incident from their younger days.

"I remember once, when Dick was in high school, and my bedroom was next to his. About three in the morning I heard this awful pounding coming from Dick's room. I ran in. He was bent over a calculus book and was pounding on the desk as he tried to work out a problem.

"Needless to say he got it, and that, I think, should tell you a lot about Dick Ambrose," who was once known as "Bam-Bam," but is now Richard Ambrose, Esquire.

The 'most courageous' player

There were a lot of things Bill Nelsen couldn't do because of continual knee problems, which is why the Browns were able to get him in a 1967 trade with Pittsburgh.

But one thing Nelsen could do was lead a team, which he did very well for the Browns from 1968 through 1972.

Nelsen took the Browns to three division and two conference titles before his knees - which were surgically repaired four times - finally said enough already.

Team physician Dr. Vic Ippolito called Nelsen "the most remarkable and courageous player in the game today."

It was an assessment few could dispute.

Even fewer would dispute that it was Nelsen's gutsy field generalship that was a major reason the Browns won 34 of the 50 games he played for them in four seasons.

A tenth round draft choice out of the University of Southern California in 1963, Nelsen became Pittsburgh's starting quarterback in 1965, replacing veteran Ed Brown.

Knee injuries forced him to miss parts of the next three seasons, however, and the Steelers installed young Kent Nix in Nelsen's place.

Thus Nelsen was traded to Cleveland for another quarterback, Dick Shiner, and defensive tackle Frank Parker in 1968.

Bill Nelsen

At the time the Browns were only looking for someone to backup Frank Ryan, who was then 32 and playing his eleventh season in the National Football League, and seventh in Cleveland.

But when the Browns lost two of their first three games in 1968, then-coach Blanton Collier rushed Nelsen into the starting lineup and a new era - if only a too-brief one - began.

With Nelsen at the controls, the Browns won nine of their next 10 games to capture the Century Division championship.

They beat Dallas, 31-20, for the Eastern Conference title, but lost, 34-0, to Baltimore, which went on to Super Bowl III.

Ryan retired and Nelsen continued his outstanding play the next three seasons, despite those constantly aching knees.

In 1969, with Mike Phipps as Nelsen's understudy, the Browns repeated as division and conference champions, but lost the NFL championship game to Minnesota, 27-7.

Nelsen was still the starter when the 1972 season began, but he was intercepted twice in a 26-10 loss to Green Bay and another changing of the guard took place as Phipps replaced his mentor.

The Browns went 7-6-1 under Phipps in 1972, and Nelsen, who threw only 31 passes, completing 14 for 141 yards, limped into retirement when the season ended.

His 10 year totals show that Nelsen passed for 14,165 yards and 98 touchdowns, on 963 completions in 1,905 attempts, and earned the highest praise from owner Art Modell:

"Very few football players, if asked, would agree to play 60 minutes on both offense and defense, but Nelsen was one who would," said Modell.

"Team success over individual laurels was not a cliche with Nelsen, it was an obsession."

It was another assessment of Nelsen that few could dispute.

'Not bad for a blocking back'

It was literally an emergency measure that brought unheralded Ernie Green to Cleveland in 1962. But despite the circumstances that made it necessary, the deal turned out to be a very good one for the Browns.

That was the year the Browns previously traded future Hall of Famer Bobby Mitchell and their (second) first round draft pick to the Washington Redskins for the rights to Ernie Davis, the All-America running back from Syracuse University.

Ernie Green

However, when Davis was diagnosed as having leukemia during the College All-Star Game in July, Brown was desperate for a running back to block for Jim Brown, and to return kickoffs and punts.

Among the clubs he contacted in an attempt to make a deal was Green Bay, whose general manager and coach, Vince Lombardi, was Brown's long-time friend. Obviously, Lombardi felt he owed the Browns a debt for previous favors, and offered Green, then a rookie who'd been the Packers' 14th round draft choice out of the University of Louisville.

Green was expendable because, in Lombardi's opinion, he had little chance of playing much with the Packers - or even surviving the final cut.

At the time they had Jim Taylor, Paul Hornung and Tom Moore in their backfield.

So the deal was made. Green cost the Browns a conditional draft choice and was used primarily as a kick returner that first season as the Browns went 7-6-1. But Green settled in as Jim Brown's running mate in 1963, the first of his six seasons as a starter.

And though he always played in the shadow of, first, Jim Brown, from 1963-65, and then another Hall of Famer, Leroy Kelly, from 1966-68, Green wound up his career as the Browns' sixth all-time leading rusher. He gained 3,204 yards in 668 carries for a 4.8 average, and only Brown, Kelly, Mike Pruitt, Greg Pruitt and Kevin Mack rushed for more yardage in the Browns 50 year history.

"Not bad for a blocking back," Green quipped in a newspaper article after his retirement.

Not bad, indeed. Especially not bad for an "emergency" acquisition.

With Green as Brown's running mate, the Browns won their last NFL championship in 1964 and reached the title game in 1965, but lost to Green Bay.

When Green teamed with Kelly, the Browns won the Century Division in 1967 (but lost in the first round of the playoffs) and 1968, when they went on to defeat Dallas for the Eastern Conference championship, but lost the title game to Baltimore.

Green was twice selected to the Pro Bowl (1967 and 1968), and was co-captain of the Browns (with Jim Houston) in 1968 before an injury to his left knee that required extensive surgery and rehabilitation prematurely ended his playing career.

During his seven years with the Browns he was their representative in the NFL Players Association, and also served briefly as vice president and also secretary of the union.

After his retirement as a player, Green remained with the Browns as an assistant coach in 1969, and later worked as a player agent before going into business in Dayton, Ohio where he is president of E.G.I. (Ernie Green Industries).

Fourteen years and 203 games

Art Modell said it best on the occasion of Doug Dieken's retirement after 14 seasons as only the fourth offensive left tackle in Browns history.

"Maybe he hasn't played on a championship team, but Doug Dieken is a true champion," Modell said on April 17, 1985. Which was 100% accurate.

Dieken won the prestigious Byron (Whizzer) White Humanitarian Award in 1983, presented annually by the National Football League Players Association, and is recognized as one of the most giving professional athletes who ever played in Cleveland.

Doug Dieken

A sixth round draft choice out of the University of Illinois in 1971, Dieken, then a tight end who had been the second leading career pass receiver for the Illini, was switched to offensive tackle by the Browns.

He played every one of the team's next 203 games and, despite numerous injuries, started a Browns record 194 consecutive games. The amazing streak began with the tenth game on November 21, 1971, and continued through 1984, his final season.

Not bad for a guy who admittedly was afraid to unpack his suitcase upon reporting to his first training camp because he expected to be cut.

The 6-5, 252-pound Dieken was preceded at offensive left tackle by only three others in Browns history: Jim Daniell in 1946, Lou Groza from 1947 through 1958, and Dick Schafrath from 1959, until Dieken arrived 12 seasons later.

And only Groza played more games, 216, for the Browns than Dieken, their offensive captain in 1976, 1977 and 1982.

After his retirement as a player, Dieken became a "voice" of the Cleveland Browns. He was the "analyst" and color commentator on the Browns radio network until the team moved to Baltimore.

Though he was renowned as a practical joker and fun-lover, Dieken had tears in his eyes as he poignantly reminisced on his stellar career while delivering an emotional retirement speech.

"Walking in here today was a lot tougher than those bus trips from Pittsburgh," where the Browns never won during Dieken's career, he said.

"I really like this city, which I call my home, a city of much pride, determination and sincerity. As an athlete, I've admired its desire to gain respect. Obviously, this is a city that cares."

Then, injecting some levity, Dieken cracked, "I am somewhat embarrassed that, 'Holding, No. 73,' has become something of a household phrase. "(But) I am proud that, in 14 years, we haven't seen a quarterback carried off the field from a blind side hit."

Dieken regretted that his two goals as a player were not met - beating the Steelers in Pittsburgh and a National Football League championship - but easily recalled his greatest individual thrill as a member of the Browns.

It was in a 25-19 overtime victory against Houston in 1983. Near the end of the first half with the Browns trailing, 10-3, Dieken caught a 14-yard touchdown pass from quarterback Paul McDonald on a fake field goal.

"It'll be a long time before I forget it," he said - and it also will be a long time before Browns fans forget Doug Dieken.

An amazing coaching odyssey

You could say without equivocation that Lou Saban was born to coach. and coach and coach some more.

Everywhere.

An original member of the Browns in the old All-America Football Conference, Saban was captain, linebacker, and sometimes fullback and quarterback for four years. He also served as the backup placekicker in case of injury to Lou Groza.

Lou Saban

After four championship seasons in the AAFC, and just about the time the Browns were being invited to join the National Football League, Saban inexplicably quit the team.

He became head football coach at Case Institute of Technology (which later merged with Western Reserve University and is now called Case Western Reserve).

Thus began an odyssey by Saban that included coaching football teams at all levels, including high school.

A football and track star at Indiana University from 1940 through 1942, Saban served four years in the Army in World War II, much of it in the China-Burma theater. He joined the Browns upon his discharge.

More than 25 jobs are on Saban's resume, including stints as head coach of three professional teams (Buffalo, New England and Denver of the American Football League), seven colleges (Case, Washington, Northwestern, Western Illinois, Maryland, Cincinnati and Miami), as well as the U.S. Military Academy at West Point, and the presidency of the New York (baseball) Yankees.

In addition, Saban, who was born in 1921, also was an executive in the insurance industry for several years.

"Coaching presents a real challenge to me, and I'm eager to get into it," Saban said when he took the job at Case in 1950.

Quite a few years later, when asked about his penchant for job-jumping, Saban would only say, "I'm not much for dredging up the past," and he never did.

Saban began his professional coaching career with the New England Patriots in 1960 but was fired five games into the 1961 season.

Saban later coached Buffalo for four seasons, compiling a 38-18-3 record, and his teams won consecutive AFL championships in 1964 and 1965. He was the AFL Coach of the Year in 1964.

But he didn't stay long in Buffalo either. A year later Saban became general manager and coach of the Denver Broncos.

He left the Broncos in 1971 and returned to the Patriots in 1972 as head coach, and remained with New England until 1976 when he resigned at midseason to become coach of the University of Miami Hurricanes.

A year later – and, not surprisingly, some would say – Saban underwent a double coronary bypass operation.

In January 1979, Saban pulled out of Miami to take over the football program at West Point, but only for a year.

From there Saban went into high school coaching until his retirement a few years later.

A performance for the ages

William A. - better known as "Dub" - Jones is best remembered for one spectacular performance in a Browns game on November 25, 1951.

Against the Chicago Bears that afternoon, Jones scored six touchdowns as the Browns won, 42-21, in front of 40,969 fans in the Stadium. It was the eighth of 11 consecutive victories by the Browns, who finished the season with an 11-1 record, but lost the NFL championship game to the Los Angeles Rams, 24-17.

Jones scored on runs of two, 12, 27 and 42 yards, and caught touchdown passes of 34 and 43 yards from Otto Graham.

Those six touchdowns are still a Browns record, and tied an NFL mark set by Ernie Nevers in 1929 and equaled by Gale Sayers in 1965.

Dub Jones

While that probably was Jones' best game, there were many other excellent performances by the 6-4, 205-pound running back-flanker who joined the Browns in the All-America Football Conference in 1948, and played for them through the 1955 season.

Jones returned to serve as offensive backfield coach of the team under Blanton Collier from 1963-68.

A tailback at Tulane University, Jones was drafted by the Bears of the NFL and the Miami Seahawks of the AAFC in 1946. He signed with the Seahawks and, after one season, was traded to the Brooklyn Dodgers.

His acquisition by Paul Brown from Brooklyn represents one of the Browns' best deals. They traded the draft rights to Bob Chappuis, the University of Michigan star running back, to get Jones, who'd been a defensive back with the Dodgers. He was selected on the All-Pro team in 1951, and for the Pro Bowl in 1952.

However, while Jones' playing career was memorable, his coaching career with the Browns ended on a discordant note. As he was quoted in a January 1968 article in the Cleveland *Plain Dealer*, Jones said, "I thought I had resigned until I was read (a) news release from the Browns office. Man, that was rough.

"The way (the release) was written was an unnecessarily low blow. The truth is, I don't think I was fired. Or at least, I didn't until tonight. It irritates me more than anything about the whole deal. Whoever wrote it had no concern for my interests."

That was Jones' reaction upon learning that he was being replaced as the offensive backfield coach by Nick Skorich, who had been the Browns' defensive line coach. It marked the end of Jones' coaching career.

And if you wonder how Jones was nicknamed "Dub," his wife, Shumpert, explained: "We're from (Ruston) Louisiana and you know how southerners often refer to men by their initials. My husband's (initials) are W. A., and that's how 'Dub" came out - it's short for 'Double-You'," she said, making it sound very simple.

Dub's and Shumpert's son, Bert, followed his dad into professional football, after an outstanding collegiate career at Louisiana State University. A quarterback who was called the "Ruston Rifle," Bert was a first round draft choice of the Baltimore Colts in 1973 and had a ten year career in the NFL.

A legend in his own time

Parker Hall didn't play for the Browns, but it would be unfair to exclude him from among the stars that flashed across the skies in Cleveland's professional football history.

Hall played for the Rams in the National Football League before his career was cut short by World War 11, and then the Cleveland franchise was relocated in Los Angeles.

Parker Hall

But Hall became a legend in his own time.

"Never in the history of football in Cleveland - professional, collegiate, or scholastic - has there appeared a boy with the passing wizardry of the Rams' Parker Hall," a November 10, 1939 story in the Cleveland *News* extolled his talents.

Drafted No. 1 out of Mississippi, Hall led all NFL passers and won the Most Valuable Player award as a rookie in 1939, when the Rams, in the third year of their existence, went 5-5-1.

Nicknamed "Buffer," Hall was the epitome of the "triple threat" tailback as he ran, passed and kicked for the Rams in those early days of leather helmets and high-top shoes.

Actually, Hall was lucky to even be alive. He was nearly killed at the age of 15 when he was involved in an automobile accident, suffering a crushed chest and fractured ribs that pierced his right lung. He was hospitalized for six months.

Doctors advised his parents that Parker should forget playing sports. But Hall wouldn't give up the game he loved.

Not only did he return to play college football, but also baseball and basketball.

The yellowed clipping from the Cleveland *News* said it well: "Hall was a sensation at Ole Miss ... he was unstoppable on the ground and through the air."

The war, unfortunately, did stop Hall, after he'd played four seasons for the Rams.

He passed for 4,033 yards (349 completions in 711 attempts) and 29 touchdowns, ran for 1,052 yards and six touchdowns, and punted 201 times for an average of 40.9 yards in 44 games, when each NFL season consisted of only 11 games.

After Hall and other key players went into the service in 1943, the Rams suspended operations for a year.

By the time Hall became a civilian again, the Rams had a new home and a new triple-threat quarterback in Bob Waterfield. It was Waterfield who led the Rams in 1945 to their first NFL championship in the eight year history of the franchise.

A year later the Browns came into being, launching a new era of professional football in Cleveland.

Parker Hall, who might have become one of Cleveland's greatest quarterbacks instead of one of Cleveland's fabled stars of the past - caught on with the San Francisco 49ers of the All-America Football Conference in 1946.

But, rusty from three years away from the game, he played little behind Frankie Albert, the 49ers' great quarterback, and retired in 1947.

Hall was soon forgotten - except by those who remembered the sensational performances he gave when pro football was in its infancy in Cleveland.

He left his heart in Cleveland

Calvin Hill earned most of his fame during the six years he was a star for the Dallas Cowboys, but there's no doubt he left his heart in Cleveland when he retired after playing four seasons with the Browns from 1978-81.

And neither is there any doubt that the Browns - the organization and its players - were as fond of the 6-4, 228-pound running back and receiver as he was of them, and his adopted city.

Calvin Hill

"Calvin is an amazing guy," marveled then-coach Sam Rutigliano. "He has super hands, is a big target and he's good at finding a hole in the zone. It's tough to measure by statistics just what he means to us."

When Hill played his final game for the Browns, a 42-21 loss to Seattle on December 20, 1981 - a game in which he caught five passes for 49 yards and a touchdown, the 65th of his splendid 14 year professional career - his teammates presented him with a three-foot high trophy.

It was inscribed, "To one of the greatest players the NFL ever had." The presentation and adulation by Hill's teammates brought tears to the eyes of several, including Rutigliano.

The coach was quoted as saying, "It was such a great thing to see, I just sat there and couldn't help crying. It was so well deserved ... I have never met a guy like Calvin in all my life."

Another "gift" was presented to Hill during that game by the 51,435 mostly Seahawk fans in the Kingdome: a standing ovation as his retirement was announced during the final minutes.

"It was one of the most moving moments I've ever experienced, and also one of the most deserved tributes I've ever seen a man receive," Art Modell, then owner of the Browns, said after the game.

Hill, who was the NFC "Rookie of the Year" after being the Cowboys' first round selection out of Yale University in the 1969 college draft, led Dallas to the Super Bowl in 1970 and 1971, and was selected for the Pro Bowl in 1972 and 1974.

He later played two years for the Washington Redskins and one season with Hawaii in the ill-fated World Football League.

He signed as a free agent with the injury-riddled Browns on September 26, 1978 after considering offers from several other teams.

"I wanted to get into a winning situation and where I could help ... because I knew I wanted to continue my career," Hill said.

"I can't think of a better way to earn a living than playing football. Sometimes I enjoy it so much I feel like I'm stealing money. If I weren't playing pro football, I'd probably be out somewhere playing touch football, that's how much I enjoy the game."

In his four seasons with the Browns, Hill rushed for 516 yards (in 138 carries) and two touchdowns, and also caught 107 passes for 1,248 yards and 16 touchdowns. At the time of his retirement Hill was the 18th all - time leading rusher in NFL history with 6,083 yards.

Hill remained with the Browns for a year as a front office executive, working with Paul Warfield in the employment assistance program and the "Inner Circle," which was formed to help rehabilitate players with chemical and alcoholic dependency problems.

The tough and durable 'Gunner'

Few football players of any era were tougher than "The Gunner," center Frank Gatski, a charter member of the Browns from 1946 through 1956.

His record for durability is amazing.

In his 11 years with the Browns, plus four at Marshall College, three in high school in 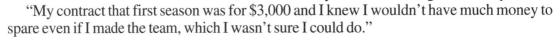 Farmington, West Virginia, and a final season with the Detroit Lions in 1957, Gatski is renowned for never having missed a team practice, let alone a game.

"You've got to be tough to play this game," Gatski once said, and nobody ever doubted him.

Elected to the Hall of Fame in 1985, Gatski was the epitome of the position he played.

That is, nobody ever notices the center on a football team until he makes a mistake, which The Gunner seldom did.

During his Hall of Fame induction ceremonies, Gatski reminisced about the start of his career, recalling that he hitch-hiked from West Virginia to Bowling Green State University where the Browns then held their training camp.

"I wasn't sure what was going to happen and I wanted to save the money," Gatski said.

At the time Gatski also was a linebacker, but played center exclusively after the season got underway.

Frank Gatski

"My contract that first season was for $3,000 and I knew I wouldn't have much money to spare even if I made the team, which I wasn't sure I could do."

Not only did Gatski make the team, he was an National Football League all-star four times, started in the 1955 Pro Bowl, and played in 11 championship games, 10 with the Browns and the other in his only season with the Detroit Lions, 1957.

He was traded to the Lions after holding out for a better contract with the Browns.

And then, ironically, in Gatski's final game he helped the Lions beat the Browns, 59-14, for the NFL championship.

As the Browns' center, Gatski had helped them defeat the Lions, 56-10, two years earlier, in 1954.

They also won the NFL title in 1950 and 1954 during Gatski's tenure in Cleveland.

A man of few words under normal circumstances, Gatski concluded his Hall of Fame acceptance speech by recalling two of the greatest games in Browns history.

"We were considered upstarts from a minor league, the All America Football Conference, when we came into the NFL in 1950, and played the Philadelphia Eagles in our first game - and beat 'em, 35-10," Gatski said with unmistakable pride.

"They called us 'sandlotters' because we passed so much. So, the next time we played 'em that season we didn't throw a single pass and we beat 'em again, 13-7."

Gatski also talked about the Browns' 30-28 victory over Los Angeles in the 1950 title game, when Lou Groza kicked a 16 yard field goal with 28 seconds remaining.

"This is the best feeling I've had since we hung it on the Rams in our first championship game," Gatski told the Hall of Fame audience,

"If I could play another game, I'd put on my togs and run all the way to California to do it."

And those who knew the Gunner, believe he would - and could - do just that.

'He won't back up from anybody'

It was a salary dispute with Paul Brown that convinced Walt Michaels, a Pro Bowl linebacker renowned as "one tough guy," to hang up his cleats and become a coach.

That was in 1962, after Michaels had played ten seasons for the Browns, and eleven years after they'd selected him seventh in the 1951 draft out of Washington & Lee University.

Brown, who seldom acknowledged making a mistake in trading a player, did so in the case of Michaels. Shortly after the draft, and before Michaels played a game for the Browns, he was dealt to Green Bay. A year later Brown re-acquired him from the Packers.

At the time Michaels was sent to Green Bay the Browns' linebacking corps included Tommy Thompson, Tony Adamle, Alex Agase and Hal Herring.

"I understood why they didn't need me," Michaels said then - but not in 1962. When he left the Browns the disgruntled Michaels was quoted as saying, "(Brown) admitted I had a good year (in 1961), but you'd never know it from the money I've been offered." He took a job as defensive line coach of the Oakland Raiders in 1962, and a year later went to the New York Jets and served as their defensive coordinator through 1972.

It was Michaels who was the architect of the defense that enabled the Jets to win Super Bowl III, 16-7, against the favored Baltimore Colts - for whom Michaels' younger brother Lou was their kicker.

Walt Michaels

Michaels went to the Philadelphia Eagles and was their defensive coordinator from 1973-75, returned to the Jets as an assistant to Lou Holtz in 1976, and took over as head coach of the team in 1977. It was a job he held for six years, through 1982, posting an overall won-lost record of 41-49-1, including 2-2 in the playoffs.

The Jets' best season under Michaels was 1981 when they went 10-5-1 and, as the AFC wild card, lost to Buffalo, 31-27, in the first round of the playoffs.

The Jets did even better in the strike-shortened 1982 season, winning six of nine games, and their first two in the playoffs, beating Cincinnati, 44-17, and the Raiders, 17-14, to advance to the AFC championship game, which they lost to Miami, 14-0.

In the wake of that defeat Joe Walton replaced Michaels, who then became coach of the New Jersey Generals of the United States Football League. With former Browns star Brian Sipe at quarterback the Generals were 14-4 in 1984 and 11-7 in 1985, after which the league folded.

During his 10 seasons as a player for the Browns the 6-0, 230-pound Michaels was recognized as one of the best linebackers in the NFL, playing in the Pro Bowl four consecutive years, 1957-60.

And though Brown was unwilling to meet his salary demand in 1962, Michaels was highly regarded by his teammates, as Thompson, an All-Pro linebacker himself, made clear in a story in the Cleveland *Plain Dealer*.

"Walt Michaels won't back up from anybody," Thompson was quoted as saying. "If Rocky Marciano and Joe Louis came at him together, Michaels wouldn't flinch. He'd swing right back. I've seen him refuse to back track from the toughest men in the game, guys much taller and bigger than he is. He's one tough guy."

111

A miscarriage of justice

One of the great mysteries - and miscarriages of justice - in professional sports has to be the way Frank Ryan was literally booed out of Cleveland in the 1960s.

The scholarly, soft-spoken Texan, who went on to earn a Ph.D. in higher mathematics and the title, "Dr. Ryan," was the only quarterback to lead the Browns to a world championship since the glory days of Otto Graham.

Frank Ryan

Ryan engineered a 27-0 victory over Baltimore in 1964, and nobody was able to do the same in the 31 seasons that followed, before the Browns moved to Baltimore after the 1995 season.

But Ryan was never really appreciated during his tenure with the Browns that began in 1962, when he was acquired from the Los Angeles Rams with halfback Tom Wilson (for defensive tackle Larry Stephens and two draft choices), until he was replaced by Bill Nelsen in 1968. He was traded to Washington in 1969.

"I don't know why," Ryan was quoted in 1977 upon his appointment as athletic director of Yale University. "I worked hard, I was a team player, and I had some pretty good years,"

All of which were indisputably true.

It got so bad at times for Ryan and his family that he often made a conscious effort to avoid being in public.

Once, during the 1964 season, Ryan said, "I made a trip to the zoo with my family. It was the only place I found a group of Clevelanders who weren't criticizing me."

A second string quarterback to King Hill at Rice University, and a part-timer with the Rams, Ryan was acquired to serve as a back-up to Jim Ninowski.

But Ninowski sustained a broken collarbone in the eighth game of the 1962 season, Ryan took over, and didn't relinquish the position until he was injured in 1968. Then the Browns made a deal to get" Nelsen from Pittsburgh.

The high-point of Ryan's career, of course, was that championship game on December 27, 1964. He fired three touchdown passes to Gary Collins to lead the "laugh champs," as the Browns were called then, in their startling upset of the Colts.

Maybe it was brain-power that made Ryan so good.

As he once said, "If you go into a game with the right frame of mind, you can be a world-beater. In our league the players are so equal physically, the difference on any given Sunday is the mental attitude.

"When I'm in the right frame of mind it seems I can think the ball right to the target. It seems so easy to pass. Then there are days it seems I'm throwing a shot put."

Ryan's name is prominent throughout the Browns' list of individual records. His 907 completions in 1,755 attempts are third only to Brian Sipe (who played three more years) and Bernie Kosar, his 134 touchdown passes are 20 fewer than Sipe threw, and his 29 in one season are second by only one to Sipe's total.

Ryan also played in three Pro Bowl games, and when he retired he was seventh on the all-time NFL list of quarterbacks in total offense.

But still, the fans booed Ryan more than cheered him, which remains one of the great mysteries - and miscarriages of justice - in professional sports.

To be the best was his quest

By his own admission during his four year career with the Browns from 1976-79, Gerald Irons had a "split personality."

The 6-2, 223 pound linebacker who was co-captain of the Browns in 1978 and their "Most Valuable Defensive Player" in 1977, was as tough as his name implied.

"I'm as aggressive on the field as I can be," he said upon being dealt to the Browns for a second round draft pick by the Oakland Raiders, for whom he played from 1970-75. Before leaving the Raiders, Irons was described by their All-Pro fullback Marv Hubbard as being "the most powerful man I've ever met in pro football."

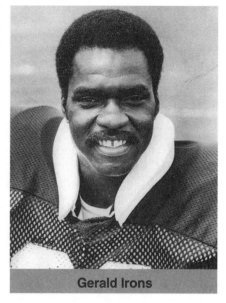
Gerald Irons

But out of uniform, Irons' personality changed from "Darth Vader" - a nickname he brought from Oakland - to "Mr. Nice Guy."

"Yes," he confirmed, "I think an appropriate description would be that I'm a mild-mannered, maybe even a meek man off the field."

Indeed, there were times - many of them - when Irons would stop a ball carrier with a tackle that nearly loosened the teeth of both players, and then get to his feet and help the other player off the ground, patting him on the back in the process. "But the minute I step off the field I become a different person. I have a split personality."

The reason he was nicknamed "Darth Vader" was because he wore so much protective equipment. "It's my armor," explained Irons, whose equipment included helmet, mouth guard, neck brace, shoulder pads with rib protectors attached, bicep pads, elbow pads, forearm pads, hand pads, hip pads, supporter, thigh pads and knee pads.

Irons was a graduate of the University of Maryland-Eastern Shore where he made the dean's list with a 3.43 grade average, and was president of the student government.

While playing for the Raiders, Irons spent six off-seasons earning a master's degree in marketing at the University of Chicago. He also wrote free verse poetry, and one of his poems summarized his attitude about playing football, to wit:

"To be the best is my quest. Athletes come and athletes go, but there's always something special about a real pro. See, he's determined to be the very best, and until he is world champion he will never rest.

"To be the best is my quest. I've learned over the years there is no shortcut, you've got to work hard at knocking your opponent on his butt.

"To be the best is my quest and execution is the only solution. While blocking and tackling is my forte, when I finish my opponent will need an x-ray.

"To be the best is my quest. From day-to-day towards my goal I will strive, while keeping my championship hopes alive. And let's not forget day-to-day concentration, for it will help make us the best in the nation.

"To be the best is my quest. Some may be happy just to make the Browns' squad, but I'll never be satisfied 'till I get that Super Bowl wad. So much happiness I know it will bring, the thrill of wearing a Super Bowl ring.

"To be the best is my quest. While everything needed I cannot mention, I hope the things I've said is not beyond your retention."

Plenty of room for doubt

Paul Brown didn't make many mistakes in his 17 years as coach of the Browns, but one that stands out was his decision to trade Bobby Mitchell to Washington on December 14, 1961.

Yes, the same Bobby Mitchell who was elected to the Hall of Fame in 1983 after seven outstanding seasons with the Redskins.

Bobby Mitchell

In that deal for Mitchell, the Browns obtained the rights to Ernie Davis, the 1961 Heisman Trophy winner from Syracuse University.

But Davis' untimely death from leukemia 18 months later was not the reason for faulting the trade.

It was Brown's evaluation of Mitchell, whom he considered a "fumbler," that made the deal a bad one.

It also was Brown's negative opinion of the former University of Illinois speedster that damaged the coach's relationship with Jim Brown.

And that problem between Paul and Jim Brown probably had a bearing on owner Art Modell's decision to fire the longtime coach on January 7, 1963.

Mitchell's reputation as a fumbler, whether it was justified or not, probably was the reason he was not drafted higher than the seventh round in 1958.

In his four seasons with the Browns, Mitchell teamed up with his best friend, Jim Brown, and often was sensational, although, to be sure, he did fumble on occasion.

With the Browns he rushed for 2,297 yards and gained 1,463 yards receiving, 607 on punt returns, 1,550 on kickoffs and scored 38 touchdowns.

'I didn't mind the No. 2 role (to Jim Brown)," Mitchell said during his enshrinement in the Hall of Fame. "Jim and I pushed each other, and the competition made both of us better."

But Paul Brown wanted two big backs, the likes of Green Bay's Jim Taylor and Paul Hornung, which is why he coveted Davis instead of the 5-9, 180 pound Mitchell.

When Mitchell was traded to the Redskins, they had never employed a black player, which also was an issue in the deal.

The first thing Mitchell did was negotiate a contract with the Redskins which, they said, equaled Jim Brown's, then the highest in the National Football League, reportedly for $40,000.

Then the Redskins switched Mitchell to flanker and he became their most prolific receiver the next seven seasons.

He retired in 1969 with 14,078 combined yards, and only Jim Brown ranked ahead of him in total yardage at that time.

Mitchell's stats also included 521 pass receptions for 7,954 yards and 65 touchdowns, and he returned 102 kickoffs for an average of 26.4 yards. His receiving and return marks placed Mitchell among the game's top 20 in both departments.

Included in his 11 year career statistics were 32 fumbles.

After his retirement, Mitchell became assistant general manager of the Redskins, so from his point of view, being traded to Washington was a good deal.

Not so for the Browns, as Modell commented. "To be honest and candid," he said, "there is plenty of room for doubt (that it was good for Cleveland). There is a question as to whether Mitchell was deployed properly here."

'What's this game coming to?'

"What's this game coming to?" exclaimed Dan Stonesifer, the defensive captain of the-then Chicago Cardinals as they prepared for a game against the Browns on October 10, 1954.

"Now we've got to play against our own scouts. What is this game coming to?" Stonesifer asked again.

And therein lies one of pro football's strangest - and best - human interest stories.

Stonesifer's remark was motivated by the sight of Browns linebacker Tony Adamle who, a week earlier - and for the previous two seasons – had been a scout for the Cardinals.

In fact, Adamle had scouted the Browns in their previous game, a 28-10 loss to Philadelphia and, a few hours after he submitted his report to Cardinals Coach Joe Stydehar, Cleveland Coach Paul Brown called.

"Tommy Thompson had just broken his leg and Paul wanted me to return to the team," said Adamle, who had retired in 1952. He began playing for the Browns in 1947, out of Ohio State University, and was their captain in 1950.

"I quit when I did because I wanted to go to medical school ... I'd always wanted to be a doctor," said Adamle. "But things weren't going too well financially at that time, and Paul (Brown) offering me a job was almost perfect

Tony Adamle

timing. I was just about at the point where I would have had to dig up a loan someplace, or quit school."

Adamle didn't accept Brown's offer immediately.

First he wanted assurance that Brown wasn't inviting him back to get his hands on Adamle's scouting report on the Browns.

"To his credit, Paul never once asked me about my scouting report; he was a perfect gentleman, a man of honor," said Adamle, who - with only four days practice – went on to play a key role in the Browns' 31-7 victory over the Cardinals.

Early in that game Ollie Matson, the Cardinals' speedy running back, tried an end sweep, but Adamle caught him from behind. "It surprised everybody, especially Matson," said Adamle, who was deceptively fast for his size.

Adamle played well the next nine games, too, until he suffered a broken leg in the second-to-last game. It was a 42-7 victory over Pittsburgh that clinched the championship of the National Football League's Eastern Conference.

It turned out to be the final game of Adamle's football career that began at Cleveland's Collinwood High School when he was a triple-threat fullback.

It continued at Ohio State in 1941 and 1946, when he was a center and linebacker before and after three years in the Air Force as a radio operator on a B-25 bomber during World War II.

That 1954 season, as the Browns won their second of four NFL championships, provided Adamle with enough money to return to Western Reserve University for the medical degree he coveted.

He graduated in 1958 and, as "Dr. Tony Adamle," was a general practitioner in Kent, Ohio thanks to his un-retirement as a scout for the team he then helped beat.

'Tommy-O' - better than Graham?

Any quarterback good enough to break Otto Graham's collegiate passing records surely must be good enough to play in the National Football League, right?

Well, maybe. But not in the case of Tommy O'Connell, who was the NCAA passing leader for the University of Illinois in 1952 when he bettered the marks set by Graham at Northwestern University in the early 1940s.

Tommy O'Connell

In his three seasons at Illinois, O'Connell completed 195 of 344 passes for 2,453 yards, and took the Illini to a 40-7 victory over Stanford in the Rose Bowl.

A cocky, confident leader who was nicknamed "Tommy-O," O'Connell started well enough for the Browns, who signed him as a free agent on October 22, 1956, after he'd been released by Chicago two games into the season.

The Bears had taken O'Connell in the 18th round of the 1952 draft, and he played briefly for them in 1953, then spent most of the next two years in the Air Force.

When then-Browns quarterback George Ratterman and his back-up, Babe Parilli, were injured midway through the 1956 season, Paul Brown eagerly signed O'Connell. He proceeded to lead the team to four victories in the final seven games, after the Browns had gone 1-4 at the start.

O'Connell was even better the next season when he was the NFL's most efficient passer with 63 completions in 110 attempts for 1,229 yards and nine touchdowns with eight interceptions for a league-leading 93.3 rating. He missed two games with a leg injury that was initially diagnosed as a sprain, but later was found to be a hairline fracture.

That was the season the Browns reached the championship game for the seventh time in their eight years in the NFL. However, they were overwhelmed by Detroit, 59-14, as O'Connell was forced out of the game early in the second quarter as he attempted to play despite his injury, and was replaced by Milt Plum.

That winter "Tommy O" was honored by the Cleveland Touchdown Club as the Browns' outstanding player. But it obviously did not influence Brown who was obsessed with the need to have an outstanding quarterback, and had lost confidence in O'Connell.

The coach felt that O'Connell, who was listed at 5-11 (but probably wasn't even that tall), was too short to be an effective NFL passer, and announced his intention to install Milt Plum as the Browns' quarterback in 1958.

O'Connell promptly retired and said that he would return to his alma mater, Illinois, as an assistant under head football coach Ray Elliot.

"My affiliation with the Browns has been the finest, but I thought this was the best time for me to step out of pro ball," O'Connell was quoted then. "I'm not the biggest fellow in the world, nor the fastest, and football is getting to be a big, fast man's game. I'm taking a financial setback, but over seven or eight years it all will balance out."

O'Connell left the Illini after one season to become head coach at Drake University in 1959, then in 1960 and 1961 returned to pro football as a player-coach of the Buffalo Bills under Buster Ramsey in the American Football League. When Lou Saban replaced Ramsey in 1962, O'Connell was not retained and left the game.

The No. 1 equipment manager

When Morrie Kono was interviewed by Paul Brown for a job with the Browns in the summer of 1946, the coach of Cleveland's new team in the fledgling All-America Football Conference asked three questions.

"First, Paul wanted to know, 'Do you like football?'" said Kono. "That was easy. I told him, 'I always got in trouble in school for reading football magazines hidden in textbooks during class.'

"The second question was, 'How soon could you leave for training camp?' I said, 'How much longer are we going to talk?'

"Then Paul asked me, 'Do you have a way to get to Bowling Green?'" where the Browns would hold their first training camp. "I answered, 'Where's the bus station?'"

Five minutes later Kono was buying a bus ticket. He in such a hurry that he didn't even bother to ask how much the job paid - which turned out to be $50 a week.

And for the next 34 years, through 1979, while Kono never scored a touchdown, threw a pass or even made a tackle for the Browns - though he claimed to have made a key block once - he was considered one of the most valuable members of the organization.

Morrie Kono

Everybody always said that the rotund, affable, humorous and hard-working Kono had the patience of a saint, which was a pre-requisite for his job, and that he could take a joke, even when he was the butt of it, which he usually was.

In a Cleveland *Plain Dealer* article in 1976, it was written, "In a world of behemoths, Kono, at 5-7, remains a small gem. And because of his sense of humor, he is probably the only equipment manager who is in demand as an after dinner speaker."

One of Kono's favorite stories involved former quarterback George Ratterman, who was renowned as a practical joker. As Kono related, "I'll never forget a game in 1956 when Paul Brown sent me to the huddle during a time out with a play to give Ratterman.

"I kept repeating it over and over so I wouldn't louse it up, and just as I reached the huddle, Ratterman turned and said, 'Who the hell are you replacing?' He shook me up so, I completely forgot the play that Paul told me to give to Ratterman."

As for that "key block" that Kono claimed he made, it occurred in a game in the late 1950s and helped the Browns beat San Francisco.

"Honest, I did," he insisted. "Don Paul (a defensive back-kick returner for the Browns) caught a punt near the sidelines where I was standing. One of the first 49ers down the field ran out of bounds to avoid a block, planning, of course, to swing back on the field to get Paul.

"But he hit me instead. Both of us went down - me out cold - and Don went for a touchdown. The guy who ran into me would have stopped him, but didn't because of me.

"I was out for about 15 minutes. When I came to, Marion Motley was giving me smelling salts. It had to be the only time in football history that a team's star fullback, a guy who went on to make the Hall of Fame, had to take care of the equipment manager."

Kono retired at the age of 68 in 1980 with enough golden memories to fill a book - and without a single regret, he said then. "The only thing I'd change, if I could, would be the scores of some of the games. But that's all. Nothing else."

The Browns' costliest mistake

The acquisition of Tom Cousineau was the Browns' most expensive transaction - and, as it turned out, their costliest mistake.

They got him in a round about deal from Buffalo, which had made Cousineau the first (overall) choice in the 1979 college draft after he'd been a highly acclaimed star at Ohio State and previously at St. Edward High School in Cleveland.

Tom Cousineau

Cousineau, a 6-3, 232-pound middle linebacker, refused to sign with the Bills and instead opted to play in the Canadian Football League for the Montreal Alouettes, who gave him a five year contract reportedly worth $2 million.

However, after three seasons north of the border, Cousineau invoked his contractual right to terminate his agreement with the Alouettes and announced his desire to play in the NFL.

It was then, partly because of Art Modell's cozy relationship with Buffalo owner Ralph Wilson, that the Browns were able to acquire Cousineau by matching an offer the Bills had made to prevent Houston from getting the right to sign the celebrated linebacker.

The offer: $3.5 million, which included a $1 million signing bonus, for five years.

It made Cousineau - at the time - the highest paid player in Browns history, and one of the wealthiest in the NFL.

Making the deal even more expensive for the Browns, they had to give the Bills their first round draft choice in 1983, their third round selection in 1984, and their fifth round pick in 1985.

Though beset by personal problems almost from the beginning of what turned out to be Cousineau's four year career with the Browns - he was rumored to be gay, which he regularly and vehemently denied, and which never was substantiated - he played well enough, but wasn't even the best all-around linebacker on the team.

Cousineau led the Browns in the strike shortened 1982 season with 72 tackles (in nine games), and in 1983 with 138, but was second with 170 in 1984, and third with 145 in 1985.

He was never an All-Pro selection nor picked for the Pro Bowl, though two of his lesser-paid linebacker-teammates were, Chip Banks (All-Pro) in 1983 and Clay Matthews (All Pro) in 1984, and Banks (Pro Bowl) in 1983 and 1984.

The fact that Banks and Matthews were out-producing Cousineau contributed to team "chemistry" problems.

Banks demanded and received a contract calling for $600,000 in 1986 and $700,000 in 1987, which led to Cousineau's eventual demise with the Browns.

They waived Cousineau during training camp in 1986, unburdening themselves of the remaining $500,000 of his salary.

As then-coach Marty Schottenheimer announced, "I have no doubt Tom will play in the NFL and probably start (but) we just had too many quality players at his position."

Thus ended the Browns most expensive deal - and their costliest mistake.

Cousineau joined San Francisco, though he was injured and unable to play that first year with the 49ers, and retired after the 1987 season.

From anonymity to the Hall of Fame

When Leroy Kelly was selected in the eighth round of the 1964 college draft out of little Morgan State University, it was primarily as a punt and kickoff return specialist, which he was for the Browns the first two years he played in the National Football League.

And, back then, it's doubtful that even Kelly's most ardent fans, including his parents or his brother Pat, a budding major league baseball player, expected that the 6-0, 202-pound halfback would wind up in the Pro Football Hall of Fame.

When he joined the Browns they had Jim Brown, the greatest runner in the NFL, and his backfield mate, Ernie Green, and Kelly was listed on the depth chart behind the long forgotten Charlie Scales and Jamie Caleb.

Leroy Kelly

However, following Brown's retirement at the end of the 1965 season, Kelly took over as Green's partner and rushed for 1,141 yards - an NFL-leading 5.5 yard average per carry - and 15 touchdowns, which also was the best in the league, and was on his way to football immortality.

After two more 1,000 yard seasons in 1966 and 1967, during which he was the was the No. 1 rusher in the NFL with 1,205 and 1,239 yards, and the league scoring champion in those three consecutive seasons, Kelly signed a four year contract worth a total of $320,000, then the most money ever paid a Browns player.

And in 1994, 21 years after he left the Browns, Kelly, the lightly-regarded - by some - kick returner/running back was elected to the Pro Football Hall of Fame, the 13th member of the franchise to be so honored.

At the time of his retirement, after an unsuccessful training camp trial in 1974 with the Oakland Raiders, who claimed him from the Browns on waivers, Kelly spent one season as a coach with the Philadelphia Bell in the ill-fated World Football League.

Then he ended his football career and entered the business world as a restaurateur in Philadelphia.

In his 10 seasons with the Browns, Kelly rushed for 7,274 yards (in 1,727 carries), then the fourth best total in the NFL, behind Jim Brown (12,312), Jim Taylor (8,597), and Joe Perry (8,378). He was an All-Pro selection five times (1966-69, 1971), and played in six Pro Bowl games (1966-72).

Kelly had 27 100-yard rushing games in his career and is the fifth leading scorer in team history with 90 touchdowns (74 rushing, 13 pass receiving) for 540 points, behind Brown (second with 756), and kickers, Lou Groza (1,349), Don Cockroft (1,080), and Matt Bahr (677).

All of Kelly's accomplishments made a prophet of Dub Jones, the former Browns running back who was the team's backfield coach when Brown indicated he was planning to retire. In a story that appeared in the Cleveland *Plain Dealer* in December 1965, Jones was quoted as saying:

"I'd be willing to match Leroy's potential with any of the much publicized backs coming out of college this year. He's way above average. In fact. He eventually may move in with the 'super' players."

Which Kelly quickly did, spectacularly well.

'I should be thankful to Wiggin'

A bargain, that's what Cleo Miller was to the Browns. A *real* bargain, and credit for his acquisition in 1975 - though inadvertent - must be given to another former member of the Browns, Paul Wiggin, a defensive end who played here from 1957-67.

However, while Miller was happy to join the Browns, he was unhappy about the circumstances that made it possible for him to come to Cleveland. "I guess it could be said I should be thankful to Paul Wiggin, or should I?" Miller said in a first person story that appeared in *Browns News Illustrated*.

Cleo Miller

Thankful, because it led to his opportunity to play for the Browns through 1982.

But unhappy, even embittered, because of what he considered unfair treatment by Wiggin, who was then coach of the Kansas City Chiefs.

Miller, a 5-11, 214-pound running back at the University of Arkansas-Pine Bluff, signed as a free agent with Kansas City, when he was not selected in the 1974 draft. At the time the Chiefs' coach was Hank Stram, who liked what he'd seen of Miller.

Miller played briefly for the Chiefs that season but, in his opinion, was virtually ignored by Wiggin, who replaced Stram as head coach in 1975.

"(Wiggin) said I was going to be his starting fullback," said Miller. But that was before the Chiefs traded for MacArthur Lane and Wiggin installed him at fullback.

"After our third regular season game - we had just beaten the Raiders and I still hadn't seen any action - I went into (Wiggin's) office the next day and asked him again if I could play," continued Miller. "He flew off the handle and started cursing, screaming and shouting at me. He told me that I couldn't let him be a winner for one day without spoiling it for him, and that I wasn't going to play.

"Before I realized what I was saying, I let him have it. I told him that he had spoiled every day I had since he had been there. I then came to my senses and told him to trade me, play me or put me on waivers.

"Wiggin said he had tried to trade me but nobody wanted me. He said I no longer fit into their plans and that he was releasing me."

Which led to Miller joining the Browns.

"The only reason I came to Cleveland was that, of all the teams that called me, the Browns were the only team that was playing against the Chiefs that year, and I wanted to play against them. I wanted to show them that they had made a big mistake."

Unfortunately for Miller, when the Chiefs came to Cleveland for the second last game of the season, Miller played only on special teams because of an ankle injury, but was elated to be part of the Browns' 42-10 victory.

Miller stayed with the Browns for seven more seasons, starting 26 consecutive games at fullback between 1976-78. In 1977 he rushed for 768 yards, including 117 in 21 carries in a 27-16 victory over Buffalo, and also led the team with 41 pass receptions for 291 yards.

He wound up his playing career in 1982 in ninth place on the Browns all-time rushing list with 2,297 yards in 546 carries - thanks to Paul Wiggin.

Twice chosen, twice rejected

Jim Ninowski came to the Browns in 1958 with a big reputation as the Big Ten passing champion at Michigan State, and high expectations.

As it turned out, Ninowski's claim to fame is that he was one of the few members of the Browns alumni who were picked by Paul Brown twice, and rejected twice.

A fourth round draft choice, Ninowski was traded to Detroit after seeing limited duty in 1958 and 1959 playing behind Milt Plum.

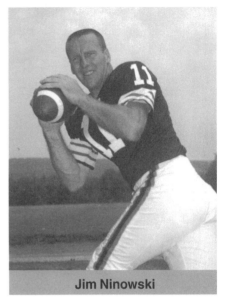

He was the starter for the Lions in 11 games in 1960 and 13 in1961, then was re-acquired by the Browns in another deal with Detroit in 1962.

In the first transaction, the Browns received the Lions' No. 1 pick in the 1961 draft, which they used to select tight end Bobby Crespino. Then, to bring Ninowski back to Cleveland, the Browns sent their eighth round draft choice in 1962 to the Lions.

The flurry of activity that eventually involved six quarterbacks in the next six years started with the retirement of future Hall of Famer Otto Graham, who hung up his cleats after the 1955 season.

Longtime understudy, George Ratterman, with Babe Parilli in reserve, initially replaced Graham. However, both were injured in 1956 and, in desperation, the Browns

Jim Ninowski

signed free agent Tommy O'Connell, who'd played for Chicago in 1953, but spent most of the next two years in the Air Force. He rejoined the Bears in 1956, but was cut after two games.

O'Connell took over for the Browns in the final seven games in 1956, winning four of them. They finished 5-7, the first losing record in the history of the franchise.

O'Connell was the Browns quarterback in all but one game in 1957, and was the NFL's top-rated (93.3) passer, completing 63 of 110 passes for 1,229 yards and nine touchdowns. He led the team to a 9-2-1 record and the Eastern Division title.

However, when the Browns lost the championship game to Detroit, 59-14, Brown was determined to make a change. Milt Plum, who'd played behind O'Connell, was installed at quarterback. O'Connell, despite his league-leading rating, was waived.

But the next four seasons were no better with Plum at the controls, during which the Browns made it to the playoffs only once, losing, 10-0, to the New York Giants in 1958. That's when Brown made the decision in the spring of 1962 to re-acquire Ninowski, who'd been a substitute behind Earl Morrall with the Lions.

To do so, Brown sent Plum, Tom Watkins and Dave Lloyd to Detroit, for Ninowski, defensive end Bill Glass and running back Howard "Hopalong" Cassady.

Ninowski started the 1962 season at quarterback for the Browns, but suffered a broken collar bone in the eighth game and was replaced by Frank Ryan, who'd been acquired in a deal with the Los Angeles Rams, strictly as a back-up.

But Ryan played so well, eventually leading the Browns to their third – and last – NFL championship in 1964, that Ninowski never started another game.

He remained with the Browns, playing behind Ryan through 1966, after which he was traded to Washington, where he also saw little action the next two seasons, and in 1969 wound up his career - which had started so promisingly – on New Orleans' bench.

The 'best tight end' - until Ozzie

Three years before the arrival of Ozzie Newsome, the "best tight end" in the history of the Browns, as anointed by the team's publicity director in the 1975 media guide, was a 6-4, 250-pound giant from the University of Massachusetts named Milt Morin.

It was said of Morin that he "resembles a bull on a rampage when he catches the ball in the open and starts bowling over defensive backs."

Nobody at that time disagreed with the extravagant praise for Morin, one of the best - and best-liked - players on the team.

Morin caught 271 passes for 4,208 yards and 16 touchdowns in his ten years with the Browns, and was a Pro Bowler in 1968, 1969 and 1972. His best seasons were 1968, when he had 43 receptions for 792 yards, and 1971, with 40 for 581 yards.

In his own words, in the media guide, Morin said of his dedication to the team and the game: "I owe it to the younger guys to drive myself. When they look at an established NFL player they want to see the best, and I want to show them the best.

"If you just go at a normal pace, you won't stick out even if you have talent. You have to drive yourself on every play, and though you run 40 to 50 plays a game, you'll be remembered for only your three best and three worst."

Milt Morin

Several injuries, including a herniated disc, robbed Morin of speed and dexterity later in his career. In 1975 he was replaced by rookie Oscar Roan and caught only one pass.

In training camp the following season Morin was waived by then-coach Forrest Gregg, after which Browns co-captain Doug Dieken paid tribute to Morin in a story that appeared in the Cleveland *Plain Dealer*. "It's a shame. Milt is a wonderful guy and a squad just can't have too many like him," Dieken said.

And, as the *Plain Dealer* story went on: "Morin's value to the club can't be measured in years or yards. He contributed certain intangibles as a member of the squad and the Cleveland community. His rapport with the fans was earned through countless appearances all over Ohio. He had a particular fondness for children, which was reciprocated fully."

Morin admitted, when he was handed his release, "I shouldn't be too surprised, though you never really expect it to happen. Every football player realizes this day will come ... still, it's a shock. Maybe I shouldn't have been, but I was kind of optimistic. I wanted to be part of this team."

When the Browns made Morin their No. 1 draft choice in 1966, he also was selected by the San Diego Chargers of the-then American Football League. He came close to signing with the Chargers because, he said, he liked the idea of playing on the West Coast where the weather was better, though the competition was not as good.

Morin eventually chose the Browns, and said of his decision: "The Browns are the Browns. You think of them as champions, and I just wanted to play with that type of team."

It was a choice he never regretted, and neither did the Browns, because Morin also was a champion - and the best tight end that ever played for the franchise, until the arrival of Ozzie Newsome.

He refused to call it a 'game'

There were a couple of things about Bernie Parrish that distinguished him from most of his teammates when he was a member of the Browns from 1959-66.

First, he proved to be an outstanding defensive back, much better than anyone expected when he was drafted in the ninth round in 1958, a year before he was to graduate from the University of Florida.

Second, but definitely not *least*, Parrish was very opinionated – perhaps even *too opinionated* for his own good.

Parrish was especially outspoken in 1971 when he wrote, *They Call It A Game*, a book promoted as "an indictment of the pro football establishment."

During his playing career Parrish also was a leader in the formation of the NFL Players Association, which did not endear him to management.

But the man could play football, which he did very well for the Browns.

Bernie Parrish

Parrish was a starter at left cornerback his first six seasons in Cleveland, was a key member of the Browns' defense that shut out Baltimore, 27-0, in the NFL championship game in 1964, was selected to play in the Pro Bowl in 1961 and 1964, and is fifth among the team's all-time interception leaders with 29 (for 557 yards and three touchdowns), though three of the four defensive backs ahead of him played longer.

A halfback as well as a defensive back in college, Parrish earned a total of 16 letters at Florida, four each in football, track, basketball and baseball, and in the latter sport won All-America honors as a third baseman-outfielder in his senior year.

After being selected by the Browns, Parrish also was picked by Cincinnati in baseball's amateur draft and quit college in his senior year to accept a $30,000 bonus contract from the Reds. He played two seasons in their farm system, then decided to concentrate of a professional football career.

In a letter to Paul Brown prior to reporting to training camp in 1959, Parrish wrote, "Being drafted by the Browns was the greatest honor I ever received in football. I like running the ball, but I think my best position might be defensive back."

Which proved to be correct.

In 1966, after seven seasons as one of the leaders of the Browns' defense, Parrish threatened to retire, but changed his mind when then-coach Blanton Collier made him a player-coach. "Bernie knows as much or more about football than any other player in the NFL, and this year he will be coaching the defensive backs as well as playing with them," Collier said then.

Parrish also helped the Browns by recommending in 1960 that they make a deal with the then-Chicago Cardinals to acquire Don Fleming, another who proved to be an outstanding defensive back. Fleming, who was killed in an off-season accident in 1963, briefly was Parrish's roommate at the University of Florida.

Parrish's career with the Browns ended after one game in 1966 when he was waived and picked up by Houston. He played 11 games for the Oilers that season, then retired from football to concentrate on other endeavors, including writing his controversial book that was critical of the professional football establishment.

The 'Kentucky Rifleman'

He was called the "Kentucky Rifleman" and, back there in 1956, Vito "Babe" Parilli was supposed to be the Browns' "next Otto Graham."

Even Paul Brown, who was not one to make rash, hyperbolic statements, was quoted in the 1973 book, *The Cleveland Browns*, as saying, "Much of our future is wrapped up in this young man (Parilli)."

Vito "Babe" Parilli

But something happened to the quarterback who was as famous in his day at the University of Kentucky as Tim Couch was for the Wildcats in 1998. In 1951, Parilli set a then-collegiate record by throwing 23 touchdown passes, and scored five himself.

Parilli, who was Green Bay's No. 1 draft choice in 1952, played well enough for the Packers that season and the next, but spent 1954 and 1955 in the service and played, by his admission, "only touch football," which might have been part of the problem.

Whatever, Brown, then seeking a quarterback to replace Graham, who had retired, acquired Parilli in a trade with the Packers. They didn't think they needed Parilli; their quarterback then was the accomplished Tobin Rote.

The Browns had George Ratterman, who'd been Graham's understudy since 1952, but Brown clearly favored - and *expected* - Parilli to take the team back to the NFL championship game where they'd been all six of their seasons in the league.

When he didn't, when Parilli failed to even come close to the stardom he'd established for himself in college, the theories as to why he couldn't were plentiful.

The best might have been expressed by future Hall of Famer Mike McCormack, then offensive captain and tackle on the team, in *The Cleveland Browns* book: "Babe and Paul just couldn't get along. Babe had the hives because he was nervous and then he got hurt. After George (Ratterman) also got hurt, Paul put in a call for Tommy O'Connell ... (which) really saved us from having a complete washout of a season."

The Browns in 1956 suffered their worst year since entering the NFL in 1950, their record falling to 5-7 for fourth place in the Eastern Conference.

Ratterman started the season as the No. 1 quarterback, primarily because of his familiarity with the Browns' system, but injured a knee in the fourth game (three of which were losses) and was finished for the year. That opened the door to Parilli, but he struggled, too, and the Browns lost two of the next three, before Parilli went down with a separated shoulder.

That's when Brown signed free agent and former Chicago Bear O'Connell, and Parilli never played another game for the Browns. His stats in five games, three as a starter: 24 completions in 49 attempts for 409 yards and three touchdowns, with seven interceptions.

Parilli was traded back to Green Bay the winter of 1956-57 in what has to be considered one of Brown's worst deals. In addition to Parilli, he gave the Packers defensive end Carlton Massey, defensive back John Pettibon, running back Billy Kinard, and linemen John Macerelli and Sam Palumbo, all for quarterback Bobby Garrett.

Parilli played for Green Bay in 1957 and 1958, then enjoyed an outstanding ten year career in the American Football League with Oakland in 1960, the then-Boston Patriots from 1961-67, and the New York Jets in 1968 and 1969.

The big addition of 'Little Mo'

Dick Modzelewski was a 6-0, 250-pound defensive tackle, but still was known as "Little Mo," while his smaller brother Ed, a 6-0, 217-pound, pile-driving fullback, was nicknamed "Big Mo."

"I guess it's because Dick is older. That's the only reason I can give," Modzelewski told the Cleveland *Plain Dealer* when he was acquired by the Browns from the New York Giants in a trade for tight end Bobby Crespino in 1964.

The deal for Crespino was a good one for Cleveland, if only briefly, as Modzelewski was a key factor in the Browns winning the NFL championship in 1964, the last time they reached the pinnacle of pro football.

He played only three seasons for the Browns, was selected for the Pro Bowl in 1965, and ran his consecutive games played streak to 180 before retiring at the end of the 1966 season.

Dick "Little Mo" Modzelewski

Modzelewski scouted for the Browns in 1967, served as an assistant coach for the next ten seasons under Blanton Collier, Nick Skorich and Forrest Gregg, and wound up in 1977 as the team's head coach - although for only one game.

"Little Mo" took over as interim coach when Gregg resigned under fire with one game left in 1977. The Browns lost that final game to Seattle, 20-19, and when Modzelewski was not given consideration as Gregg's replacement in 1978, he resigned and looked elsewhere - unsuccessfully - for a head coach's job, ending his football career.

"I think I have head coaching ability. I felt I was ready four years ago, and I certainly feel I'm more ready now," he said then. Modzelewski also had applied for the job after the 1974 season when Skorich was fired and Gregg was hired.

Modzelewski, who was 33 when he came to Cleveland, started in the NFL in 1953 with Washington as a second round draft choice out of the University of Maryland. He was traded to Pittsburgh in 1955, and then to the Giants for whom he was a star from 1956-63 as a member of the "Fearsome Foursome," one of the best defensive lines in football that also included Andy Robustelli, Jim Katcavage and Rosey Grier.

Modzelewski said that he almost retired when he was traded to Cleveland. He was disappointed to be leaving the Giants, who'd won the Eastern Division championship three consecutive seasons, 1961-63, though they lost the NFL title game each year.

Another factor was that the Browns had always been one of the chief rivals of the Giants. As he said then, "I can't remember a game when we weren't up for the Browns ... it wasn't anything personal, it's just that the Browns were always breathing down our necks."

But Modzelewski changed his mind, he said, "Because now I won't have to tackle that No. 32 anymore." No. 32, of course, was Jim Brown.

And upon joining the Browns, Modzelewski brought what he called a "winning habit" from the Giants. On the first day of training camp, Modzelewski gave the same speech that, he said, his mentor, Robustelli, used to give to the Giants.

"It went something like this: 'We start winning the division championship right now.' Then, 'I'll pause ten seconds so anyone who doesn't agree can get out now.'"

It worked for the Browns in 1964 - although, unfortunately, not thereafter.

The failed 'Game-Buster'

He was nicknamed "Hopalong," because of a famous cowboy movie star with the same last name. But despite his outstanding collegiate career as a running back at Ohio State, Howard "Hopalong" Cassady never attained the fame predicted for him in professional football.

The winner of the Heisman Trophy in 1955, when he also was elected "Male Athlete of the Year" in a poll by the Associated Press, Cassady played - but only sparingly - just one year for the Browns.

Howard "Hopalong" Cassady

That was in 1962, after he'd been acquired by the Browns in a trade with the Detroit Lions, who had drafted him No. 1 in 1956 after his three superb seasons for Ohio State, during which he led the Buckeyes to two Big Ten championships. Cassady played six seasons - also without great success - for the Lions, and in 1962 was traded to the Browns, with quarterback Jim Ninowski and defensive end Bill Glass, for quarterback Milt Plum, halfback Tom Watkins, and linebacker Dave Lloyd.

But Cassady couldn't crack the starting lineup with the Browns. He was third on the depth chart behind running backs Tom Wilson and Charley Scales.

When the season ended, Cassady was traded to Philadelphia, but didn't fare well with the Eagles either, suffering a broken leg in the fourth game that ended his football career.

Ah, but "Hopalong" was a superstar during his three seasons with the Buckeyes.

The late Woody Hayes, then Ohio State's coach, called Cassady "Hoppy the Game Buster," and he often lived up to that nickname – in college, if not in the NFL.

According to the A.P. story in 1956, announcing that he had won the "Male Athlete of the Year" award:

"Cassady wasn't the best all-around football player of the 1955 season. Even his coach (Hayes) admitted that. But there was one thing he could do superlatively - that was take the ball and run with it, eluding tacklers or bowling them over, until he reached the goal line. And he had the knack of turning in his finest performances in the clutch games.

"At the end of the season Cassady was selected for the All-America team for the second year, was awarded the Heisman Trophy as the outstanding football player of the year, and was named the Most Valuable Player in the Big Ten.

"Unquestionably, he was the driving force behind Ohio State's second straight championship team, as well as its leading point-getter."

Cassady's fame perhaps was best illustrated in his winning of the "Male Athlete of the Year" award, considering the caliber of the players he outdistanced in the poll.

Cassady, who also was a highly regarded baseball player at Ohio State, received 257 points, including 53 first place votes, to easily beat out runner-up Rocky Marciano, then heavyweight boxing champion, whose point total was 161 with 35 first place votes.

Johnny Podres, the Brooklyn Dodgers pitching star of the 1955 World Series, was third with 16 first place votes and 90 total points; Otto Graham, who'd led the Browns to the NFL championship, was fourth; followed by basketball star Bill Russell, then of San Francisco University; American League batting champion Al Kaline, Detroit Tigers; Texas Christian halfback Jim Swink and welterweight boxing champion Carmen Basilio.

'He knew what he didn't know'

In the Browns' first 50 years there haven't been many – perhaps not any – better success stories than one fashioned by Vince Costello, whose friends called him the "Pride of Magnolia" when he was signed as an undrafted free agent in 1956.

Costello wasn't given much of a chance when he joined the Browns after a four-year career at Ohio University, and his stock didn't improve when he suffered a leg injury in his first training camp.

Instead of playing that season with the Browns, Costello limped home to Magnolia, Ohio and took a job coaching a high school team in Big Walnut.

However, the following summer Costello returned to the Browns for another trial and this time his perseverance paid dividends. He took over at middle linebacker, replacing the incumbent, Walter Michaels, who was switched to the outside, and continued as the starter for ten seasons, through 1966.

Many observers of the Browns during the mid-1950s and early-1960s rate Costello as the best middle linebacker in the history of the team.

He played for the New York Giants in 1967 and 1968, then served as an assistant coach for Cincinnati from 1969-73, and Kansas City in 1975 and 1976.

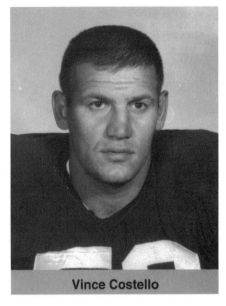

Vince Costello

One of Costello's best games – perhaps THE best he ever played – helped the Browns beat the Giants, 52-20, in the finale of the 1964 regular season, to win the Eastern Division. It vaulted them into the NFL title game in which they beat Baltimore, 27-0, the last time they won the league championship.

In that victory over the Giants, according to an article in the Cleveland *Plain Dealer*, it was written that the Browns "had heroes galore ... but none stood out more prominently than Costello.

"He hounded (quarterback) Y.A. Tittle the way Sam Huff always was credited with hounding Jim Brown, and generally made life miserable for the New York receivers and runners trying to invade his territory."

And, just as he played the game on the field, Costello didn't pull any punches in his remarks when he was the featured speaker at a Pro Football Hall of Fame luncheon a few years ago.

When asked who he thought was NFL's all-time greatest player, Costello said, as reported in a story that appeared in the Canton *Repository*: "I don't think there ever will be another Jim Brown." Costello and Brown joined the Browns the same year, and played together through 1965, when Brown retired.

Costello went on to say of Brown: "He is the best running back of all-time, and always will be. If you compare him to (Chicago Bears Hall of Famer) Walter Payton, there is no comparison. Brown averaged 5.2 yards per carry, and Payton 4.4."

Costello also rated his former coach, Paul Brown – but prefaced his remarks by saying: "There are two kind of coaches. Those who know not and knows he knows not, who is ignorant but can be taught, and those who know not and DON'T know they know not." Of the coach in the latter category, Costello said, "He is a fool ... pray for him."

Of Brown, Costello said, "He knew what he didn't know. He was not an X's and O's type of guy, but he had guys on his staff like Bill Walsh who was. He knew how to pick people. It was both of those reasons that made (Brown) such a great coach."

The longest of longshots

He was the longest of longshots, the greatest of underdogs, an undrafted free agent who'd played college football at Drake University and – finally – got a chance to accept an NFL tryout because ... well, "I might as well. It can't hurt anything."

Which eventually brought Felix Wright to the Browns in 1985 and, though he didn't become a starter at free safety until midway through 1987, led the entire NFL with nine interceptions in 1989 after switching to strong safety.

Felix Wright

When Wright ended his six year career with the Browns, he had picked off 26 passes, tying him with Tommy James and Hanford Dixon in eighth place on the franchise's all-time list of interceptions.

So how was it that Wright was overlooked by every team in the NFL in 1981, and his agent finally was able to get him invitations for tryouts with the then-Houston Oilers and Detroit Lions in 1982?

"I'm not sure, all I know is that I received a letter from my agent and I thought, 'What the heck, I might as well give it a shot,'" Wright was quoted in an Akron *Beacon Journal* story. At the time, he was coaching football at a high school in Joplin, Missouri.

Because both tryouts by the Oilers and Lions were held the same day, he chose the former and was one of three defensive backs – out of a field of 200, he said - to be offered a contract and reported to Houston's training camp.

But his pro football odyssey didn't end there. It was just the beginning.

"All of a sudden I was gone, cut," he was quoted in the paper. "My partners in the secondary couldn't believe it. They thought it was crazy."

However, it led to a job in the Canadian League and Wright played for the Hamilton Tiger-Cats from 1982-84, helping them win the Gray Cup in his third season north of the border, and that in turn resulted in a successful training camp trial with the Browns.

When Wright reported to camp, he said, "First, I was worried about just making the team. Second of all, I said to myself, 'OK, I'm going to make it. Now I want to start. I've never played a backup role before. That would be tough for me to do. But if that's what I have to do, then that's what I have to do. Wait for my chance.'" It came, though not immediately.

Wright was a special teams player from 1985 until the seventh game of 1987, when he replaced Chris Rockins (who'd been a second round draft pick in 1984).

As then-coach Marty Schottenheimer was quoted, "We knew (Wright) was a good player, but he's better than I thought he'd be," which seemed to be a defining characteristic of Wright's entire career.

His value to the Browns was enhanced, as Schottenheimer made clear, by the fact that Wright could play cornerback as well as free and strong safety.

But apparently not enough.

Though Wright went on to start 55 consecutive games through 1990, he staged an extended holdout during training camp and, when the season ended, he left the Browns as a free agent and signed with Minnesota.

He played for the Vikings in 1991 and 1992, then retired, satisfied that he'd proved himself, that he was no longer the longest of long shots, the greatest of underdogs.

'The best move I ever made'

How long was genial Leo Murphy associated with the Browns as their trainer?

Well, to put Murphy's length of service in perspective, be advised that he served the team longer than any player on the roster was alive at the time of his retirement – 43 years, from 1950, when he was hired by Paul Brown, through 1992.

Which speaks eloquently about, not only Murphy's ability to help heal the myriad of injuries that every NFL team incurs, but also, his impeccable character and sparkling personality.

Known for his marvelous sense of humor, it often has been speculated that Murphy could have been a hit as a stand-up comic, had he chosen to be a professional entertainer instead of a trainer. He also is an accomplished pianist, and it is hard to believe that anybody knows more and funnier jokes – or can tell them better.

Murphy, who grew up in Buffalo, New York, was a jack-of-all-trades with the Browns. Not only was he their trainer, in the early years of the franchise he often helped line the practice and game fields, and performed a multitude of other tasks that helped the Browns.

Nobody worked for the team longer – or more diligently, it also can be said without fear of contradiction – than Murphy. He joined the Browns the year they were

Leo Murphy

admitted to the NFL, after serving as the trainer for the Chicago Rockets and then the New York Yankees of the defunct All-America Football Conference from 1947-49.

A 1947 graduate of Notre Dame where he played basketball and was the football team's assistant trainer, and the son of a physiotherapist, Murphy "semi" retired from the Browns in 1989, but stayed aboard as "trainer emeritus" through the 1992 season.

As testament to the high regard in which he was held by his peers, Murphy was inducted into the National Athletic Trainers Association Hall of Fame in 1982.

He also was named "Pro of the Year" by the Fairview Park (Ohio) American Legion in 1989, and that same year was honored by the Cleveland Touchdown Club which presented him with the "Pro Recognition Award."

Murphy was hired by Paul Brown, then general manager and coach of the Browns, when the team's trainer, Wally Bock, left to take a similar position with the Cleveland Indians.

The job offer came as a surprise, Murphy said in a Cleveland *Plain Dealer* story at the time of his retirement as head trainer.

"My wife Betty and I were having breakfast at the old Bellevue-Stratford Hotel in Philadelphia where the NFL owners were meeting, when Paul Brown came to our table and asked if he could sit down," Murphy was quoted in the article.

"Dick Gallagher (then an assistant coach with the Browns) was with him, and Paul said he needed a trainer. I'd had some other feelers, but Paul made me promise not to do anything until I heard from him.

"Two days later Brown called and offered me the job. I jumped at the opportunity … it was the best move I ever made."

It also could be said – again without fear of contradiction - that it was one of the best decisions Paul Brown and the Browns ever made.

Invaluable on the sidelines

He never threw a pass, caught one or ran with the football, nor did he ever make a block or a tackle for the Browns. But John Bergfeld was an invaluable member of the team on the sidelines before the franchise moved to Baltimore in 1995.

Bergfeld, a.k.a., "Dr. John," joined the team in 1976 as an "orthopedic consultant" to Dr. Vic Ippolito, then the Browns' physician. When Ippolito re-

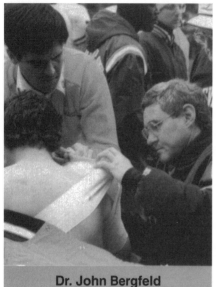

Dr. John Bergfeld

tired in 1978, he was replaced by Bergfeld, who held the position for 13 seasons, and returned to the new Browns as their doctor in 1999. Having intimately known – and treated – the Browns from 1976-95, the obvious questions for Dr. Bergfeld were:

• Who was the toughest, and
• What was the worst injury suffered by a member of the team?

First, he said, "All of (the players) are tough. You have to be tough to play in the NFL."

Then, when pressed to be specific, he responded, "I'd have to say that Brian Sipe (the Browns quarterback from 1974-83) probably was the mentally toughest. He got banged up an awful lot, but played hurt. He refused to give in to a lot of his injuries."

Then, two others immediately came to mind, Dr. Bergfeld said.

"It was practically impossible to keep (offensive tackle) Doug Dieken out of a game. He played over 200 consecutive games (actually 203) without missing one, which should tell you how determined he was to stay on the field.

"The other player – I'd call him a 'Warrior' – was (center) Mike Baab. He was big, strong … a really tough guy. Once I did arthroscopic surgery on his knee and, I think it was two days later, he was back on the field, practicing. An amazing guy."

The worst injury during Bergfeld's earlier service with the Browns was suffered by Robert L. Jackson in training camp 1977. The linebacker from Texas A&M, who had been the team's No. 1 draft choice, went down with battered knee.

Jackson underwent reconstructive surgery and was on Injured Reserve all that season. He returned in 1978, but re-injured his knee and was never the same. He played for the Browns into 1982, and ended his NFL career that season with Atlanta.

Tom DeLeone, a center for the Browns from 1974-84, probably best summarized the players' attitude toward Dr. Bergfeld, as reported in the Cleveland *Plain Dealer*: "He cares about everything. He cares about the way the stitches go in. You might say he's a perfectionist at his job. A lot of doctors can shorten your career. (But) whatever he says is gospel with me. You hear all those horror stories with other teams sending athletes out on the field after injuries, but it doesn't happen here."

Dr. Bergfeld resumed his position as the team physician when Al Lerner purchased the expansion Browns, while continuing in to be in charge of Sports Medicine of the Cleveland Clinic Foundation, where he began his medical career in 1965. He served in the U.S. Navy with the rank of Commander at the U.S. Naval Academy in Annapolis, Maryland from 1970-73.

And though he never played professional football, Dr. Bergfeld knows the game. As an undergraduate at Bucknell University, he played three years on the football team as an offensive lineman and linebacker, and he earned his medical degree at Temple University in 1964.

The best of the Browns ...
... in the Hall of Fame

Paul Brown (1946-1962)
Enshrined in 1967

An exceptionally successful coach at all levels of football, Brown organized the Browns in the AAFC in 1946 after being hired by the team's original owner, Arthur B. (Mickey) McBride. Brown built a great Browns dynasty with a 158-48-8 record, winning four championships in the AAFC, and three in the NFL. His teams suffered only one losing season in the 17 years he was their coach. Brown was recognized as a revolutionary innovator with many coaching firsts to his credit, and was elected to the Pro Football Hall of Fame before his tenure with Cincinnati Bengals began. He was born September 7, 1908 in Norwalk, Ohio and died August 5, 1991.

Otto Graham (1946-1955)
Enshrined in 1965

A college tailback in the old single wing formation, Graham was switched to a T-formation quarterback when he was drafted by the Browns in 1946. He guided the Browns to 10 division or league championships in 10 years, topped the All-America Football Conference passers four years and National Football League passers two years, and was named to the AAFC and NFL all league teams in nine of his 10 seasons. Graham threw four TD passes in winning the 1950 championship game, and ran for three TDs and passed for three more in the 1954 title game. He passed for 23,584 yards and 174 TDs in his career, and scored 276 points on 46 TDs. Graham was born December 6, 1921 in Waukegan, Illinois.

The best of the Browns ...

Marion Motley (1946-1953)
Enshrined in 1968

A deadly pass blocker and peerless runner on the Browns famed trap play, Motley also played linebacker early in his pro football career. He was the all-time AAFC rushing champion, and the leading NFL rusher in 1950, his and the Browns first year in the league. Motley won All-AAFC honors in three of his four seasons in that league, was an All-NFL selection in 1950, and played in the 1951 Pro Bowl. He averaged 5.7 yards per carry – an NFL record - during his pro career (4,720 yards in 828 carries), and caught 85 passes and scored 234 points in nine years. Motley was born June 5, 1920, in Leesburgh, Georgia.

Jim Brown (1957-1965)
Enshrined in 1971

Brown won All-America honors at Syracuse University, and was the Browns' No. 1 pick in the 1957 college draft. He was the most awesome runner in pro football history, and led the NFL rushers eight years while winning All-NFL honors in eight of his nine seasons with the Browns. Brown was the NFL's most valuable player in 1958 and 1965, and was Rookie of the Year in 1957. He played in nine straight Pro Bowls, and posted career marks of 12,312 yards gained rushing, 262 pass receptions, 15,495 net yards, and 756 points scored. Brown was born February 17, 1936, in St. Simons, Georgia.

Lou Groza (1946-59,1961-67)
Enshrined in 1974

Groza was the last of the original Browns to retire after serving as the team's regular offensive left tackle from 1947-1959. A back injury forced him out of football in 1960, and returned as a kicking specialist only from 1961-67. He was an All-NFL tackle six years, the NFL player of the Year in 1954, and played in nine Pro Bowl games. It was Groza's last second field goal that won the 1950 NFL title game for the Browns. He played in four AAFC and nine NFL championship games, and scored 1,608 points in his 21 seasons with the Browns. Groza was born January 25, 1924, in Martins Ferry, Ohio.

... in the Hall of Fame

Dante Lavelli (1946-56)
Enshrined in 1975

Lavelli played only three college games (at Ohio State) and served in the U.S. Army as an infantryman before joining the Browns in 1946. He was the leading AAFC receiver as a rookie, scored the winning TD in the championship game in 1946, and caught 11 passes in the 1950 NFL title game. He won All-AAFC honors in 1946 and 1947, and was All-NFL in 1951 and 1953. Lavelli, nicknamed "Gluefingers," had a record 24 receptions in six NFL championship games, caught 386 passes for 6,488 yards and 62 touchdowns in his career, and played in the Pro Bowl three times. Lavelli was born February 23, 1923, in Hudson, Ohio.

Len Ford (1950-57)
Enshrined in 1976

Ford caught 67 passes as a two-way end with the Los Angeles Dons in 1948 and 1949. However, after the AAFC folded, he was acquired by the Browns and converted to defensive end and his exceptional pass rushing skills caused opposing defenses to be altered. Ford overcame serious injuries in 1950 and went on to earn All-NFL honors five times, from 1951-55, and played in four Pro Bowls. Ford recovered 20 opponents' fumbles in his 10 year professional career. He was born February 18, 1926, in Washington, D.C., and died March 14, 1972 at age 46.

Bill Willis (1946-53)
Enshrined in 1977

An All-America tackle at Ohio State, Willis played on both sides of the ball, but excelled as a defensive middle guard. His lightning quickness was Willis's trademark that earned him a job in his first pro scrimmage. He made a touchdown-saving tackle against the New York Giants to preserve the Browns' 1950 NFL title drive. Willis was a member of the All-AAFC team three years, was an All-NFL selection each season from 1950-53, and played in the first three Pro Bowls. He was born October 5, 1921, in Columbus, Ohio.

The best of the Browns ...

Bobby Mitchell (1959-61)
Enshrined in 1983

Blessed with exceptional speed, balance and faking ability, Mitchell split his career as a Browns halfback and Washington Redskins flanker. He was noted for spectacular long distance scoring plays, amassing 14,078 combined net yards while catching 521 passes and scoring 91 touchdowns, eight on kick returns. Mitchell was the NFL's leading receiver in 1962 with the Redskins, and surpassed 50 receptions six years. He made the All-NFL team two times. and played in four Pro Bowls. He was born June 6, 1935, in Hot Springs, Arkansas.

Paul Warfield (1964-69,76-77)
Enshrined in 1983

The No. 1 pick of both the Browns and AFL Buffalo Bills in 1964, Warfield was a Cleveland fixture before a controversial trade in 1970 sent him to Miami where he became a key element in the Dolphins' offense. Warfield's mere presence on the field forced defensive adjustments because of his speed, sure handedness, and ability to run super smooth, precise patterns. He also was an excellent blocker. Warfield caught 427 passes for 8,565 yards and 85 touchdowns, and his 20.1 yards per catch average is the best ever. He was an All-NFL selection five years, and played in seven Pro Bowls. Warfield was born November 28, 1942, in Warren, Ohio.

Mike McCormack (1954-62)
Enshrined in 1984

McCormack was drafted by the 1951 New York Yankees and played in the first of six Pro Bowls as a rookie. While serving in the U.S. Army from 1952-53 he was traded to the Browns in a 15 player deal. McCormack played defensive middle guard, and in the 1954 championship game stole the ball to set up a key TD. Thereafter he excelled as an offensive right tackle for eight years, 1955-62, helping the Browns win the 1964 NFL title. McCormack was equally adept as a rushing a passer, and as a pass protector. He was born June 21, 1930, in Chicago, Illinois.

... in the Hall of Fame

Frank Gatski (1946-56)
Enshrined in 1985

Gatski anchored the powerful offensive line during the Browns' dominant years in the AAFC and NFL as a strong, consistent, exceptional pass blocker who never missed a game or practice in high school, college, or pro football. He played in 11 championship games in 12 years with his teams winning eight times. Gatski was a linebacker early in his career, and after switching to center, won All-NFL honors four years, and played in the 1957 Pro Bowl. Gatski was born March 13, 1922, in Farmington, West Virginia.

Leroy Kelly (1964-73)
Enshrined in 1994

An eighth round draft choice in 1964, Kelly's career with the Browns began as a kick returner became a regular running back in 1966 and was a 1,000 yard rusher three consecutive seasons, 1964-66, winning the NFL rushing title in 1967 and 1968 with 1,205 and 1,239 yards, respectively. Kelly also was a two-time punt return champion, in 1975, when he led the entire NFL, and 1971, when he led the AFC. He was an All-NFL running back five years (1966-69, 1971), and played in six Pro Bowls (1966-72). Kelly was fourth on the NFL all-time rushing list with 7,274 yards when he retired. Kelly was born May 20, 1942 in Philadelphia, Pennsylvania.

Ozzie Newsome (1978-90
Enshrined in 1999

A second No. 1 draft choice (23rd overall) in 1978, Newsome was a starter his entire 13 year career with the Browns after being switched from wide receiver, the position he played at the University of Alabama. Newsome's 662 receptions for 7,980 yards and 47 touchdowns placed him fourth among the NFL's all-time receivers, and he also was the No. 1 receiver in the history of the Browns. Newsome was voted All-Pro in 1979 and 1984, and played in the Pro Bowl in 1981, 1984 and 1985. He was born March 16, 1956 in Muscle Shoals, Alabama.

BROWNS ALL-TIME TEAMS

It is subjective and debatable – *very debatable* – amongst longtime Browns fans, but here's one man's opinion of the Browns' all-time All-Offense and All-Defense teams:

ALL-OFFENSE		ALL-DEFENSE	
Wide Receivers:	Dante Lavelli	**Defensive Ends:**	Len Ford
	Paul Warfield		Bill Willis
Tight End:	Ozzie Newsome	**Defensive Tackles:**	Jerry Sherk
Tackles:	Lou Groza		Bob Gain
	Mike McCormack	**Middle Linebacker:**	Vince Costello
Guards:	Gene Hickerson	**Outside Linebackers:**	Clay Matthews
	Jim Ray Smith		Jim Houston
Center:	Frank Gatski	**Cornerbacks:**	Hanford Dixon
Quarterback:	Otto Graham		Warren Lahr
Running Backs:	Jim Brown	**Safeties:**	Don Paul
	Marion Motley		Don Rogers
Placekicker:	Lou Groza	**Punter:**	Horace Gillom
		Kick returner:	Greg Pruitt
		Coach:	Paul Brown

Agree or not, some of the choices are no-brainers: who else but Graham at quarterback … or Brown as one of the running backs … or Lavelli, old "Glue Fingers," as one of the receivers … or Newsome at tight end … or Ford as one of the defensive ends … or Sherk and Gain as the defensive tackles … or Rogers at strong safety?

And some of the others are, well … flip a coin: Motley over Hall of Famer Leroy Kelly … Warfield over Gary Collins or Ray Renfro or Mac Speedie … Groza and McCormack, two Hall of Famers, over Dick Schafrath and/or Doug Dieken … Willis, another Hall of Famer who could have made the offensive team as a guard or the defensive team as a linebacker, over Paul Wiggin … Gain over Michael Dean Perry … Hickerson over Abe Gibron … Matthews and Houston over Galen Fiss and/or Walt Michaels … and Dixon and Lahr over Frank Minnifield and/or Tommy James?

It's also difficult to ignore four quarterbacks who did so much for the Browns in their first 50 years: Frank Ryan, who led them to their last NFL championship; or Bill Nelsen, the peerless leader who did remarkable things on a pair of knees that sometimes barely held him upright; or Brian Sipe, the thrilling triggerman of the "Kardiac Kids," or fan favorite Bernie Kosar?

There also were Bobby Mitchell, another Hall of Fame running back, though he gained most of his recognition as a receiver after he was traded to the Washington Redskins … and cornerback Erich Barnes and guard Joe DeLamielleure, all of whom were included among the "Three Hundred Greatest Players in the History of the NFL," as selected by *Total Football*.

Again, the lists are subjective and debatable.

And, most of all, memorable.

BROWNS COACHES 1946-1995

It all began with **Paul Brown**, in 1945 a 35-year old lieutenant in the Navy who, a year later, became general manager and coach of the Cleveland Browns in the fledgling All-America Football Conference. Brown had coached in high school (1932-40), Ohio State (1941-43), and at the Great Lakes Naval Training Station (1944-45). He coached the Browns from 1946-49 in the AAFC, and in the National Football League from 1950-62. His teams won four AAFC championships and two in the NFL. Brown was fired by Art Modell on January 9, 1963, then coached the Cincinnati Bengals from 1968-75. He died in 1991 at age 82. Brown's overall professional record: 167-53-8, including 9-5 in playoff games, and 120-49-5, and 3-5 in playoff games, in the NFL.

Blanton Collier, who'd been an assistant under Brown during the team's early years, took over as head coach of the Browns on January 16, 1963, and was at the helm of the team through 1970, winning one – and the team's last – NFL championship in 1964. He died in 1983 at age 76. Collier's record: 79-38-2, including 3-4 in playoff games.

Nick Skorich, a former head coach of the Philadelphia Eagles who'd been an assistant under Collier, replaced his retired mentor and coached the Browns from 1971-74, when he was fired by Modell. Skorich's record: 30-26-2, including 0-2 in playoff games.

Forrest Gregg, offensive line coach under Skorich in 1974, became head coach of the Browns in 1975 and served until the final game of 1977, when he resigned and was replaced by defensive coordinator Dick Modzelewski. Gregg's record: 18-23.

Sam Rutigliano, a longtime NFL assistant coach, was hired as the Browns head coach on December 27, 1977, and served from 1978 through the first eight games of 1984, when he was fired on October 22 by Modell. Rutigliano's record: 47-51, including 0-1 in playoff games.

Marty Schottenheimer, the Browns defensive coordinator under Rutigliano since 1980, was appointed head coach on October 22, 1984 and served through 1988, when he resigned and became head coach of the Kansas City Chiefs. Schottenheimer's record: 46-31, including 2-4 in playoff games.

Bud Carson, another longtime NFL assistant, was head coach of the Browns from 1989. through the first eight games of 1990, when he was fired and replaced on an interim basis by offensive coordinator Jim Shofner (who coached the team the final eight games). Carson's record: 12-14-1, including 1-1 in playoff games.

Bill Belichick, an assistant with the New York Giants, was hired as the eighth full-time head coach of the Browns on February 1, 1991. He coached the Browns through 1995, after which Modell moved the team to Baltimore, renamed it "Ravens," and Belichick was replaced by Ted Marchibroda. Belichick's record: 37-45, including 1-1 in playoff games.

It almost was Frank Leahy

How different it undoubtedly would have been if Arthur B. "Mickey" McBride had not changed his mind about Frank Leahy.

Leahy, the toast of college football in the early-1940s because of his success at Notre Dame, was McBride's first choice to build and coach Cleveland's franchise in the new All-America Football Conference in 1945. Not Paul Brown.

McBride and Leahy, then serving in the Navy, even shook hands on the deal. "Frank Leahy is my kind of coach," McBride, a Notre Dame alumnus, bragged.

In the final analysis, however, it was McBride's loyalty to Notre Dame that led to Brown being hired, on the advice of a Cleveland sportswriter.

Notre Dame asked McBride to not take Leahy. McBride reluctantly agreed and set out again to find another coach.

Enter John Dietrich, who covered Ohio State for the Cleveland *Plain Dealer*. He recommended Brown, 36, who had been a successful high school coach at Severn (Maryland) Prep and Massillon, Ohio and had turned the Ohio State program around in 1941. Brown's 1942 Buckeyes won the national championship, and his three year record at Ohio State was 18-8-1.

Paul Brown

Brown entered the Navy and coached football in 1944 and 1945 at the Great Lakes Naval Training Station where his teams went 15-5-2, and beat Notre Dame in 1945.

Heeding Dietrich's advice, McBride contacted Brown and quickly hired him.

"I could have signed (Brown) for $15,000, but I wanted to make a big splash for publicity, so I gave him $25,000." McBride was quoted in an early history of the franchise. "I wanted to say my team had the highest paid coach in America."

It also had the best coach in America, as it turned out.

Brown's contract, which also paid him $1,000 a month for the duration of World War II, was signed on February 8, 1945.

Brown established his doctrine early. "At Ohio State, I asked nothing of my players that I wouldn't ask of my own sons, and that's the way I planned to run the Browns." he said.

"The two things I insisted upon were that I would be in charge of the football end of the business, and that I would have an absolute free hand in selecting my players. I was determined that I wanted them to be high class, and I picked them on the basis of personality as well as ability. I had always lived by the rule that you don't win with dogs, and to me it is a rule that has never changed."

It was Brown's insistence upon total control that led to his being fired in January 1962 by then - owner Art Modell.

But there's no disparaging Brown's remarkable record as coach of the team that bore his name: 167-53-8, a winning percentage of .759, unmatched by any of his successors.

In Brown's 17 seasons at the helm of the Browns, they won the AAFC championship all four years of its existence, and played for the National Football League title seven times, winning it in 1950, 1954, and 1955.

Nobody, not even Frank Leahy, could have done it better.

A great coach and a great man

Otto Graham, the best quarterback the Browns ever had - and many believe, the best ever in the National Football League - credits one man for making him as good as he was.

"Blanton Collier taught me everything I know about quarterbacking," Graham once said of the man who died in 1983 at the age of 76.

Blanton Collier

Collier was an assistant under Paul Brown from the inception of the Browns in 1946 and Graham's mentor.

When Brown was fired, he was replaced by Collier, who led the Browns to their first National Football League championship in 1964. He retired after the 1970 season.

Collier's eight-year record was 79-38 2, a winning percentage of .675, second only to Brown's .759 (167-53-8).

Of the eight head coaches in the Browns first 50 years, there is no doubt Collier was Art Modell's favorite.

As testimony to Collier's character, he initially refused the head coach's job when Brown, his friend, was fired. He finally accepted after Brown convinced Collier he should take it.

Collier was the coach who introduced "option" blocking, which gave blockers and runners more freedom of movement - and which is universally used in college and pro football today.

Quarterbacks also were given more leeway in play calling under Collier, as opposed to the rigid discipline in effect under Brown - and which was significant in the development of Frank Ryan as a championship quarterback after he'd been a second-stringer all of his college and pro career.

Collier was the antithesis of coaches such as Vince Lombardi, George Halas, Forrest Gregg, even Brown himself, who were gruff and impersonal in their dealings with players.

It sometimes led to the suggestion that the gentlemanly, soft spoken, warm and sensitive Collier might have been "too soft" to be an effective coach in professional football.

But the people who knew Collier best, his players, refuted that speculation in no uncertain terms.

Veteran defensive lineman Dick Modzelewski, who became an NFL assistant coach, said of Collier: "He's not the type who jumps up and down or raises the devil.

"Blanton makes a few calm statements and, to me, this does the most good. He is the teacher-type, easy to play for. We're all adults and he chews you out in his own intellectual way. He knows how to get the best out of every player."

And this from Jim Brown, whose career flourished under Collier, and who said at the time of Collier's retirement: "I don't know how anybody could think (Collier) is too soft, as successful as he's been.

"The greatest thing about Blanton is that he knows how to utilize his forces. He gets more from individuals because he understands their talents.

"Paul Brown tried to teach everybody to do the same thing exactly the same way. But we're not all made the same. Blanton recognizes this and takes advantage of it.

"He's a great coach - and a great man."

Indeed Blanton Collier was.

Two tough acts to follow

It was a tough act – make that *two tough acts* – that Nick Skorich had to follow when he was hired as head coach of the Browns in 1971.

His predecessors were, first, Paul Brown, who'd led the Browns to seven championships (four in the All-America Football Conference and three in the National Football League) from 1946-62, and then Blanton Collier, whose teams went 79-38-2 (.675) from 1963-70, and won the franchise's last NFL title in 1964.

Nick Skorich

Skorich had been an assistant to Collier, and previously had played in the NFL as a 5-9, 197-pound guard-linebacker for the Pittsburgh Steelers from 1946-48 after being a 15th round draft choice in 1943 (prior to entering the service).

He later was an assistant with the Steelers, Green Bay and Philadelphis, and was the unfortunate and ill-fated head coach of the Eagles from 1961-63.

Skorich replaced Collier, who retired, in 1971, and his head coach's career with the Browns started impressively. They won the AFC Central Division with a 9-5 record, but were beaten by Baltimore, 20-3, in their first playoff game.

The Browns were even better in 1972, going 10-4, finishing second to Pittsburgh and winning a wild card berth in the playoffs, only to lose to Miami, 20-14.

But then they fell to 7-5-2 and third place in 1973, and, in 1974 when they won only four games while losing ten, Skorich was replaced by assistant coach Forrest Gregg.

His tenure with the Browns was a difficult time for Skorich as he was breaking in a new quarterback, Mike Phipps, to replace the aging – but peerless leader – Bill Nelsen.

And though Phipps played well in 1972, when the Browns went 8-1 after losing three of their first five games, it became obvious that he wasn't the answer.

Brian Sipe took over in 1976, but by then Skorich was gone, even though, in 1973, he'd been given a new, three year contract by Art Modell, "in appreciation for a job well done."

His firing after the 1974 season ended a 21-year NFL coaching career for Skorich.

Skorich's first job as a head coach, in Philadelphia in 1961, began with unexpected turmoil as the Eagles' then-quarterback (and NFL MVP in 1960) Norm Van Brocklin publicly complained that he had been promised the head coach's job.

However, with Sonny Jurgensen replacing Van Brocklin at quarteback, the Eagles went 10-4 in 1961, though they failed to win the NFL Eastern Conference, in part because they lost to the Browns, 45-24. Their record was a half-game behind the champion New York Giants, who went 10-3-1. (Sudden death overtime was not part of the NFL rules at that time.)

Jurgensen went down with a knee injury early in 1962 and the Eagles fell to 3-10-1, after which more trouble plagued Skorich. Jurgensen and backup quarterback King Hill walked out of camp in contract disputes in 1963. They finally returned, but the team was in chaos, and when the Eagles' record fell to 2-10-2, Skorich was fired.

That's when he joined the Browns as an assistant coach, replaced Collier eight years later and, after he was fired by Modell, Skorich went to work for the NFL as a supervisor of officials until his retirement.

The coach who was too tough

It is ironic that the very reason Art Modell hired Forrest Gregg as the Browns' fourth head coach in 1975, turned out to be a factor in the termination of the Hall of Famer's career in Cleveland, one game short of three seasons later.

Modell wanted an aggressive, fiery leader to replace Nick Skorich after the Browns had

Forrest Gregg

stumbled to a 4-10, fourth place finish in the AFC Central Division of the NFL in 1974. Included were four losses in as many games to Cincinnati and Pittsburgh, which represented serious trouble for any coach who worked for Modell.

The Browns regressed under Gregg in his first year, winning only three games while losing 11. They rebounded big in 1976, with a 9-5 record, and Gregg was named AFC "Coach of the Year" by the Associated Press, but one game short of a full season later, the Browns reverted to their woeful ways. Their record fell to 6-7 and Gregg resigned - though he would have been fired had he not chosen to quit.

It was his strict, heavy-handed system of discipline, as well as a widely-reported shouting match between Gregg and the owner, that sealed the abrupt demise of the coach.

That stormy argument with Modell - in which, according to the *Plain Dealer,* Gregg "forcefully" requested a raise and extension of his contract - damaged what had been a cordial relationship between the two men.

Modell also was upset with Gregg over an incident that transpired in the Browns locker room in the third last game in 1977.

It happened in San Diego as the Chargers coasted to a 37-14 victory after jumping out to a 27-0 half-time lead. It was the Browns' worst loss of the season and Gregg was humiliated. "You're cowards," he reportedly shouted at his players afterwards. "You quit on me. I don't even want to pray with you."

When Houston beat the Browns, 19-15, the following week for the 23rd loss in 41 games under Gregg, Modell decided that a coaching change was necessary.

But Gregg, aware of Modell's intention, didn't wait to be fired. He resigned five days before the final game, a 20-19 loss to Seattle, and Dick Modzelewski served as interim head coach.

So ended Gregg's career in Cleveland, though not in football.

The man whom Vince Lombardi called "the greatest player I ever coached" was elected to the Pro Football Hall of Fame in 1977. He was the Packers' second round draft pick in 1956 and, after spending 1957 in the service, was an offensive tackle for the Packers through 1970.

Gregg won All-Pro honors eight times and played in nine Pro Bowls, and was on three Super Bowl championship teams, Green Bay in 1967 and 1968, and Dallas in 1971, when he was a player-coach for the Cowboys. He was an offensive line coach for San Diego in 1972 and 1973, and joined the Browns as an assistant coach in 1974.

After his resignation from the Browns, Gregg coached Toronto in the Canadian League in 1979, the Cincinnati Bengals from 1980-83 (taking them to Super Bowl XVI, which they lost to San Francisco, 28-21), and Green Bay from 1984-87, after which he returned to coach his alma mater, Southern Methodist University.

'It's still only a game'

It was Sam Rutigliano's professional and philosophical resemblance to Blanton Collier that initially endeared him to Browns owner Art Modell.

"I feel I have a new Blanton Collier. Sam is a teacher by background, he relates with today's athletes," is the way Modell praised Rutigliano in December 1977.

That's when Rutigliano was hired as the fifth coach of the Browns, replacing Forrest Gregg.

Six-and-a-half years later Modell changed his opinion, as owners are wont to do when losses begin to outnumber victories, and Rutigliano was fired on October 23, 1984.

But there's no doubt Rutigliano was an early favorite as his Browns went 8-8, 9-7 and then 11-5 in his first three seasons, 1978-80.

His teams came to be known as the "Kardiac Kids" because they won so many games in the final minute, and Sam was called – more than once and by more than one person – a "miracle worker."

"(Rutigliano) has captured this town in a personal sense," Modell said then. "No one in sports had done this in the 20 years I've been here. The elite, as well as the steelworkers, they all love him."

Sam Rutigliano

During that time Modell made Rutigliano a vice president and gave him a new five year contract. "It shows my high regard for him as a coach and a person. It demonstrates my feeling for him, professionally and personally," Modell said.

But the fortunes of the Browns began going bad on a sub-freezing day at the Stadium in the 1980 playoffs. They lost to the Oakland Raiders, 14-12, in the final seconds on a controversial play called "Red Right 88."

Brian Sipe was intercepted in the Raiders end zone after Rutigliano disdained what seemed would be a chipshot, game-winning field goal by Don Cockroft.

Rutigliano later explained that, first, he doubted that Cockroft, who had not been kicking well, would be able to make a field goal at the open end of the wind-swept Stadium.

And second, Sipe was under orders to "throw the ball into the bleachers" if intended receiver Ozzie Newsome was covered.

The Browns fell to 5-11 in 1981 and to 4-5 in the strike-torn season of 1982. They rebounded to 9-7 in 1983, but when seven of the first eight games in 1984 were losses, Rutigliano was fired.

"I was disappointed, but not devastated," Rutigliano said of his dismissal. "I never had a fear of failure. When I came to Cleveland, I knew the only thing I had to lose was my address."

Rutigliano always was a winner, but never was consumed with winning. He'd lost a child in an automobile accident in 1963, which re-shaped his outlook on life.

It was during Rutigliano's tenure – and primarily through his efforts – that the Browns' "Inner Circle" was formed to cope with the growing drug problem in professional sports. It involved counseling and rehabilitation, and became the basis of similar programs instituted by other teams.

And so, while "Red Right 88" may forever live in infamy in the annals of the Browns, Rutigliano was able to walk away with his head held high, remembering the philosophy he espoused:

"I've never played a game that was labeled 'must.' It's still only a game, even at this level."

Marty's goal, still un-reached

"We talk about only one thing here," Marty Schottenheimer was quoted as saying early in his career as the sixth fulltime head coach of the Browns from mid-1984-88.

"That's the Super Bowl championship. That's the only thing we want and anything less than that will not satisfy us. And when we win that first one, and I'm convinced we're heading in the right direction, we'll do everything we can to continue winning NFL titles."

Marty Schottenheimer

But the best the Browns could do under Schottenheimer was to get close in 1986 and 1987 - and are still seeking their first berth in a Super Bowl.

So is Schottenheimer as a coach.

He resigned – though there's evidence that, had he not quit, he would have been fired – after the Browns lost to Houston, 24-23, in the 1988 playoffs.

Immediately thereafter Schottenheimer was hired as head coach of the Kansas City Chiefs, though he was no more successful with them than he'd been in Cleveland.

And when Kansas City failed to reach the Super Bowl for a tenth consecutive year in 1998 under Schottenheimer, he resigned despite being under contract through 2001, his avowed goal still unrealized.

The most frustrating times for Schottenheimer had to be in the 1986 and 1987 playoffs when the Browns were beaten in AFC championship games, both times by Denver.

The first was a 23-20, overtime loss that long will be remembered – and lamented – by Browns fans as "The Drive." A year later they were defeated, 38-33, in a game referred to as "The Fumble," which they seemed to be winning in the final minute.

Schottenheimer came to the Browns as their defensive coordinator in 1980. He previously served as an NFL assistant with the New York Giants from 1975-77, and Detroit from 1978-79, after beginning his coaching career with Portland in the World Football League in 1974.

When the Browns lost seven of their first eight games under Sam Rutigliano in 1984, Schottenheimer took over as head coach with a five year contract, and the team went 4-4 to finish with a 5-11 record.

Schottenheimer was named AFC "Coach of the Year" in 1986 by *United Press International*, and in 1987 his contract was extended by three more years, through 1991.

Though he was popular with the media early in his career with the Browns, Schottenheimer's sometimes imperious attitude was often resented in later years.

As written in an Akron *Beacon Journal* column after his departure, "Schottenheimer has yet to admit any of his mistakes, and there were many."

Among the alleged errors: Schottenheimer's mishandling of 1987 No. 1 draft choice Mike Junkin, his too-limited use of the Browns' two top draft picks in 1988, Clifford Charlton and Van Waiters; his too-absolute control of the offense, and that he flatly refused to make changes on his staff of assistants as requested by Art Modell, which reportedly resulted in his decision to resign.

During Schottenheimer's tenure with the Browns they were 4-4 in 1984, 8-8 in 1985, 12-4 in 1986, 10-5 in 1987, and 10-6 in 1988, and he left with an overall won-lost record of 44-27 - without reaching his avowed goal.

'We are ... confident' about Carson'

When he hired Bud Carson on January 27, 1989 as the seventh fulltime coach of the Browns, then-owner Art Modell was certain he'd picked the right man.

"We are absolutely confident that Bud Carson is the right man to help us make the next step, which is to win the league championship and, hopefully, more than one," Modell said when choosing the successor to Marty Schottenheimer.

"I have never been more involved in a more exhaustive talent search for a coach. We wanted to make sure we studied the whole field and, when we did, Carson became the clear-cut choice."

Carson, when offered the job, accepted even before Modell outlined the financial terms, according to Hal Lebovitz in the Lake County *News Herald.* "Don't you want to know the salary?" Modell asked. Carson reportedly replied, "No. I leave that up to you."

It was a three-year contract "in the neighborhood of $1.2 million," Modell said.

And, after the Browns' first regular season game under Carson's tutelage, it seemed that Modell had been accurate in his assessment of Carson.

The Browns blanked the Pittsburgh Steelers, 51-0, in Carson's debut on September 10, 1989, although not everything that followed was quite so pleasing.

Bud Carson

Oh, the Browns went on to win the AFC Central Division with a 9-6-1 record. They beat Buffalo in the divisional playoffs, 34-30, only to lose to Denver, 37-21, for the AFC title - and a berth in Super Bowl XXIV - the third time in four years the Broncos had beaten the Browns for the conference championship.

But, no matter. As Carson himself predicted during training camp in 1990, "we'll be a better team than we were last year."

However, instead of improving, they got worse. Much worse. They won the opener, again beating the Steelers, this time, 13-3, but lost the next three before a 30-29 victory over Denver on October 8.

Four more losses followed, the last one a 42-0 shutout by Buffalo, and Carson was fired after nine weeks with a 2-7 record.

He was replaced on an interim basis by Jim Shofner, who had been the team's offensive coordinator, but the situation only worsened. Under Shofner the Browns won one of their final seven games and he, too, was summarily dismissed.

For Carson, then nearing 59, it was a particularly distressing turn of events. He'd been an assistant coach in college and professional football for 33 years.

Prior to joining the Browns, Carson served as an NFL assistant – earning a reputation as a "defensive genius" – for sixteen seasons. He'd previously worked for the New York Jets, Kansas City, Baltimore Colts, Los Angeles Rams and Pittsburgh.

In eleven of those seasons Carson's teams made the playoffs and played in the Super Bowl three times, and was the architect of Pittsburgh's famed "Steel Curtain" defense in the 1970s.

But somewhere along the line Carson apparently forgot all he'd learned and Modell fired the man he had been – only 22 months earlier – so "absolutely confident" was the coach who would "help the Browns make the next step."

The coach the fans loved to hate

If hard work and long hours were keys to success, Bill Belichick probably would have been declared a genius when he was coach of the Browns from 1991-95.

But they weren't enough for Belichick and, by the time he was fired by then-owner Art Modell upon the re-location of the franchise to Baltimore, the eighth fulltime head coach of the Browns was one of the most disliked coaches in NFL history. Certainly, Belichick was the most disliked coach in the history of the Browns.

Bill Belichick

Belichick's biggest fault probably was his inability to relate to people. He was perceived by the fans, media and even many of his players as arrogant and domineering, and when the Browns moved to Baltimore, Belichick was blamed almost as much as Modell for Cleveland losing its NFL team.

Never a head coach previously, Belichick came to Cleveland after twelve years as an assistant with the New York Giants, and his Browns teams went 6-10 in 1991, 7-9 in 1992 and 1993, 11-5 in 1994, and 5-11 in 1995, for an overall won-lost record of 36-44

However, in addition to his lack of success as coach of the Browns, Belichick probably was resented as much by the fans because of the insensitive manner in which he dealt with Bernie Kosar in 1993.

Although the Browns were 5-3 and still in the hunt for a playoff spot that season, Belichick fired Kosar in the wake of a 29-14 loss to Denver, citing what he called the popular quarterback's "diminishing skills."

It didn't help Belichick's persona in the eyes of the media and fans when the Browns lost six of their last eight games that season under Vinny Testaverde and Todd Philcox - or when Kosar, after getting his release, joined the Dallas Cowboys for the final four games, and helped them win Super Bowl XXVIII.

To paraphrase a caller to a Cleveland talk radio station who complained on the air to Belichick as he was taking questions from the fans: "You have no rapport with the players. You have no rapport with the media. Your play calling stinks. Just what are your strengths?"

Needless to say, Belichick did not attempt to answer the question.

Through it all, Modell steadfastly supported Belichick – until the team moved.

When Modell was asked by *Browns News/Illustrated* early in Belichick's tenure what prompted him to hire the former Giants defensive coordinator under Bill Parcells, the owner replied, "Gut instinct."

Modell then went on to say, "If I made a mistake on Bill Belichick from what I already know, I would seriously consider getting out of the game."

That was in 1991. Five years later Modell fired Belichick and replaced him with Ted Marchibroda who, ironically, had been Belichick's first football mentor.

Then, in 1975, Belichick served as a "special assistant" to Marchibroda with the-then Baltimore Colts, who said of the 23-year old aspiring coach, "He was a young man who was willing to work around the clock."

But hard work and long hours were not enough for Bill Belichick to become successful – a lesson that even Art Modell eventually learned.

The Interim Coaches

Dick Modzelewski, a former Browns' defensive tackle who then served as an assistant coach for ten years under Blanton Collier, Nick Skorich and Forrest Gregg, took over as interim head coach for the final game in 1977, a 20-19 loss to the Seahawks in Seattle at the old Cleveland Stadium. Modzelewski left the organization at the end of the 1977 season when he was not given consideration to become the new head coach, a job that went to Sam Rutigliano instead.

Jim Shofner, who'd been the Browns' No. 1 draft choice as a defensive back out of Texas Christian University in 1958, played for them through 1963. He served as an NFL assistant for four teams before rejoining the Browns as quarterbacks coach in 1978-80. Shofner returned to the Browns as offensive coordinator in 1990 and that season replaced the fired Bud Carson as interim coach for the final eight games, seven of which were losses.

MEMORABLE GAMES

It is a subjective list, of course, and few Browns fans would agree in its entirety. But among the 739 games played by the Browns from their inception in 1946 through 1995 – 437 of which were victories, 289 losses and 13 ties for an overall winning percentage of .602 - twenty stand out, for one reason or another, as being particularly memorable.

Included in the total games played were 685 in the National Football League – 390 victories, 285 losses and 10 ties for a winning percentage of .578. Their record in 59 games the All-America Football Conference from 1946-49 was 47-4-3 = .922.

Not all were victories, nor were they all classics; in fact, of the twenty most memorable games, the Browns lost five.

But all were unforgettable – perhaps even by fans who were too young to see them and have only read about them - because of the impact they had on the franchise at the time, through those first 50 years.

In chronological order, the most memorable games were:

1. September 6, 1946   Browns 44, Miami Seahawks 0
2. November 21, 1948   Browns 34, New York Yankees 21
3. November 25, 1948   Browns 31, Los Angeles Dons 14
4. November 28, 1948   Browns 31, San Francisco 49ers 28
5. September 16, 1950   Browns 35, Philadelphia Eagles 10
6. December 24, 1950   Browns 30, Los Angeles Rams 28
7. December 26, 1954   Browns 56, Detroit Lions 10
8. November 1, 1959   Browns 38, Baltimore Colts 31
9. December 27, 1964   Browns 27, Baltimore Colts 0
10. September 23, 1970   Browns 31, New York Jets 21
11. October 11, 1970   Browns 30, Cincinnati Bengals 27
12. November 8, 1970   Oakland Raiders 23, Browns 20
13. December 21, 1980   Browns 27, Cincinnati Bengals 24
14. January 4, 1981   Oakland Raiders 14, Browns 12
15. January 3, 1987   Browns 23, New York Jets 20, double overtime
16. January 11, 1987   Denver Broncos 23, Browns 20, overtime
17. January 17, 1988   Denver Broncos 38, Browns 33
18. December 10, 1994   Browns 19, Dallas Cowboys 14
19. December 17, 1995   Browns 26, Cincinnati Bengals 10
20. December 24, 1995   Jacksonville Jaguars 24, Browns 21

The first victory September 6, 1946

The date was September 6, 1946, and 60,135 curious fans crowded into Cleveland Stadium to see a new team called the "Browns" play in a new league called the "All-America Football Conference."

And what a beginning it turned out to be.

Mickey McBride's and Paul Brown's collection of World War II veterans and former underpaid National Football League players methodically routed the Miami Seahawks, 44-0, and a new era in sports was begun.

The Seahawks were shocked, and so was Daniel F. Reeves, then-owner of the Los Angeles Rams.

The previous season in Cleveland the Rams had won their only National Football League championship in their eight-year existence, but played before only 73,000 fans in five home games.

Reeves claimed an operating loss in 1945 of $50,000, and when a crowd of just 32,178 turned out at the Stadium for the championship game against Washington, his mind was set.

McBride's vigorous promotion of the new team also had much to do with Reeves' decision to flee.

But many eyes were opened when the Browns' debut was reported. The crowd was a professional football

Paul Brown and Otto Graham

record (broken two weeks later when 71,134 paid their way into the Stadium), as the fledgling Browns, in the fledgling AAFC, were absolutely awesome.

And would continue to be during the four year existence of the AAFC.

The rout of the Seahawks began four minutes into the inaugural game when Cliff Lewis fired a 19-yard touchdown pass to Mac Speedie. Lewis was the Browns' safety, but started at quarterback because Otto Graham was still unfamiliar with the offense.

Graham had played in the annual preseason exhibition between the College All Stars and the NFL champion two weeks earlier - leading his team to a 16-0 victory over the Rams - and missed much of the Browns training camp.

After Lewis' scoring pass to Speedie, Graham got into the act, connecting with Dante Lavelli for six points, fullback Marion Motley hammered away on the ground, and Lou "The Toe" Groza kicked three field goals.

But it wasn't just the offense that dominated the game. The Browns' defense completely throttled the Seahawks, holding them to just 28 yards passing and minus one yard rushing.

The Seahawks won just three of 14 games and, when the season ended, the franchise moved to Baltimore and eventually folded, while the Browns flourished.

They won seven straight games before losing to San Francisco 34-20, and finished 12-2. Then they beat the New York Yankees, 14-9, for the first of four consecutive AAFC championships.

Attendance for the Browns' seven home games was 339,962, which had to further impress the Rams and Reeves - and especially Elmer Layden, then commissioner of the NFL.

When he was initially informed of the creation of the new league, Layden sneered, "Let 'em go get a football."

Which the AAFC - and the Browns - did. Very well.

A memorable week November 21-28, 1948

It wasn't just one game – there were three in three cities in seven days – that long will be recalled among the greatest memories in Browns' history.

They took place during the week of November 21-28, 1948, and were victories over the Yankees in New York, 34-21, on November 21; the Dons in Los Angeles, 31-14, on November 25; and the 49ers in San Francisco, 31-28, on November 28. Then, as the two-time defending champion of the All-America Football Conference the Browns were working on a ten game winning streak, and 19 without a loss, including the final nine games of 1947.

Dante Lavelli

As recalled by Hall of Famer Dante Lavelli, who played a prominent role in the Browns' success during his eleven year career in Cleveland, "At the time, we didn't think anything of it. Anytime we took the field, we felt we would win." Which they did - most of the time.

In that first game, in front of 52,518 fans in Yankee Stadium, the Browns broke a 14-14 tie on a pair of Otto Graham touchdown passes and a 12-yard run by Marion Motley, to win going away.

Four days later, on Thanksgiving Day in the Los Angeles Coliseum – after a 16 hour trip from New York with stops in Chicago and Denver – the Browns found themselves again in a 14-14 tie at halftime.

But Graham scored on a quarterback sneak as the Browns took the lead for keeps early in the third quarter. They scored again on another touchdown pass, this one from Graham to Edgar "Special Delivery" Jones, and Lou Groza added a field goal while the defense was shutting out the Dons in the second half. It was the second time the Browns had beaten Los Angeles that season – they won the opener, 19-14 - eliciting the comment from Dons coach Jimmy Phelan: "The Browns are unquestionably the best team in pro football, and probably the greatest team ever assembled."

After beating the Dons, the Browns traveled up the California coast to San Francisco where, three days later, they played their arch rival 49ers, whose record at the time was 11-1. San Francisco's only previous loss had been administered by the Browns, 14-7, two weeks earlier in Cleveland.

Graham, playing despite a painful knee injury, fired four touchdown passes - to Lavelli, Motley, Dub Jones and Edgar Jones – as the Browns rallied to overcome a 21-10 deficit to beat the 49ers in front of 59,785 fans in Kezar Stadium. Afterwards, Coach Paul Brown called the victory over the 49ers Graham's "greatest performance," and, as was the case with Phelan's assessment, few would have disagreed.

When Groza was asked how difficult it was to win three games in seven days, he replied, "The toughest thing was to make three game plans in one week."

The Browns went home from that three-game, three-city journey to beat the Brooklyn Dodgers, 31-21, capping a 14-0 season, becoming the first professional football team to go undefeated.

Then they routed Buffalo, 49-7, for their third (of what would become four straight) AAFC championships, and didn't lose again until the sixth game in 1949, stretching their unbeaten streak to an amazing 29 games (of which two were ties).

The first 'World Series'

It was called the first "World Series of Football."

The date: September 16, 1950.

The place: Shibe Park, Philadelphia.

The teams: the 1949 National Football League champion Philadelphia Eagles and the 1949 All-America Football Conference champion Cleveland Browns.

More than 71,000 – mostly smug - fans were on hand to see the AAFC put in its place.

But instead, as it turned out, it was the other way around.

The Browns, playing their first game in the NFL, humiliated the Eagles, 35-10, to launch a new era in professional football.

The Browns were fresh from winning four consecutive championships in the AAFC, losing only four of the 54 regular season games they'd played.

Their domination of the AAFC was so complete, the league folded at the end of the 1949 season and three of its teams were taken in by the NFL - Cleveland, Baltimore and San Francisco.

Philadelphia had dominated the NFL almost as handily as the Browns did the AAFC.

Mac Speedie

The Eagles had won back-to-back titles in 1948 and 1949, behind the bruising running of Steve Van Buren, the passing of Tommy Thompson and a strong defense headed by Chuck Bednarik.

But the game, which also could have been called the NFL's first Super Bowl, turned into a rout for the Browns in the second half, after the Eagles scored early on a 15 yard field goal.

After Lou Groza was hurt and his replacement as a kicker, Chubby Grigg, missed a 25-yard field goal, Otto Graham connected with Dub Jones on a 59-yard touchdown pass late in the first quarter. It put the Browns ahead, 7-3, a lead they never relinquished.

Still, the Eagles came close and the turning point might have been a magnificent goal line stand by the Browns' defense midway through the second quarter.

It was spearheaded by none other than fullback Marion Motley, who was inserted at linebacker when the Eagles drove to a first down on the Cleveland six.

Motley made four consecutive tackles, the Eagles gained but three yards, and the Browns took over the ball and control of the game.

Graham passed to Dante Lavelli for a touchdown and a 14-3 halftime lead, then hit on another scoring pass to Mac Speedie, and the rout was on.

The resounding victory was most gratifying to Paul Brown,

"(It) was the highest emotional game I ever coached," he was quoted later. "We had four years of constant ridicule to get us ready."

The Browns went on to win the NFL championship that season.

Bert Bell, the NFL commissioner who had been responsible for some of that ridicule, was a believer by the time the final gun sounded in Philadelphia.

"Cleveland is the best football team I have ever seen," Bell said - and few among those who witnessed this "World Series of Football" would disagree.

'The greatest game ever' December 24, 1950

Some called it the greatest game ever played. Maybe it was.

Certainly it had to be the Browns' most satisfying victory when they beat the Los Angeles Rams, 30-28, at the Cleveland Stadium on December 24, 1950.

It won the National Football League championship in the Browns' first season in the estab-

Warren Lahr

lished league, and of all the people who had to eat crow, the late Bert Bell was the one who probably found it most distasteful.

Bell was commissioner of the NFL then, and earlier had referred to the Browns as champions of "that Humpty Dumpty League," a.k.a. the All-America Football Conference that played its final season in 1949.

But after the Browns went 10-2, beat the New York Giants, 8-3, for the NFL's American Conference championship, and defeated the National Conference champion Rams in the title game, the forerunner of the Super Bowl, Bell changed his opinion.

In fact, when the Browns prevailed on Lou Groza's 16-yard field goal with 20 seconds remaining in the game, Bell called them "the greatest team to ever play football."

What's more, he referred to the Browns' comeback victory over the Rams as "the greatest, most exciting football game ever played," which probably was an exaggeration - but not much.

Paul Brown himself said later, "Looking back, it was the greatest game I ever saw, not because of the game itself, but because of the tremendous exhibition of passing by both teams.

"Both of us were the leaders in a modern-day revolution of switching the emphasis from running to passing. I think back and recall the pass catchers who played, and all you can say is that it was a star-studded cast."

It also was a spectacular show, especially by Otto Graham, who passed for 298 yards and four touchdowns, two to Dante Lavelli, and one each to halfbacks Dub Jones and Rex Bumgardner.

Bob Waterfield, the Rams quarterback who got his start when the team was based in Cleveland five years earlier, also played well, but didn't match Graham.

Waterfield threw for 312 yards and one touchdown - an 82-yard pass to Glenn Davis, "Mr. Outside" of West Point fame - but was intercepted four times.

The key theft was made by Warren Lahr midway through the fourth quarter when the Browns were trailing, 28-20.

They turned it into a touchdown on Graham's 14 yard pass to Bumgardner, cutting the Rams' lead to 28-27, though only 4:35 remained and it didn't look good for the Browns.

They forced the Rams to punt, however, took over on their own 32 with 1:50 left, and Graham went into action.

First he ran for 14 yards, then passed to Bumgardner for 15, to Jones for 16, and again to Bumgardner for 12, to the Rams' 11 with less than a minute to go.

Then, to be sure the ball was in good position, Graham ran it to the middle of the field and was downed at the 10.

From there Groza made his clutch kick, and the Browns were the champion of the NFL - instead of the "Humpty-Dumpty League."

Revenge was never sweeter

Revenge always is sweet – and it never was sweeter for the Browns than December 26, 1954, when they overwhelmed, not merely *beat* the Detroit Lions, 56-10, to win their second NFL championship in their fifth year in the league.

It was particularly sweet for the Browns who, not only lost to the Lions, 14-10, in the final regular season game a week earlier, they also were defeated by Detroit in the two previous seasons championship games, 17-16 in 1953, and 17-7 in 1952.

As reported on Page One of the Cleveland *Plain Dealer*: "What a difference a week made.

"Down and being counted out only seven days back, the Browns unloaded years of pent up frustration on the Detroit Lions at the Stadium to take over as the new champions of the National Football League.

Ray Renfro

"Paced by an almost unbelievable bow-out performance by quarterback Otto Graham, Paul Brown's finest football team of all humiliated the defending champion Lions with a tremendous offensive display."

The "humiliation" was witnessed by a crowd of 43,827, and several thousand of them invaded the field and tore down both goal posts in a display of bedlam seldom seen in professional football.

It capped a 9-3 season for the Browns, who lost two of their first three games, then won eight straight before losing the finale to the Lions a week before the title game.

In his post-game meeting with the Browns, Brown told the players, "On this given day you were the finest team I have ever coached. I've got to take my hat off to you."

Brown's counterpart, Lions coach Buddy Parker, whose teams had never lost to the Browns in eight previous games, lamented, "I saw it but still hardly can believe it."

And Lions quarterback Bobby Layne succinctly summarized the loss by saying, "They just beat the hell out of us."

Despite the Browns' awesome offensive display, the game ball was awarded to safety Warren Lahr, whose play sparked the defense, which intercepted six of Layne's passes and recovered three fumbles, two of which resulted in touchdowns.

Graham, the future Hall of Famer who had planned to retire but returned for a final season in 1955, "reached new heights in his illustrious career," according to the *Plain Dealer*. He scored three touchdowns, an NFL record, and passed for three others.

It all happened after the Lions had taken a 3-0 lead on Doak Walker's 36-yard field goal in the first quarter.

The Browns scored twice in the first quarter for a 14-3 lead, increased it to 35-10 at halftime, and coasted, 49-10, going into the final quarter.

The rout got underway six plays after Walker's field goal as Graham and Ray Renfro collaborated on a 37-yard touchdown pass. Graham also threw a 31-yard scoring pass to Renfro, and a 10-yarder to Darrell "Pete" Brewster, and ran for three scores himself.

For the Browns, who were 2 1/2 point underdogs going into the game, the victory was worth $2,478.57 per player as the winners' share, compared to $1,585.42 for the losers, according to the *Plain Dealer*.

Jim Brown's greatest game

Jim Brown had many great games during his nine-year career with the Browns, but the best might have been on November 1, 1959, when he scored five touchdowns in a 38-31 victory over the NFL defending champion Baltimore Colts, who would win the title again later that season.

Jim Brown

"I guess this was my most satisfying day," the future Hall of Famer was quoted in the Cleveland *Plain Dealer*.

"I do my best all the time, but I just may have been hitting with a little something extra out there today."

Among the many who would have agreed with Brown was Coach Weeb Ewbank of the Colts, who made a point of personally congratulating the Browns' fullback in the Cleveland locker room a half hour after the game.

"We knew you were quite a runner, but you're even better than we thought," Ewbank told Brown. "I hope you're back in December," meaning he hoped the Browns would win the NFL Eastern Conference, and that the Colts would win the Western Conference and play for the championship.

As it turned out, the Browns' victory over the Colts that day was their fourth of what would be six in eight games. However, they lost three of their final four to finish with a 7-5 record, three games behind the New York Giants. The Colts went on to win nine of their twelve games and beat the Giants, 31-16, for the championship.

After personally paying homage to Brown, Ewbank, an assistant coach with the Browns before he took over the Colts in 1954, told the *Plain Dealer,* "(Jim Brown) is everything everybody's said, and more. We didn't tackle as well as usual, but maybe that's because we were trying to bring down Jim Brown."

Brown, who ran for 178 yards, scored his first touchdown on a 70-yard jaunt after taking a pitch out from quarterback Milt Plum, who also played one of his best games, out-shining Colts' future Hall of Famer Johnny Unitas.

Brown's first touchdown put the Browns ahead, 10-3, in the second quarter, and they were never headed thereafter, though the score was tied twice, and the victory wasn't wrapped up until 1:32 remained. That's when Brown smashed into the end zone from one-yard out giving the Browns a 38-24 margin, which withstood the Colts' final touchdown.

Between his first and fifth touchdowns, Brown scored on a 17-yard run midway through the second quarter, breaking a 10-10 tie, and twice crossed the goal in the third quarter on plunges of three yards and one yard.

Plum didn't match Unitas in yardage, but his 14 completions in 23 attempts for 200 yards, including several key third down plays that were key factors in the upset by the Browns, who were seven point underdogs going in.

Unitas unleashed 41 passes and connected on 23 for 397 yards and four touchdowns. Raymond Berry and Lenny Moore, both of them also future Hall of Famers, were Unitas's favored targets. Berry caught 11 balls for 156 yards, and Moore hauled in five for 115 yards.

But nobody was as good on this day as Jim Brown, in what was the best game of his remarkable career as one of the greatest players in the history of the NFL.

How sweet it was December 27, 1964

How sweet it was ... and how long it has been.

More than a quarter of a century. Thirty-five years.

Lyndon Johnson was President, and Ralph Locher was mayor of Cleveland.

The Super Bowl had not yet been born and it became easier to put a man on the moon than for the Browns to win another National Football League championship.

But they did it in style in 1964.

Galen Fiss

Jim Brown ... Frank Ryan ... Gary Collins ... Galen Fiss ... Lou Groza ... and Blanton Collier, the great coach who brought them all together.

The date: Dec. 27, 1964.

The place: Cleveland Stadium.

The event: the NFI, championship game, forerunner of the Super Bowl.

And the score: Browns 27, Baltimore Colts 0.

The Colts, coached by Don Shula, a Collier protege and former member of the Browns and a star at John Carroll University, were supposed to win big. All the experts said they would.

But after a scoreless first half, Groza - whose 16-yard field goal 14 years earlier won the Browns' first NFL championship - kicked a 43-yarder early in the third quarter and the Browns were off to the races.

Collins, the flanker from the University of Maryland who wasn't supposed to be good enough to play professional football, caught three touchdown passes from Ryan, the mathematics whiz who would become Dr. Frank Ryan, athletic director of Yale University.

Ryan completed 11 of 18 passes for 197 yards, and Brown, football's greatest running back, ran 27 times for 114 yards. And the defense was superb, which it had to be to shut out the Colts, whose quarterback was the great John Unitas.

But this day Unitas passed for a mere 92 yards. The Colts' running game was even more impotent as the Browns held them to only 89 yards.

The second half was absolutely one-sided after the Browns scored on Groza's first field goal and on Ryan's 18-yard touchdown pass to Collins.

The Colts gained only 54 yards in 22 offensive plays after the intermission and, as it turned out, the game never officially ended.

With 26 seconds left on the clock, fans from the crowd of 79,544 swarmed onto the field and tore down the goal posts.

It wasn't the greatest day in Browns history, only their fourth NFL championship, beginning with a 30-28 victory over the Los Angeles Rams in 1950, a 56-10 beating of Detroit in 1954, and a 38-14 trouncing of the Rams in 1955.

But this one against Baltimore was special for many reasons, not the least of which was the fact that the Browns were given almost no chance to pull it off.

And after it was over, after the experts were proved wrong, a headline in the Cleveland *Plain Dealer* the next day suggested that a new sports dynasty had been born.

Unfortunately, it was wrong.

But how sweet it was 35 years ago. And how long it has been since then.

159

Monday night fever September 21, 1970

It was only a novelty, an *experiment,* if you will, in which no team wanted to be involved in 1970 when the NFL and ABC television network agreed to schedule a Monday night game that would be shown around the country.

And even though it was to be hosted by two well-known broadcasters – Howard Cosell and Keith Jackson, teamed with former NFL quarterback Don Meredith – the proposal by ABC's Roone Arledge was frowned upon by virtually all the teams.

Gary Collins

Browns then-owner Art Modell, chairman of the NFL's television committee, finally agreed to put his team in front of the national spotlight, with the condition that the game would be played in Cleveland. His friend, Sonny Werblin, principal owner of the New York Jets, agreed (with reluctance) to provide the opposition.

The game was scheduled for September 21, the opener of the 1970 season, and turned out to be a great success, so great that today teams and their players clamor for the opportunity to play in what has become ABC's weekly "MNF" special.

Spurred on, perhaps, by the presence of Joe Namath, the Jets' heralded quarterback, a crowd of 85,703 filled the old Cleveland Stadium on a hot and humid night, and were not disappointed by any aspect of the game. Especially the outcome.

The Browns won, 31-21 – though it was much closer than the score indicates – and, according to the Cleveland *Plain Dealer* the morning after the game, "large corporations reported excessive tardiness and absences," which were blamed on the fact that so many fans either attended in person, or stayed up late to watch on television.

The significance of that first Monday night game is underscored by *Total Football*, the unofficial encyclopedia of the NFL, which rates it as the ninth (of 25) "Most Memorable Regular Season Games" in the history of the league.

A major reason, of course, is that Monday Night Football has become so popular since that first game in Cleveland three decades ago.

But the Browns' victory itself also was a factor, exciting as it was from start to finish, as reported in *Total Football* by sportswriter/author Jack Clary:

"The Browns took a 14-0 lead in the first quarter on Bill Nelsen's touchdown pass to Gary Collins and Bo Scott's two-yard plunge, and led 14-7 at the half. Cleveland's Homer Jones returned the second half kickoff 94 yards for a touchdown before Emerson Boozer's second touchdown run of the game pulled the Jets to within 21-14 in the third quarter.

"It was 24-14 until Namath's 33-yard touchdown pass to George Sauer trimmed New York's deficit to three points later in the game. With two minutes to play, the Jets forced Cleveland to punt, but safety Mike Battle misjudged the ball. Instead of catching it at the Jets' 30-yard line, he allowed it to roll dead at the four with 90 seconds to play.

"Namath (who had an otherwise spectacular game, completing 18 of 29 passes for 284 yards) tried to pass the Jets downfield, but linebacker Billy Andrews intercepted a pass and returned it 25 yards for the clinching score."

So ended the first Monday night game – and launched a weekly event in the NFL.

The great grudge game  October 11, 1970

It was one of the NFL's all-time great "grudge" games – the Browns vs. the Cincinnati Bengals on October 11, 1970 at the Stadium – and became one of the team's most satisfying victories for then-owner Art Modell.

It was the first regular season meeting between the established Browns and the expansion Bengals whose president, general manager and coach was Paul Brown, who'd been the first general manager and coach of the Browns 24 years earlier, and had been fired by Modell on January 9, 1963.

With Blanton Collier, Brown's former assistant, on the sidelines as the Browns coach, they beat their downstate rival, 30-27, though the victory didn't come easily, and not without some anxious moments for Modell, as well as the 83,520 fans in attendance.

The decision still was in doubt until the last two seconds, though quarterback Bill Nelsen did a masterful job of running out the clock as the Browns sat on their three point lead before turning the ball over to the Bengals.

Then defensive end Jack Gregory slashed through the Bengals' line to sack quarterback Virgil Carter for a 12-yard loss, ending the grudge game.

As the players trotted off the Stadium turf, both Brown and Collier headed directly to their respective locker

Jack Gregory

rooms, disdaining the customary post-game congratulatory hand-shake although, later, each insisted their friendship was still intact.

And though Nelsen, playing on two injured knees, fullback Bo Scott and running back Leroy Kelly were the stars for the Browns, the game ball was awarded to Modell, which he probably still treasures above all other mementos of his 35 years in Cleveland..

Perhaps the single most important play in the Browns' victory came with 1:50 left.

It was an eight yard pass to Gary Collins – Nelsen's 17th completion in 19 attempts – on a third and five on their own 38. It provided a first down, enabling the Browns to retain possession instead of having to punt.

"If we had been forced to punt, then it was almost like playing for a tie the way their kicker (Horst Muhlman) was kicking," Collier was quoted in the Cleveland *Plain Dealer.* "We decided we had to throw the ball."

Then Collier praised the three players who played the most prominent roles in the victory, despite injuries that would have kept most players on the sidelines..

"It was quite a display of courage on the part of all three," he said, referring to Nelsen, Scott and Kelly. "It took courage to play when they hadn't worked much during the week."

Nelsen passed for 218 yards and two touchdowns, while Kelly ran for 84 yards in 29 carries, and caught a pass for a touchdown, and Scott gained 44 yards in 10 carries.

The Browns were behind most of the way, trailing 10-0, and then 10-2 in the first quarter, 17-16 at the half, and 20-16 through three periods.

Touchdowns by Kelly and Scott put them ahead, 30-20, and proved to be enough despite a late score by the Bengals, as the Browns controlled the ball in the final minutes.

It gave Modell the victory he had long coveted, and in the 26 seasons from 1970-95, the Browns won 27 of the 51 games between the two Ohio teams.

A most memorable defeat

Actually, the Browns' game in Oakland on November 8, 1970, was one their fans would prefer to forget, as it was more memorable to the Raiders – and especially to their-then 43 year old place kicker and substitute quarterback, George Blanda.

It is included here because the game was deemed one of the 25 "greatest" played in the

Bill Nelsen

National Football League since its inception in 1922. The Oakland Raiders beat the Browns 23-20.

The list was compiled by a panel of thirteen historians, and published in *Total Football*, which is considered to be the encyclopedia of professional football.

It was Blanda's late heroics, as both a passer and kicker – and the fact that it meant so much to both teams - that made the game so noteworthy.

The Browns that season finished with a 7-7 record, and the loss to the Raiders cost them a chance to tie Cincinnati for the AFC Central Division title and probably a place in the playoffs.

On the other hand, the victory enabled the Raiders to win the AFC Western Division with an 8-4-2 record as they finished one game ahead of Kansas City (7-5-2).

Memorable? It sure was – for Oakland.

Blanda was playing because of an injury to regular quarterback Darryl Lamonica early in the fourth quarter with the Browns clinging to a 17-13 lead.

It appeared the Browns would prevail when, with 4:10 left in the game, Don Cockroft kicked a field goal, to the dismay of 54,463 fans in the Oakland Coliseum. It boosted the Browns lead to 20-13 and, with Lamonica on the bench, the Raiders' hopes were waning as they returned the ensuing kickoff to their own 30.

That's when Blanda, the grizzled, future Hall of Famer whose professional career began 21 years earlier with the Chicago Bears, got hot.

He completed a 22-yard pass to Warren Wells, and three plays later, on fourth-and-16 with 1:55 to play, scrambled and fired a 17-yard pass to Fred Biletnikoff for a first down on the Cleveland 17. Then Blanda hit Wells in the end zone with 1:34 left on the clock, and kicked the extra point, tying the score at 20-20.

The Browns took the kickoff, but were immediately stopped as Bill Nelsen's first down pass intended for tight end Milt Morin was intercepted by the Raiders' Kent McCloughan.

At that point it seemed the game would end in a tie as the Raiders were unable to gain any yardage in their first two plays, and then, on third down at the Browns' 49 with only 34 seconds remaining, were whistled for an illegal procedure penalty.

But, as *Total Football* reported, "Astonishingly, the Browns accepted (the penalty)," and instead of fourth-and-20 ... the Raiders had a third-and-25 at their own 46.

"(The Browns) weren't going to let us throw to get out of bounds," Blanda explained later, "but Hewitt (Dixon) kept saying, 'Give it to me, give it to me, I can get out.'" Blanda did, firing a nine-yard pass to Dixon, who got out of bounds at the Browns' 45 with seven seconds to play.

It was enough time only for a field goal attempt, and Blanda booted the ball 52 yards through the uprights for the Raiders' three point, "most memorable" victory – though it was memorable to the Browns because it was such a costly loss.

162

The first - and last - step

It was the culmination of a remarkable season, and seemed to be the first step along the road to the Browns' initial appearance in a Super Bowl.

They rallied for a 27-24 victory over the Cincinnati Bengals, achieved on a 22-yard field goal by Don Cockroft with 1:25 left in the game, on December 21, 1980 at Riverfront Stadium to win the AFC Central Division championship.

It was the Browns' – a.k.a. "Kardiac Kids" – 11th victory in 16 games, and fifth of the season in the waning minutes, for their first division title since 1971, after overcoming an 0-2, and then a 2-3 start in 1980.

In beating the Bengals, after trailing 10-0 in the second quarter and 17-10 in the third, the Browns qualified for the playoffs for the first time in seven years.

"I don't care who we play, or when," said then-coach Sam Rutigliano, who was carried off the field on the shoulders of his players. "We can play Carnegie Tech, for all I care. I just want to enjoy this accomplishment."

As it turned out, they played Oakland in the playoffs that were supposed to be culminated by winning Super Bowl XV, but lost to the wild card Raiders, 14-12, though that defeat didn't – at least until later - detract from the victory over the Bengals.

Sam Rutigliano

The turning point of the game, as elaborated by quarterback Brian Sipe, was a most unlikely one, coming on the play in which the Bengals went ahead, 17-10, on Ray Griffin's touchdown on a 52-yard pass interception 34 seconds into the second half.

"I got mad," said Sipe, the trigger-man of the Kardiac Kids. "I think we all did. After Griffin ran it back, I felt more aggressive than I had at any time in the game, and I was determined they wouldn't beat us," he was quoted in the Cleveland *Plain Dealer.*

Two minutes after Griffin scored, Sipe fired a 35-yard touchdown pass to Ricky Feacher, tying the game at 17-17, and 2 ½ minutes later, they collaborated for another touchdown, this one a 34-yard pass, and the Browns led for the first time, 24-17.

But not for long. With 14 seconds left in the third quarter the Bengals deadlocked the game again, 24-24, on a 59-yard pass from Jack Thompson to Pat McInally.

The score stayed that way until 13:35 of the fourth quarter when Cockroft clicked on his field goal after the Bengals were forced to punt and the Browns took over on their own 46.

Eight plays advanced the ball to the Bengals' five yard line, where the Browns had a first down with two minutes remaining. Two more running plays by Mike Pruitt gained two yards and, on third down with 1:39 left, Sipe tried what Rutigliano called a "feast or famine" bootleg.

"It would be feast or famine," said Rutigliano, "but we knew we still had Cockroft to kick the field goal if Brian didn't get it."

Sipe didn't. In fact, he lost three yards. But as Rutigliano said, the Browns still had Cockroft, and he kicked the field goal, for a three-point lead, though the Bengals, after the ensuing kickoff, still had a chance with 1:18 to play and the ball on their 32.

They reached the Browns 34 with 11 seconds to go. One last aerial to Steve Kreider gained 20 yards. Kreider, however, couldn't get out of bounds as he was tackled by cornerback Ron Bolton, and the clock ran out giving the Browns the victory.

'Red Right 88' January 4, 1981

It's not a *favorite* memory, but Browns fans will long remember – and surely long lament – what happened on the frozen turf of the old Cleveland Stadium on January 4, 1981.

Then, in front of 77,655, the Browns, a.k.a. the "Kardiac Kids," came within 49 seconds of pulling off another miracle, which they'd done five times in the final minute earlier in the season in winning the AFC Central Division with an 11-5 record.

Brian Sipe

Oakland, which reached the playoffs as the AFC wild card, was leading, 14-12, as the Browns took possession of the ball on their own 15 with 2:22 remaining in the game. Brian Sipe, who would be the NFL's consensus "Most Valuable Player" for 1980, hit on a couple of passes to the Raiders' 28 with 1:12 left to play. After an incompletion, fullback Mike Pruitt burst up the middle for 14 yards and a first down at the Oakland 14.

Another plunge by Pruitt put the ball on the 13 and, with the clock down to 49 seconds, Coach Sam Rutigliano huddled with Sipe and quarterbacks coach Jim Shofner.

With a third-and-nine it was expected that the Browns would either boot a field goal, or run the ball to set up a better angle for a fourth down kick by Don Cockroft.

They did neither. Instead, Rutigliano chose a play called "Red Right 88," a pass to Ozzie Newsome in the end zone. It was intercepted by the Raiders' Mike Davis and, that quickly, the Browns' hopes for their first NFL championship since 1964 ended.

In that crucial game the Browns scored first, midway through the second quarter, when Ron Bolton intercepted a Jim Plunkett pass and returned it 42 yards. After Cockroft missed the extra point, the Raiders retaliated with 18 seconds left in the first half as Mark Van Eeghan scored on a one-yard plunge that put Oakland ahead, 7-6.

Cockroft, who was nursing a sore back and an injury to his left knee, kicked two third quarter field goals of 30- and 29-yards (though he also missed 47- and 30-yarders), which regained a 12-7 lead for the Browns, who by then appeared to be in control.

They held off the Raiders until 5:38 of the fourth quarter when Van Eeghan scored again from one yard out, after an 80-yard march, for Oakland's two point lead.

The Browns took the ensuing kickoff but were forced to punt, and the Raiders advanced to the Cleveland 15 where they were stopped after disdaining a field goal attempt.

It gave the Browns one last chance. They drove 72 yards in 1:33, to the Oakland 13, where they had a third-and-nine. That's when Rutigliano ordered "Red Right 88."

The play was called, Rutigliano said, because there was time for Sipe to try one more pass, though he told the quarterback, "If Ozzie is covered, throw the ball to the blonde in the bleachers." Then Cockroft would try for the game-winning field goal. When it was over – and ever since that frigid day in 1981 – Rutigliano insisted his call was a logical one.

And, without criticizing Cockroft, he said, "It was so cold, kicking a football was like kicking a cement block. And not to have an opportunity to win the game with the league MVP (Sipe) didn't make sense."

Years later Rutigliano was still sure that "Red Right-88" was a good call.

"There is no question in my mind that I'd do the same thing if I had it to do all over again," he told the Touchdown Club in a 1999 speech.

The first time in 18 years

Mark Mosely would have been the saddest – and, perhaps, even the most *hated* – man in Cleveland if he had not succeeded after being given another chance for atonement.

The 38-year old place-kicker, playing only his fifth game for the Browns after replacing injured Matt Bahr, booted a 27-yard field goal 2:02 into the second overtime period for a 23-20 victory over the New York Jets in a divisional playoff in front of 78,106 fans at the Stadium on January 3, 1987.

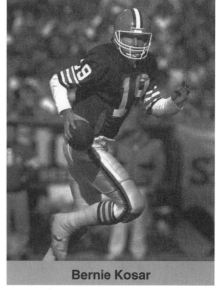

Earlier, with a chance to beat the Jets in the first overtime period, Mosely blew a 23-yard kick, prolonging the battle that became the third-longest game in NFL history.

It went into the first overtime as the Browns overcame a 20-10 deficit in the fourth quarter with a touchdown by Kevin Mack and a 22-yard field goal by Mosely, all in the final minute. Mack scored on a one-yard plunge and then, after the ensuing kickoff the Browns forced the Jets to punt with 1:03 on the clock.

Gerald "Ice Cube" McNeil returned the kick 11 yards to the Browns 33. Three plays and a 25-yard pass interference penalty against the Jets advanced the ball to the New York five-yard line with 11 seconds left and Mosely kicked the tying field goal.

"I think we all had an opportunity to experience one of the finest games in the history of this sport … I have

Bernie Kosar

never experienced or seen a comeback like that," Browns coach Marty Schottenheimer was quoted in the Cleveland *Plain Dealer*.

It was the Browns' first playoff victory in 18 years and, as reported in the *Plain Dealer,* "The best and worst moments Browns history unfolded in one exhilarating afternoon of football," as the fans were chanting, "Super Bowl! Super Bowl."

It was the sixth straight victory for the Browns, who were 12-4 in the regular season to win the AFC Central Division. It positioned them to play Denver, the AFC West winner, in what became a gut-wrenching loss in the game dubbed "The Drive."

The Browns' furious rally against the Jets was led by quarterback Bernie Kosar, who set playoff records with 33 completions in 64 attempts for 489 yards - though he also was intercepted twice in the fourth quarter.

The first, with the Browns trailing, 13-10, came in a third-and-two situation at the Jets' two-yard line, on a pass intended for Webster Slaughter that was picked off in the end zone by Russell Carter. Nine plays and 4 ½ minutes later, after the Browns had forced a punt, Kosar was intercepted again, this time on a first-and-ten from the Cleveland 17. Jerry Holmes stole the ball and the Jets scored on their first play, a 25-yard run by Freeman McNeil, increasing the Browns' deficit to 20-10.

And, while it was devastating turn of events for the fans, it apparently motivated the Browns, especially Kosar.

As left tackle Paul Farren testified, after the Browns took over on their 32 with 4:08 remaining, "Bernie comes into the huddle and says, 'We're going to take this game.' It's incredible the way he brought us together as a unit, one play at a time," according to the *Plain Dealer.*

Which the Browns did, though not without several more anxious moments, especially Mosely's failed field goal, before he got another chance for atonement, and went from goat to hero.

165

'The Drive' January 11, 1987

With less than six minutes left in the game, Browns fans, especially 79,915 of them in the old Cleveland Stadium, were sure that, at long last, their team was Super Bowl bound.

The date was January 11, 1987, and the Browns, coming off a 12-4 season and a 23-20, double overtime victory against the New York Jets in the divisional playoff, were beating the Denver Broncos, 20-13, for the AFC championship.

They had the Broncos pinned back on their own two-yard line and only had to stop John Elway to capture their fifth NFL title and first in 23 seasons.

But stopping Elway, as it always was difficult to do, turned out to be an impossible task this day.

The Hall of Fame-bound quarterback engineered a 15 play, 98-yard drive in five minutes and six seconds to get a game-tying touchdown and extra point with only 37 seconds remaining.

Then, after the Browns won the coin toss to receive the kickoff in overtime, the Broncos forced a punt, took over the ball and again refused to be denied, finally winning the game, 23-20. It was achieved on a 60-yard drive that was culminated by a 33-yard field goal by Rich Karlis at the 5:48 mark in the sudden death session.

Mark Mosely

It was, and long will be remembered as one of the cruelest losses ever suffered by a Browns team - just as it was, and long will be remembered as one of Elway's greatest clutch performances, playing as he was on a sprained ankle that limited his mobility.

The first 54 minutes of the game was a see-saw battle featuring Bernie Kosar and Mark Mosely of the Browns, and Elway and Karlis of the Broncos.

The score was tied, 10-10, at halftime, on Kosar's six-yard touchdown pass to Herman Fontenot and Mosely's 29-yard field goal, and Gerald Wilhite's one-yard plunge for a Denver touchdown and Karlis's 19-yard field goal.

Karlis booted another field goal, a 26-yarder, for a 13-10 Denver lead in the third quarter, but again the Browns retaliated, this time on Mosely's 24-yard field goal. It deadlocked the game again, 13-13, at 2:22 of the fourth quarter.

Then, after Denver took the kickoff but was forced to punt, Kosar hit Brian Brennan on a 48-yard touchdown bomb and, with 5:33 left on the clock, Browns fans began to chant, "Super Bowl! Super Bowl!"

The cheers became even louder – though they soon would be quieted – when the Browns kicked off and pinned the Broncos back on their two-yard line.

But, as so often has been the case, that's when Elway was at his best. Fourteen plays later, including five completed passes in eight attempts, the Broncos had a third-and-one on the Browns' five, from where Elway hit Jackson for the touchdown that set up Karlis's extra point and sent the game into overtime.

After the Browns won the coin toss, their first possession stalled on their own 38. They punted and Elway took over on the Denver 25.

He got the Broncos to the Browns' 33 in nine plays and, on fourth down, Karlis was called upon to kick his third field goal of the game, a 33-yarder that vaulted Denver into Super Bowl XXI – and sent Browns fans into mourning.

'The Fumble' January 17, 1988

How many times can a heart be broken?

That's what Browns fans were asking on January 17, 1988, in the wake of another gut-wrenching loss to the Denver Broncos for the second year in a row in the AFC Championship game, this time, 38-33, with a trip to Super Bowl XXII at stake.

The critical turning point, on a play called "Trap 13," came on a fumble by Earnest Byner at the Denver three yard line with 65 seconds remaining.

They were closing in on what would have been a game-tying touchdown, 38-38, after they'd trailed the Broncos, 14-0, in the first quarter, and 21-3 at halftime.

Byner, normally one of the NFL's sure-handed running backs and a star of the Browns team that had gone 10-5 under Coach Marty Schottenheimer, fumbled when he was hit by Broncos' cornerback Jeremiah Castille.

Making it even more frustrating for the Browns is that Byner already had gained enough yardage for a first down, and only Castille was between him and the goal line.

Castille pounced on the loose ball, which preserved the victory.

Reggie Langhorne

Byner's fumble was the second costly turnover by the Browns as Bernie Kosar was intercepted in the opening minutes which set up the first of John Elway's three touchdown passes. It was an eight yard strike to Ricky Nattiel, 3:38 into the game, and the Broncos made it 14-0 on Steve Sewell's one-yard plunge with 3:54 left in the first quarter.

The Browns got on the scoreboard with a 24-yard field goal by Matt Bahr at 1:42 of the second quarter, only to have the Broncos quickly retaliate on another one-yard plunge by Gene Lang. It put Denver ahead, 21-3, with 8:01 left in the first half.

Kosar cut the deficit to 21-10 with an 18-yard touchdown strike to Reggie Langhorne at 3:44 of the third quarter, though the Broncos roared back on an 80-yard scoring pass and run from Elway to Mark Jackson, restoring Denver's 18-point lead.

It didn't, however, stop Kosar, who completed an AFC championship game record 26 of 41 passes for 356 yards. He connected with Byner on a 32-yard touchdown pass at 8:10 of the third quarter, and 3:05 later, Byner barreled into the end zone from four yards out to cut the Browns' deficit to 28-24.

Before the third quarter ended, Rich Karlis booted a 38-yard field goal for a 31-24 Broncos' lead, but the Browns culminated their comeback at the 4:12 mark of the fourth quarter as Kosar's four yard touchdown pass to Webster Slaughter tied the score, 31-31.

But it didn't stay that way long. With 4:01 left in the game, Elway's third touchdown pass, this one a 20-yarder, landed in the hands of Sammy Winder and the Browns faced another mountain to climb in their quest to reach the Super Bowl.

They mounted a drive that took them within the shadow of Denver's goal post, only to have Byner lose the ball.

Then, to ensure the victory, Broncos' punter Mike Horan ran out of the end zone for a safety with eight seconds remaining. It gave the Browns two points that cut their deficit to five - but also allowed the Broncos to escape from the shadow of their goal post and finalized the gut-wrenching defeat that always will be remembered by Browns fans as "The Fumble."

A little luck ... and tenacity December 10, 1994

There weren't many memories to savor during the mostly-unpleasant regime of Bill Belichick from 1991-95, though there was one in particular that deserves mention.

It was a 19-14 victory over the two-time defending Super Bowl champion Dallas Cowboys in Texas Stadium on December 10, 1994, a game that few gave the Browns a chance of winning, probably not even their mothers. They were 10 ½ point underdogs.

Eric Turner

It also was a game that, as it turned out, the Browns had to win to make it into the playoffs as an AFC wild card team.

"We were like giant killers. It was like Ali beating up Sonny Liston and shaking up the world," linebacker Pepper Johnson was quoted in the Cleveland *Plain Dealer.*

And cornerback Antonio Langham said, "It felt like we won the Super Bowl."

According to the paper, "Even the normally stoic Belichick could not hide his elation. 'Nobody gave us a chance to come in here and beat the Cowboys, but this team believes in itself,' he said."

The key play, the one that made it possible for the Browns to beat the Cowboys, came at the end of the game, precisely as time ran out, thanks to a little luck and a lot of tenacity on the part of Browns safety Eric Turner.

Cowboys' tight end Jay Novacek was stopped – partly because he slipped on the artificial turf, and also because of a tackle and hold by Browns safety Eric Turner – inches short of the goal line after catching a six-yard pass from Troy Aikman. The drive by the Cowboys began at their own 49-yard line with 1:49 left to play.

It gave the Browns a 10-4 record and kept them in contention for the AFC Central Division championship. However, they subsequently lost it the following week when they were defeated by Pittsburgh, 17-7, and settled for a wild card berth in the playoffs.

They went on to beat Seattle, 35-9, in the season finale, and New England, 20-13, in the first round of the playoffs, but lost again to the Steelers, 29-9.

Credit also had to be given to the entire Browns' defense, which forced four Dallas turnovers (two pass interceptions and two fumble recoveries), and don't overlook Matt Stover's contributions.

Stover, who grew up in Dallas, kicked four field goals – of 34, 32, 43 and 32 yards, three of which were set up by turnovers - without which, of course, the Browns almost certainly would have lost and, in the end, failed to make the playoffs.

The Cowboys scored first, on a seven yard pass from Aikman to Emmitt Smith at 10:49 of the first quarter. The Browns tied it on the final play of the period on a two-yard touchdown pass from Vinny Testaverde to Michael Jackson.

Stover's first field goal came at 3:56 of the second quarter for a 10-7 lead, that became 13-7 and 16-7 at 1:46 and 3:16 of the fourth quarter. Smith scored on a four yard run with 6:21 left in the game to close the Cowboys' deficit to two points.

But Stover came through with his fourth field goal with 1:49 left, giving him 20 consecutive successful three-pointers, and the Browns held off the Cowboys for the victory - though it required a little luck and geat tenacity by Turner.

'I didn't want it to be over'

The Browns beat the Cincinnati Bengals, 26-10, on December 17, 1995, but few of the 55,875 fans in the old Stadium, enjoyed the victory.

They had something else on their minds as they paid their respects to a cherished old friend - the team that was moving to Baltimore and would play as the "Ravens".

And just as the fans had mourned the decision of then-owner Art Modell to desert Cleveland in favor of what he believed would be millions of dollars in profits in Baltimore, Browns players also were saddened to be leaving.

"I didn't want it to be over," an emotional Tony Jones, the Browns' starting left tackle since 1988, was quoted in the Cleveland *Plain Dealer.* "We don't know what tomorrow brings for us yet, but wherever we are, we want Cleveland to know – thanks for everything. We couldn't ask for any better fans in the world."

And, as Earnest Byner said, "When I came here the first time, I didn't know the legacy I was stepping into. Later, I began to appreciate it more and more. Jim Brown, Bobby Mitchell, Leroy Kelly and Ernie Green played my position here. There is something proud here, something I'm proud to be part of."

Matt Stover

When the game ended many of the players, instead of trouping off the field, made their way around the perimeter of the Stadium, especially at the "Dawg Pound," to shake hands with the fans – even to embrace some of them.

Mike Brown, president of the Bengals and son of the late Paul Brown who helped Mickey McBride organize the Browns in 1946, also was quoted in the paper.

"In a way, the event outweighed the game," Brown said. "We were not trying to please (the fans), we were trying to win the game. We might have made them happy, but they earned it.

"When it was all over, I was angry until I thought that maybe this was the best way. They (the Browns) go out on a high note. The crowd loves them, hugs the players, if you will, and then it's over."

Among those who didn't shake hands or hug the fans - and who made very clear his feelings - was Andre Rison, the wide receiver. It was his five year, $17 million contract that had much to do with the financial problems that Modell claimed made it necessary to move the franchise.

"Why would I want to go (to the Dawg Pound)," Rison asked, verbally thumbing his nose at the fans. "I just got booed for three hours. I'm glad to be getting out of here."

For the record, the Browns said farewell with one of their best performances of the lame duck season, snapping a five game losing streak, giving them a 5-10 record with one game remaining.

Quarterback Vinny Testaverde completed 22 of 32 passes for 241 yards and two touchdowns to Frank Hartley and Keenan McCardell. Testaverde was 16-of-19 for 162 yards at the half, when the Browns led, 17-3, Matt Stover was 4-for-4 on field goals, and the Browns outrushed Cincinnati, 159 yards to 65.

Byner was the workhorse, handling the ball on 38 of 73 plays, including 31 runs for 121 yards, and seven receptions for 36 yards.

It should have been one of the Browns most satisfying victories – but wasn't.

The end of an era December 24, 1995

It seemed to be appropriate that the Browns – no longer the *Cleveland* Browns – would lose their 1995 finale in Jacksonville to the Jaguars, 24-21, giving them the dubious distinction of having been swept by an expansion team whose record went to 4-12..

Not only did the loss reduce the Browns' record to 5-11, the worst by the franchise since

Bennie Thompson

1990, it also proved to be Bill Belichick's last game, despite the fact that Art Modell had said much earlier that Belichick would be the last coach he'd hire.

When the former Browns, re-named the "Ravens," opened the 1996 season in Baltimore, their coach was Ted Marchibroda, ending Belichick's often stormy five year tenure in Cleveland with an undistinguished 37-45 won-lost mark.

It also ended Belichick's "five-year plan" that was supposed to bring an NFL title back to Cleveland by 1995. It would have been the Browns' first in 31 seasons.

Though it mattered little to the fans who felt they'd been betrayed by Modell, the Browns were beaten by the Jaguars on Mike Hollis's 34-yard field goal as time expired, enabling Jacksonville to snap a seven game losing streak.

Adding to the Browns' frustration was that Hollis got a second chance to kick the game-winning field goal. His first attempt from 39 yards hit an upright and fell back. But two Browns, Bennie Thompson and Johnny Thomas, were called for being off-sides, giving Hollis a second kick, which he made.

Belichick, who seldom spoke with much enthusiasm regardless of how his team fared, was quoted in the Cleveland *Plain Dealer* as saying, "This game typified the way our whole season went. Unfortunately, it's been that type of year and I don't have much to say about it."

Matt Stover, one of the few players left from Belichick's first team, was more talkative, though his remarks were no more enlightening. "Can you believe it?" he asked. "It's humbling," he said of the loss, as quoted in the newspaper.

Veteran linebacker Carl Banks, who previously played on two New York Giants teams that won Super Bowls, went even further, and in so doing issued, if ever so subtly, an indictment against Belichick.

"The thing that makes it so tough," his comments were reported, "is that this is the most talented team I've ever been around. Ever. Collectively, this is the best team I've been on."

When asked where it all went wrong, Banks spelled out his answer.

"A-t-t-i-t-u-d-e," he said. "Collectively, we didn't have the right attitude. And I refuse to single out, or exempt anyone."

The Browns trailed most of the way, but closed to within one point of the Jaguars with 1:13 left in the game, on a one-yard sneak by Vinny Testaverde, who completed 28 of 45 passes for 325 yards and two touchdowns with three interceptions.

When Belichick was asked if he considered going for a two-point conversion that would have put the Browns ahead by one, he replied, "No," again without elaboration.

The Jaguars needed less than a minute to take the ensuing kickoff and march to within the shadow of the Browns goal post for Hollis to kick his field goal.

And so ended the season and the franchise that had begun so well 50 years earlier.

THIS DATE IN BROWNS HISTORY

January 2, 1966: The Green Bay Packers hold Jim Brown to only 50 yards rushing on a sloppy field and defeat the Browns, 23-12, to win the 1965 NFL championship.

January 3, 1958: Rookie running back Jim Brown finishes in a tie with Baltimore Colts quarterback Johnny Unitas for second place behind San Francisco 49ers quarterback Y.A. Tittle in the balloting for 1957 NFL "Most Valuable Player" award.

January 3, 1987: The Browns defeat the New York Jets, 23-20, in double overtime for their first playoff game victory since 1969, as Bernie Kosar completes 33 of 64 passes for a club record 489 yards.

January 4, 1970: Appearing in their eighth NFL championship game, the Browns are beaten by the Minnesota Vikings, 27-7, in Minnesota.

January 4, 1981: "The Play," Red Right 88, a pass by Brian Sipe intended for Ozzie Newsome, is intercepted in the end zone by Mike Davis with 49 seconds remaining in the opening round of the playoffs, costing the Browns a 14-12 loss to the eventual Super Bowl XV champion Oakland Raiders.

January 9, 1963: With the three Cleveland newspapers on strike, Browns owner Arthur B. Modell fires 54-year old general manager and coach Paul Brown, who compiled a 17 year won-lost record of 158-48-8, and whose teams captured four championships in the All-America Football Conference and three in the NFL.

Paul Brown

Sam Rutigliano

This date in Browns history

January 11, 1987:   The Browns' Super Bowl hopes are killed by "The Drive," as the Denver Broncos, led by John Elway, march 98 yards in 15 plays to tie the game at 20-20 with 37 seconds remaining, then win on a 33-yard field goal 5:38 into sudden death overtime by Rich Karlis in the 1986 AFC championship game in front of 79,915 fans in the Stadium.

January 12, 1946:   The defending NFL champion Cleveland Rams announce their decision to move to Los Angeles, rather than compete with the Browns in the newly-formed All-America Football Conference.

January 12, 1958:   Jim Brown is named the winner of the NFL 1957 "Player of the Year" award by the Associated Press and United Press-International.

January 14, 1990:   Under Bud Carson as the team's eighth head coach, the Browns lose to Denver, 37-21, for the 1989 AFC title, their third conference championship game appearance in four years.

January 16, 1963:   Blanton Collier is named head coach of the Browns, succeeding Paul Brown as the second coach in the team's then 18-year history.

January 17, 1988:   "The Fumble," the game in which the Denver Broncos beat the Browns in the 1987 AFC championship game, 38-35, in front of 75,993 fans in Mile High Stadium when, with less than two minutes to play, a fumble by Ernest Byner on the Broncos' three-yard line is recovered by Denver's Jeremiah Castille with 65 seconds remaining.

January 21, 1949:   Paul Brown receives a five-year contract extension to coach the Browns through 1955 at a reported salary of $25,000 a season.

Art Modell   **Bud Carson**

This date in Browns history

January 22, 1975: Forrest Gregg is hired as the fourth coach in Browns history, replacing Nick Skorich, whose four year won-lost record was 30-26-2.

January 27, 1970: After trading up to the third pick in the NFL draft by sending receiver Paul Warfield to the Miami Dolphins, the Browns select Purdue quarterback Mike Phipps.

January 27, 1989: Bud Carson is hired as the eighth coach in Browns history, replacing Marty Schottenheimer, whose five year won-lost record was 46-31.

February 1, 1983: Paul Warfield is elected to the Pro Football Hall of Fame.

February 5, 1957: Browns players vote unanimously to endorse the newly formed NFL Players Association.

February 8, 1945: Mickey McBride, owner of Cleveland's new entry in the All-America Football Conference, signs a five year deal with Great Lakes Naval Training Station coach Paul Brown, 36, making him the team's general manager and coach.

February 10, 1954: Blanton Collier resigns as an assistant coach of the Browns to become head coach at the University of Kentucky, where he replaces Paul "Bear" Bryant.

February 12, 1959: Cleveland Indians general manager Frank Lane offers Jim Brown a contract to play baseball, but it is rejected and Brown gets an $8,000 raise from the Browns.

Mickey McBride   **Paul Brown**

This date in Browns history

March 3, 1946:   Immediately following his discharge from the Navy, Paul Brown attends the All-America Football Conference meeting in Chicago in his new role as general manager and coach of the Browns.

March 9, 1981:   Peter Hadhazy resigns as general manager of the Browns upon losing a power struggle with Tommy Prothro, director of player personnel.

March 11, 1954:   After what Paul Brown calls "his best year last season (1953)," Browns quarterback Otto Graham signs a one year deal for a reported $20,000, making him the highest paid player in the NFL.

March 16, 1954:   Future Hall of Famer Bill Willis announces his retirement after nine seasons with the Browns.

March 21, 1961:   New York television and advertising executive Arthur B. Modell purchases the Browns for a reported $3.9 million.

March 22, 1983:   Blanton Collier, who coached the Browns from 1963-70, compiling a 79-38-2 won-lost record that included the NFL championship in 1964, dies of cancer in Houston at the age of 76.

March 25, 1953:   The largest trade in the history of the National Football League, involving 15 players, is made by the Browns and Baltimore, with future Hall of Famer Mike McCormack and four other players coming to Cleveland in exchange for Don Shula and nine others going to the Colts.

March 30, 1945:   Otto Graham, who won All-America honors as a tailback at Northwestern University, is the first player signed by the Browns in the newly-formed All-America Football Conference.

Blanton Collier

Don Shula

This date in Browns history

April 5, 1976: Future Hall of Famer Paul Warfield returns to the Browns as a free agent after a six year absence, during which he starred for the Miami Dolphins from 1970-74, and played in the defunct World Football League in 1975.

April 13, 1957: George Ratterman, who replaced Otto Graham as the Browns quarterback in 1956, only to suffer a severe knee injury in the fourth game of the season, announces his retirement.

April 19, 1956: Future Hall of Famer Dante Lavelli, who played for the Browns from their inception in 1946 through 1955, announces his retirement.

April 24, 1982: Linebacker Tom Cousineau signs with the Browns after being acquired in one of the team's costliest deals.

April 25, 1978: The rights to former Ohio State punter Tom Skladany are traded by the Browns to the Detroit Lions for a third round draft choice (that is used to select running back Larry Collins).

April 28, 1982: Running back Greg Pruitt and defensive end Lyle Alzado are traded to the Los Angeles Raiders for draft choices.

May 3, 1977: Mike Phipps is traded to the Chicago Bears for a fourth round draft choice in 1977 and a first in 1978 (the latter was used to select Ozzie Newsome).

May 10, 1969: The Browns join the expansion Cincinnati Bengals, Pittsburgh and Houston in the Central Division of the NFL's American Conference.

Cleveland Browns 1954 coaching staff
Howard Brinker, Fritz Heisler, Paul Brown, Ed Ulinski, Paul Bixler

This date in Browns history

May 14, 1968: Bill Nelsen is acquired in a four player trade with the Pittsburgh Steelers that turns out to be one of the Browns' best deals.

May 15, 1955: Fullback Marion Motley, the all-time rushing champion of the All-America Football Conference who had retired in 1954, announces his plan to return to the Browns in 1955 as a linebacker (though he subsequently is traded to the Pittsburgh Steelers for fullback Ed Modzelewski on September 8, 1955).

May 18, 1963: Ernie Davis dies at the age of 23 after a long battle with leukemia, and the number he would have worn, 45, is retired by the Browns, even though he never played a game.

May 31, 1983: First round draft choice Ron Brown, a wide receiver from Arizona State, rejects the Browns' $900,000, four year contract to run track in an attempt to qualify for the 1984 Olympics.

June 4, 1944: Arthur B. "Mickey" McBride posts a $10,000 fee establishing the Browns as a charter member of the All-America Football Conference.

June 4, 1963: Defensive back Don Fleming is electrocuted in an industrial accident on a construction job in Florida; later his uniform No. 46 is retired by the Browns.

June 8, 1945: Cleveland's new team in the All-America Football Conference is given the nickname "Panthers," but it is rejected and "Browns" subsequently is chosen.

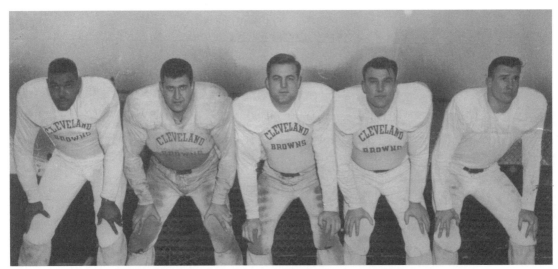

The 1954 defensive line. Left to right: RE Len Ford, RT Don Colo, MG Mike McCormack, LT John Kissell, LE Carlton Massey

This date in Browns history

June 8, 1957:   Jim Brown signs a $15,000 contract for 1957 after being the Browns first round draft choice out of Syracuse University.

June 10, 1953:   Arthur B. "Mickey" McBride sells the Browns for $600,000 to a group of Clevelanders led by David R. Jones, and including Homer Marshman, Saul Silberman, Ellis Ryan and Ralph DeChiaro, with Robert Gries, previously a minority partner of McBride, retaining his financial interest.

June 17, 1983:   Art Modell undergoes quadruple bypass coronary surgery.

June 30, 1953:   End Mac Speedie signs with Regina of the Canadian Football League, ending an outstanding, seven-year career with the Browns.

July 6, 1953:   Future Hall of Famer Otto Graham accepts a cut in salary and signs for $20,000, ending his brief holdout.

July 12, 1960:   Defensive end Willie Davis, who would be elected to the Pro Football Hall of Fame in 1981, is traded by the Browns after two seasons in Cleveland, to the Green Bay Packers for receiver A.D. Williams (who played for the Browns one year).

July 12, 1962:   Quarterback Frank Ryan and halfback Tom Wilson are acquired in a trade with the Los Angeles Rams for defensive tackle Larry Stephens and two draft selections (though Ryan was obtained primarily as a backup to Jim Ninowski, he soon took over as the starter and led the Browns to the NFL championship in 1964).

1953 Cleveland Browns

This date in Browns history

July 14, 1966: Future Hall of Famer Jim Brown announces his retirement from football to devote his time to working for the Negro Industrial and Economic Union, and on his acting career.

July 14, 1967: Future Hall of Famer Lou Groza, the only member of the original Browns still playing, signs his 22nd contract with the team.

July 17, 1956: For the first time since 1946, when the Browns came into being, Otto Graham and his favorite receiver, Dante Lavelli, are no longer with the team as training camp opens at Hiram College in Hiram, Ohio.

July 17, 1982: The Los Angeles *Times* reports that Charles White, the Browns' No. 1 pick in the 1980 draft, spent about a month in the Care Unit Hospital in Orange County, California, undergoing treatment for drug abuse (which leads to the formation of the "Inner Circle" by the Browns).

July 22, 1967: Five players – future Hall of Famer Leroy Kelly, linebacker Sid Williams, defensive back Mike Howell, offensive tackle John Brown and guard John Wooten – strike the Browns training camp for better contracts (though Wooten already is signed), on the advice of attorney and Cleveland mayoral candidate Carl Stokes (they are threatened with $100 per day fines until they report for practice, and return to duty August 7.)

July 23, 1946: Halfback Gaylon Smith becomes the fifth former member of the Cleveland Rams to sign with the Browns (the others were running backs Tom Colella and Don Greenwood, center Mike Scarry and offensive tackle Chet Adams).

Al Baker

Antonio Langham

This date in Browns history

July 23, 1956:   Future Hall of Famer Dante Lavelli changes his mind about retiring and returns to the Browns for another season.

July 26, 1946:   The newly formed Browns assemble for the first time in training camp at Bowling Green State University.

August 2, 1982:   Abe Abraham, a.k.a. "the Man in the Brown Suit," who became a fixture at Browns games since 1946 by catching field goals and extra points behind the goal post at the closed end of the Stadium, dies at the age of 74.

August 5, 1946:   Bill Willis gets a tryout with the Browns and the Cleveland *Press* headline reports, "Willis Tries Out with Browns - May Open the Way For Negro Players" (he makes the team and, along with Marion Motley, become the first black players to play for the Browns; both were subsequently elected to the Pro Football Hall of Fame).

August 6, 1965:   Future Hall of Famer Paul Warfield, the Browns' No. 1 pick in the 1964 college draft, suffers a broken collarbone in a 24-16 victory over the College All-Stars and misses all but one game that season.

August 11, 1961:   Guard Gene Hickerson suffers a broken leg in a pre-season game and is lost to the Browns for the season.

August 12, 1955:   The (1954) NFL defending champion Browns, playing for the first time without quarterback Otto Graham, who retired and was replaced by George Ratterman, lose to the College All-Stars, 30-27, in front of a crowd of 75,000 at Soldier Field in Chicago.

Chet Adams

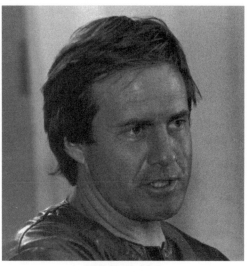

Bill Belichick

This date in Browns history

August 12, 1979:   Defensive end Lyle Alzado is acquired by the Browns in a trade with the Denver Broncos.

August 24, 1946:   Otto Graham leads the College All-Stars to a 16-0 victory over the defending (1945) NFL champion Los Angeles Rams, then joins the Browns to begin his professional career that is culminated with his election to the Pro Football Hall of Fame in 1965.

August 29, 1946:   A federal judge rules that offensive tackle Chet Adams can remain with the Browns, the team to which he jumped when the Rams left Cleveland and relocated in Los Angeles.

August 30, 1946:   Although trailing, 13-6, at halftime, the Browns, playing in their first All-America Football Conference game (an exhibition), rally to beat the Brooklyn Dodgers, 35-20, before a capacity crowd of 35,694 in Akron's Rubber Bowl.

August 30, 1951:   Defensive tackle Art Donovan, who'd been a fourth round draft choice of the Browns in 1951, and would be elected to the Pro Football Hall of Fame in 1968, is traded to the New York Yankees for a third and eighth round draft picks in 1952.

September 1, 1991:   The Browns, under Bill Belichick, making his debut as the tenth head coach in Browns' 46 year history, lose to the Dallas Cowboys, 24-16.

September 3, 1944:   Chicago *Tribune* sports editor Arch Ward announces the formation of the All-America Football Conference and awards the Cleveland franchise to taxicab magnate and entrepreneur Arthur B. "Mickey" McBride.

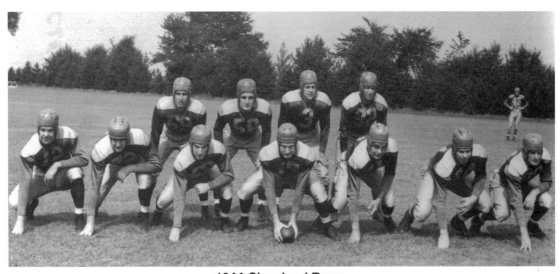

1944 Cleveland Rams

This date in Browns history

September 3, 1955: In the wake of the Browns' third of four exhibition game losses with George Ratterman at quarterback, it is announced that Otto Graham will end his retirement and return to the team for one final season.

September 3, 1978: Sam Rutigliano, who replaced interim coach Dick Modzelewski, makes his debut as the sixth head coach of the Browns in a 24-7 victory over the San Francisco 49ers.

September 4, 1954: Bobby Garrett, a quarterback from Stanford University who had been the Browns' first choice as a "bonus pick" in the 1954 draft, announces his retirement without having played a single game because of a speech impediment that caused him to stutter.

September 6, 1946: Quarterback Cliff Lewis, a Lakewood High School and Duke University graduate, throws the first touchdown pass in Browns history to Mac Speedie as they beat the Miami Seahawks, 44-0, for their first victory in the All-America Football Conference in front of 60,135 fans in the Stadium, then the largest crowd in Cleveland professional football history.

September 10, 1965: Otto Graham becomes the first Browns player to be elected to the Pro Football Hall of Fame.

September 15, 1950: Washington Redskins owner George Preston Marshall is quoted as saying that "the Browns will be lucky to win one game" upon their being admitted into the NFL.

September 15, 1956: Coach Paul Brown uses a radio transmitter to talk to quarterback George Ratterman in a pre-season game against the Detroit Lions.

1948 Cleveland Browns

This date in Browns history

September 16, 1950: In their first game in the NFL, the Browns dominate the defending champion Philadelphia Eagles in a 35-10 victory as Otto Graham passes for three touchdowns in front of 71,237 shocked spectators in Philadelphia's Municipal Stadium.

September 16, 1960: Place-kicker and offensive tackle Lou Groza, the last of the original Browns, announces his retirement (though he agrees a year later to return to the team and plays from 1961-67, and is elected to the Pro Football Hall of Fame in 1974).

September 19, 1971: Nick Skorich, who replaced Blanton Collier as the third coach in the then-25 year history of the Browns, coaches his first game, a 31-0 victory over the Houston Oilers.

September 20, 1954: Future Hall of Famer Marion Motley announces his retirement after eight seasons with the Browns, leaving four members of the original team still playing – Otto Graham, Dante Lavelli, Lou Groza and Frank Gatski (though Motley subsequently un-retired and attempted a comeback as a linebacker).

September 21, 1956: Coach Paul Brown goes back to messenger guards to carry in plays to the quarterback when his radio communications system breaks down.

September 21, 1970: The Browns beat Joe Namath and the New York Jets, 31-21, in front of 85,703 fans in the Stadium in the first Monday Night Football Game, with Keith Jackson, Howard Cosell, and Don Meredith behind the television microphones.

1961 Cleveland Browns coaching staff. Front row: Fritz Heisler, Howard Brinker, Paul Brown, Ed Ulinski, Paul Bixler Back row: Dick Evans, Lou Groza

This date in Browns history

September 21, 1975: Forrest Gregg, who replaced Nick Skorich to become the fourth coach in the then-29 year history of the Browns, coaches his first game, a 24-17 loss to the Cincinnati Bengals.

September 23, 1962: Running back-flanker and future Hall of Famer Bobby Mitchell returns to Cleveland as a member of the Washington Redskins and leads them to a 17-16 victory over the Browns.

September 27, 1982: The NFL Players Association goes on strike, forcing the cancellation of the first seven games of the season.

September 29, 1957: Jim Brown plays his first game for the Browns and gains 89 yards on 21 carries in a 6-3 victory over the New York Giants.

September 30, 1951: The Browns lose their season opener, 24-10, to the San Francisco 49ers (it is the only game they would lose that season until they're beaten in the 1951 NFL championship game by the Rams, 24-17).

October 1, 1950: The New York Giants hand the Browns their first NFL loss, 6-0, in front of 37,647 fans in the Stadium, as Otto Graham is intercepted four times, and Giants fullback Eddie Price scores the game's only touchdown on a three yard run.

October 4, 1952: Otto Graham sets a Browns record that will stand for 29 years by passing for 401 yards in a 21-20 victory over the Pittsburgh Steelers in Pittsburgh.

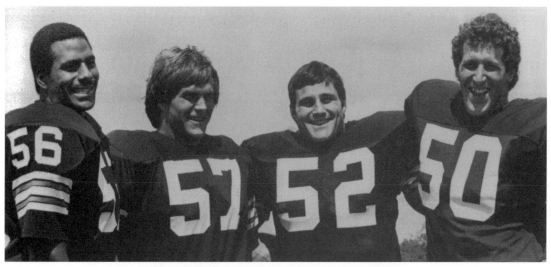

**The 1983 linebacking corps. Left to right:
Chip Banks, Clay Matthews, Dick Ambrose, Tom Cousineau**

This date in Browns history

October 4, 1953:   One of future Hall of Famer Lou Groza's extra point attempts is blocked, ending his streak of 109 successful kicks, as the Browns beat the Chicago Cardinals, 27-7 (in the same game, Horace Gillom sets a team record by punting 11 times).

October 9, 1949:   The Browns suffer their worst defeat in the All-America Football Conference, a 56-28 loss to the San Francisco 49ers in San Francisco, ending their 29 game unbeaten streak.

October 10, 1955:   Stockholders Saul Silberman, Ralph DeChiaro and A. Herman Siskind of Baltimore sell their investment in the Browns for $375,000, leaving the franchise owned completely by local businessmen – David Jones, president; Ellis Ryan and Herbert Evans, vice presidents; Homer Marshman, secretary; and Robert Gries, treasurer; in addition, general manager and coach Paul Brown is named a vice president and director.

October 11, 1952:   Paul Brown signs another five-year contract extension, keeping him with the Browns through 1960, and also is granted additional stock in the club.

October 14, 1949:   Browns' star running back Edgar "Special Delivery" Jones breaks his collarbone in a 61-14 victory over the Los Angeles Dons and never plays another game of professional football.

October 14, 1984:   Ozzie Newsome catches 14 passes for 191 yards but the Browns lose to the New York Jets, 24-20.

October 15, 1950:   Future Hall of Fame defensive end Len Ford's jaw is broken by Pat Harder of the Chicago Cardinals in the Browns' 34-24 victory at the Stadium.

Dave Logan and Brian Sipe

Dave Logan

This date in Browns history

October 15, 1961: In their first meeting with the Green Bay Packers, coached by Vince Lombardi, the Browns lose, 49-17, at the Stadium.

October 18, 1956: NFL Commissioner Bert Bell bans the use of radio helmets, which had been pioneered by the Browns.

October 21, 1956: George Ratterman's professional football career comes to an end as he suffers a knee injury in the Browns' 20-9 loss to the Washington Redskins (he is replaced in that game by Babe Parilli who completed eight of 17 passes for 93 yards).

October 22, 1950: The Browns are defeated for the second time by the New York Giants, 17-13 (on October 1 they also were beaten by the Giants, 6-0) for their only losses in their inaugural NFL season.

October 22, 1984: Following a 12-9 loss to Cincinnati, leaving the Browns with a 1-7 record, Art Modell fires Coach Sam Rutigliano, whose seven year won-lost record is 47-51, and promotes defensive coordinator Marty Schottenheimer, who becomes the seventh head coach in the club's 39-year history.

October 23, 1989: Bernie Kosar completes a pass to Webster Slaughter that goes for a club record 97 yards as the Browns defeat the Chicago Bears, 27-7.

October 25, 1981: Brian Sipe completes 30 of 41 passes for a then-club record 444 yards as the Browns beat the Baltimore Colts, 42-28.

October 27, 1946: The first loss in the history of the Browns comes after seven consecutive victories and is inflicted by the San Francisco 49ers, 34-20, in front of 70,385 fans in the Stadium.

Bernie Kosar

Bernie Kosar and Bill Belichick

This date in Browns history

October 30, 1983: Paul McDonald replaces Brian Sipe at quarterback and, in the second quarter of a 25-19 victory over the Houston Oilers, throws a touch down pass to Doug Dieken on a tackle-eligibility play.

November 1, 1959: Jim Brown scores five touchdowns in the Browns 38-31 victory over the Baltimore Colts.

November 6, 1995: Art Modell announces that the Cleveland Browns are moving to Baltimore where they become the Baltimore Ravens.

November 7, 1954: The Browns suffer their worst beating in club history, 62-3, at the hands of the Washington Redskins at the Stadium.

November 8, 1993: The Browns release Bernie Kosar as Coach Bill Belichick claims the quarterback's skills have "diminished".

November 11, 1951: Paul Brown wins his 200th game as a football coach as the Browns defeat the Philadelphia Eagles, 20-17 (included in Brown's record were 70 victories with the Browns since 1946, as well as victories at Ohio State University, Massillon High School, and Severn Prep School).

November 11, 1959: Paul Brown, considered by some to be the prime candidate to replace the late Bert Bell as commissioner of the NFL, removes his name from consideration and, eventually, Pete Rozelle, general manager of the Los Angeles Rams, is elected commissioner.

1945 Cleveland Rams

This date in Browns history

November 15, 1953: Otto Graham suffers a gashed mouth and face when he is hit by an elbow thrown by San Francisco's Art Michalik in the second quarter, but returns to the game after receiving 15 stitches during the halftime intermission and leads the Browns to a 23-20 victory over the 49ers in front of 80,698 fans in the Stadium.

November 14, 1948: In a battle of unbeaten All-America Football Conference teams, the Browns beat the San Francisco 49ers, 14-7, in front of what was then the largest crowd in professional football history, 82,769 fans in the Stadium.

November 15, 1959: Bobby Mitchell runs 14 times and gains 232 yards (five fewer than Jim Brown's NFL record set in 1957) as the Browns defeat the Washington Redskins, 31-17 (Mitchell didn't carry the ball most of the fourth quarter as Coach Paul Brown said he was unaware that Brown's record was within reach).

November l6, 1947: Chet Adams and Lou Saban are pressed into service as the Browns place-kickers as Lou Groza is injured in pre-game drills.

November 17, 1982: NFL players return to their teams after a 57 day strike, the first in NFL history that caused the cancellation of seven games.

November 19, 1961: Jim Brown rushes 34 times for 242 yards, breaking by five yards his own NFL record set in 1957, and scores four touchdowns as the Browns beat the Philadelphia Eagles, 45-24.

Parker Hall

Paul Brown

This date in Browns history

November 20, 1977: Brian Sipe is injured and replaced at quarterback by David Mays, who completes 13 of 24 passes in a 21-7 victory over the New York Giants.

November 21, 1982: The season is resumed with the Browns beating the New England Patriots, 10-7, after a 57 day strike by the NFL Players Association forced cancellation of the first seven games.

November 23, 1947: The Browns overcome a 28-0 halftime deficit to earn a 28-28 tie with the New York Yankees in Yankee Stadium as Otto Graham sets an All-America Football Conference record by passing for 325 yards.

November 24, 1949: The smallest crowd in Browns history (5,031) sees the final regular season game in the All-America Football Conference, a 14-6 victory over the Chicago Rockets in Chicago.

November 24, 1957: Rookie Jim Brown sets an NFL record by rushing for 237 yards in 31 carries, scoring four touchdowns in the Browns' 45-31 victory over the Los Angeles Rams (the previous record of 223 yards was set by the Rams' Tom Wilson in 1956).

November 25, 1951: Dub Jones scores an NFL-record six touchdowns as the Browns defeat the Chicago Bears, 42-21, in the Stadium.

November 26, 1956: Jim Brown is selected in the first round of the college draft, after the Browns lose a coin flip that would have enabled Paul Brown to take either quarterback John Brodie or Len Dawson.

November 27, 1977: The Browns lose to the Los Angeles Rams, 9-0, in what owner Art Modell called a "disgraceful" performance.

Dub Jones

Webster Slaughter

This date in Browns history

November 28, 1948: A 31-28 victory over the San Francisco 49ers is the Browns' third in a period of one week (they previously beat the Los Angeles Dons, 31-14, on November 25, and the New York Yankees, 34-21, on November 21).

November 28, 1954: Horace Gillom sets a still-standing NFL record in the Browns' 16-7 victory over the New York Giants, booming an 80-yard punt 70 yards in the air and out of the Giants' end zone, traveling a total of 95 yards from where the ball was kicked.

November 29, 1956: The NFL Players Association is organized in the home of Browns future Hall of Fame receiver Dante Lavelli (former Notre Dame star Creighton Miller is hired as the union's legal representative).

November 30, 1952: The Browns rally from a 14-0 deficit to defeat the Washington Redskins, 48-24, in Washington.

December 5, 1948: A 31-21 victory over the Brooklyn Dodgers in the final game of the season in the All-America Football Conference gives the Browns a 14-0 record to become the first team in professional football to go through a regular season undefeated since the 1942 Chicago Bears went 11-0 (but lost in the championship game to the Washington Redskins, 14-6).

December 6, 1953: With a 62-14 victory over the New York Giants, the Browns set a club scoring record (broken the following season by beating the Washington Redskins, 62-3) as George Ratterman, starting at quarterback in place of the injured Otto Graham, passes for 235 yards and three touchdowns.

Bobby Mitchell and Jim Ninowski

This date in Browns history

December 6, 1959: Thousands of New York fans swarm onto the field at Yankee Stadium, many of them trying to attack Paul Brown, as the Browns lose to the New York Giants, 48-7.

December 9, 1949: The All-America Football Conference is disbanded as the National Football League agrees to take in the Browns, San Francisco 49ers and Baltimore Colts to form the National-American Football League (though the name soon reverted to the NFL).

December 10, 1951: A 28-0 victory over the Pittsburgh Steelers is the Browns' fourth shut-out of the season, a club record that still stands (the Browns also blanked the Steelers, 17-0, earlier that season, as well as the Washington Redskins, 45-0, and the New York Giants, 10-0).

December 11, 1949: The Browns, behind the Jones boys - Edgar and Dub - and Marion Motley and Lou Groza, beat San Francisco, 21-7, in front of 22,500 in the Stadium to win their fourth and final All-America Football Conference championship.

December 13, 1977: With one game left and a 6-7 record, Forrest Gregg resigns under pressure as the fourth coach of the Browns, leaving with a three year record of 18-23 (he is replaced on an interim basis by Dick Modzelewski, who coaches the Browns in the season finale, a 20-19 loss to Seattle).

December 14, 1946: Browns captain and tackle Jim Daniell is arrested and charged with intoxication after a traffic altercation on Cleveland's east side, and is thrown off the team by Coach Paul Brown (though two other players, end Mac Speedie and tackle Lou Rymkus, who were with Daniell and charged with disorderly conduct, were allowed by Brown to remain on the team).

Bob Waterfield and Jane Russell

Gib Shanley

This date in Browns history

December 14, 1947: A 14-3 victory over the New York Yankees in Yankee Stadium gives the Browns their second straight championship in the All-America Football Conference.

December 14, 1958: Needing only a tie to reach their eighth championship game in nine years, the Browns lose their season finale to the New York Giants, 13-10, on a 49-yard field goal with 2:07 remaining by Pat Summerall, in a driving snowstorm.

December 14, 1961: Running back and future Hall of Famer Bobby Mitchell is traded to the Washington Redskins for the draft rights to Heisman Trophy winning running back Ernie Davis of Syracuse University.

December 17, 1995: The Browns beat Cincinnati, 26-10, in their final home game prior to moving to Baltimore

December 19, 1948: The Browns rout the Buffalo Bills, 49-7, to complete an undefeated (15-0) season and win their third All-America Football Conference title in front of a crowd of only 22,981 fans in the Stadium.

December 21, 1958: The New York Giants hold fullback Jim Brown to only eight yards in seven carries as the Browns suffer their first shutout in 114 games, a 10-0 loss, in the NFL Eastern Conference championship game.

December 21, 1975: A 21-10 loss to the Houston Oilers completes the Browns' worst season with a 3-11 record (though it will be broken in 1990 when they go 3-13).

1964 Browns coaching staff. Left to right: William "Dub" Jones, Fritz Heisler, Blanton Collier, Howard Brinker, Nick Skorich, Ed Ulinski

This date in Browns history

December 22, 1946: The Browns, led by quarterback Otto Graham's 16 completions for 213 yards, beat the New York Yankees, 14-9, to win their first All-America Football Conference championship game before 40,469 fans in the Stadium.

December 23, 1951: In their second NFL title game in their second year in the league, the Browns lose to the Los Angeles Rams, 24-17, ending their string of championships at five (including four in the All-America Football Conference from 1946-49).

December 24, 1950: Overcoming a fourth quarter, eight point deficit, the Browns beat the Los Angeles Rams, 30-28, on Lou Groza's 16-yard field goal with 28 seconds remaining in the NFL championship game in front of only 29,751 fans in the Stadium, as Otto Graham throws four touchdown passes.

December 24, 1995: The Browns lose to the Jaguars in Jacksonsiville, 24-21, in their final game prior to moving to Baltimore.

December 26, 1955: Otto Graham passes for two touchdowns and runs for two more in his final game for the Browns, a 38-14 victory over the Los Angeles Rams to win their second straight NFL championship and third in six seasons, in front of 87,695 fans in the Los Angeles Coliseum.

December 26, 1954: The Browns end a three year losing streak in the NFL championship game by routing the Detroit Lions, 56-10, as Otto Graham throws three touchdown passes and runs for three touchdowns.

December 26, 1955: In a 38-14 victory over the Detroit Lions, the Browns win their second straight NFL championship, and third since entering the league in 1950, while playing in their sixth consecutive title game (and tenth including four in the All-America Football Conference).

December 27, 1953: For the third straight season the Browns lose the NFL championship game, this one, 17-16, to the Detroit Lions.

December 27, 1964: Frank Ryan throws three touchdown passes to Gary Collins as the Browns upset the favored Baltimore Colts, 27-0, to win their fourth NFL championship and first since 1955.

December 27, 1977: Art Modell goes outside the organization to pick Sam Rutigliano as the Browns' sixth head coach, replacing Forrest Gregg.

December 27, 1988: Marty Schottenheimer resigns as head coach of the Browns in the wake of a 10-6 season.

This date in Browns history

December 28, 1952:   The Browns play their third NFL championship game in their three years in the league, but lose for the second straight season, 17-7, to the Detroit Lions.

December 29, 1957:   In one of their worst losses ever, the Browns are beaten, 59-14, by Tobin Rote and the Detroit Lions in the championship game, their sixth in seven seasons in the NFL.

December 29, 1968:   The Browns' Super Bowl hopes end as the Baltimore Colts, led by former Shaw High and Ohio State star Tom Matte scores three touchdowns to beat Cleveland, 34-0, in the NFL championship game in front of 80,628 fans in the Stadium.

December 31, 1959:   Future Hall of Famer Len Dawson is acquired by the Browns in a trade with the Pittsburgh Steelers for receiver Preston Carpenter and defensive back Junior Wren (though Dawson played only briefly as a backup for the Browns in 1960 and 1961, and later played 14 seasons for the Dallas Texans-Kansas City Chiefs from 1962-75, leading the Chiefs to Super Bowl I).

1995 Cleveland Browns

TOP ROW: Eric Mangini, Jerry Simmons, Ernie Adams, Pat Hill, Kirk Ferentz, Rick Venturi, Steve Crosby, Ozzie Newsome, Mike Sheppard, Jim Bates, Scott O'Brien, Jacob Burney, Chuck Bresnahan, Tom Spann, John Settle

FIFTH ROW: Joe Kim, Mark Smith, Lloyd Givan, Harold Bishop, Jed Devries, Orlando Brown, Bob Dahl, Steve Everitt, Wally Williams, Walter Reeves, Herman Arvie, Mike Frederick, Romeo Bandison, Larry Webster, Eric Moore

FOURTH ROW: Phil Savage, Ed Carroll, Bill Tessendorf, Quentin Neujahr, Rich McKenzie, Carl Banks, Rob Burnett, Anthony Pleasant, Michael Jackson, Tim Goad, Pio Sagapolutele, Craig Powell, Bob Chester, Nick Rusinko

THIRD ROW: J.J. Miller, William Sheridan, Gerald Dixon, Mike Caldwell, Dan Footman, Tommy Vardell, Eric Zeier, Don Griffin, Jim McMahon, Frank Hartley, Mike Davis, Jeff Platz, Jon Dube

SECOND ROW: Eddie Sutter, Issac Booth, Tom Tupa, Stevon Moore, Tony Jones, Vinny Testaverde, Bill Belichick, Pepper Johnson, Bennie Thompson, Eric Turner, Leroy Hoard, Brian Kinchen, Dana Hall

FIRST ROW: Earnest Hunter, Rico Smith, Derrick Alexander, Michael Bates, Earnest Byner, Antonio Langham, Andre Rison, Matt Stover, Lorenzo White, Louis Riddick, Tim Jacobs, Keenan McCardell, Johnny Thomas

No more tears for 'Big Dawg'

It all began in the mid-1980s, and while the originator was Hanford Dixon, then a Pro Bowler and All-Pro cornerback for the Browns, it was a spectator who gained most of the notoriety for what has become the home of the most rabid fans of any team in the NFL.

Dixon, for whatever reason, began barking like a dog – make that a "dawg" – after making a key play during a game at the old Stadium, and encouraged his cornerback partner, Frank Minnifield, and other teammates to do the same.

Then Dixon got the fans involved. Mainly the fans in the bleachers, exhorting them to bark their approval – and, mainly, support – of the Browns.

And, almost immediately, that section at the open end of the Stadium became known as the "Dawg Pound," filled as it usually was, by the most fanatical, vocal and loyal followers of the Browns anywhere in the world.

Quickly, too, "Big Dawg," a.k.a. John Thompson, surfaced, wearing a rubber false-face that resembled a big-eyed, bulbous-nosed, floppy-eared hound with a Browns helmet perched atop his head, and barking. Always barking.

John Thompson

Always thereafter "Big Dawg" could be found on or near the railing in front of the Dawg Pound.

It wasn't long before network television cameras spotted "Big Dawg" and beamed his image around the country, making him an instant celebrity – though few people (if any) knew what Thompson looked like under his mask.

And, so, too, was born a new nickname for the Browns.

In fact, after then-owner Art Modell moved his team to Baltimore at the end of the 1995 season, "Big Dawg" represented Cleveland fans in testifying before Congress in an unsuccessful effort to prevent the re-location of the franchise.

Naturally, "Big Dawg" was in attendance in the "Dawg Pound" on December 17, 1995, when the old Browns played their final home game in Cleveland, and beat the Cincinnati Bengals, 26-10. But the victory represented little joy for Thompson and his fellow denizens of the "Dawg Pound."

Unabashedly, "Big Dawg" admitted he saw most of the game through tears in his eyes.

"No doubt about it, that was the low point," he was quoted in a *Browns News/Illustrated* article. "I can still hear the benches and seats (of the old Stadium) being chopped up and passed over peoples' heads" as they pilfered mementos.

"As the game ended," the article went on, "Browns left offensive tackle Tony Jones, along with many of his teammates, went to the Dawg Pound and shook hands with the fans. Jones also handed a game ball to Big Dawg, who took that as a sign to take the ball and run with it – to be the leader of the pack in Cleveland's effort to get another team."

Which Thompson did, with the numerous other fans.

At least partly as a result of their endeavors – as well as, certainly, Dixon's barking exhortations on the field back in the mid-1980s – Cleveland's new Stadium includes a "Dawg Pound."

And, undoubtedly, for every Browns game it will be filled with the most rabid football fans in the world, many wearing dog masks and barking their support of their favorite team.

196

THE TRADITION CONTINUES

The new Cleveland Browns Stadium

The new Browns

Alfred Lerner, Owner and Chairman

A former minority owner of the old Cleveland Browns, Alfred Lerner was one of seven candidates applying to the National Football League to buy the new Cleveland Browns, and was awarded the franchise at a cost of $530 million on September 8, 1998.

Lerner, a 66-year old former Marine lieutenant who served on active duty from 1955-57, also is chairman of two financial institutions, MBNA Corporation, which is the second largest bank lender through credit cards in the United States, and Town and Country Trust of Baltimore, Maryland, a company that operates more than 13,000 residential apartments.

Lerner also is president and trustee of the Cleveland Clinic Foundation, vice chairman and trustee of his alma mater, Columbia University, and a trustee of Case Western Reserve University, and New York Presbyterian Hospital.

Born in Brooklyn, New York on May 8, 1933, Lerner attended New York city schools, graduated from Brooklyn Technical High School in 1951, and earned a bachelor of arts degree from Columbia University in 1955.

Lerner and his wife, the former Norma Wolkoff, whom he married in 1955, raised two children, Nancy and Randy, both of whom have earned law degrees, and have six grandchildren.

Carmen A. Policy, President / Chief Executive Officer

It wasn't until Carmen Policy made clear his interest in leaving the San Francisco 49ers and joining the new Cleveland Browns that Alfred Lerner submitted his application to the National Football League to buy the expansion franchise.

During his eight years as San Francisco's president and chief executive officer, the 55-year old Policy played a key role in shaping the course of the 49ers who were viewed as the one of the preeminent sports franchises of the 1980s and 1990s. Dating back to 1989, San Francisco won two Super Bowls and eight division titles. He was named NFL "Executive of the Year" in 1994 by both *The Sporting News* and *Pro Football Weekly*.

A native of Youngstown, Ohio, Policy, whose wife is the former Gail Moretti, grew up as a fan of the Cleveland Browns, graduated from Ursuline High School and Youngstown State University, and earned his doctorate degree in 1966 from Georgetown University Law Center.

He joined the 49ers front office in 1983 as vice president and general counsel, and worked his way up to the top administrative position in 1991.

It was Policy's creative management of the NFL's newly-implemented salary cap in 1993 that earned him recognition as "Master of the Cap," and his guidance of the annual NFL-college draft, as well as the signing of quality free agents, that were key factors in San Francisco's re-emergence as one of the league's premier organizations.

The new Browns

Dwight Clark, Executive Vice President and Director of Football Operations

Dwight Clark was one of the most popular players to ever wear a San Francisco 49ers uniform, as a wide receiver from 1979-87 after being a tenth round draft choice out of Clemson University, and then, upon retirement joined the team's front office.

Clark, 42, swiftly climbed through the ranks to become in 1995 the 49ers' executive vice president/director of football operations, after beginning as the team's marketing consultant in 1989, then executive administrative assistant from 1990-91, and coordinator of football operations and player personnel from 1992-94.

In his position as director of football operations in San Francisco – as he now is with the Browns – Clark was in charge of scouting, player personnel, contract negotiations, salary cap management, and training camp.

During his 134 game playing career with the 49ers, Clark caught 506 passes for 6,750 yards and 48 touchdowns.

According to the 49ers, Clark was the central figure of the most memorable play in the franchise's history. He made the catch that provided San Francisco with the touchdown that resulted in a 28-27 victory over the Dallas Cowboys in the 1981 NFC championship game. It sent the 49ers on to Super Bowl XVI, in which they defeated Cincinnati, 26-21.

Born in Kingston, North Carolina, Clark and his wife Ashley have three children.

Chris Palmer, Head Football Coach

A longtime National Football League, United States Football League and Canadian League assistant and former college coach noted as an offensive specialist and for his ability to develop young quarterbacks, Chris Palmer brings 27 years of coaching experience to the new Browns.

Palmer, 50, spent the past nine seasons in the NFL, with the Jacksonville Jaguars (1997-98), New England Patriots (1993-96), and the Houston Oilers (1990-92).

Previously, Palmer, a former college quarterback (Southern Connecticut State, 1968-71) himself, was head coach at the University of New Haven (1986-87) and Boston University (1988-89), an assistant at the University of Connecticut, Lehigh and Colgate, and was an aide with the Montreal Concordes in the CFL and the New Jersey Generals of the USFL.

It was during his service with the Patriots that Drew Bledsoe blossomed as a star quarterback in 1996, taking New England to Super Bowl XXXI, and Palmer also played a key role in the development of Mark Brunell with the Jaguars.

Palmer also was the quarterbacks coach and offensive coordinator for New Jersey when former Browns star passer Brian Sipe played for the Generals in the USFL.

Palmer and his wife Donna have two children.

New Browns timeline

January 25, 1995: A task force is appointed by Cleveland Mayor Michael R. White to recommend whether a new stadium for football should be built or if the existing Stadium should be renovated in order to ensure keeping the Browns.

June 5, 1995: Art Modell requests a moratorium on talks aimed at keeping the Browns in Cleveland, saying he does not want his team to be distracted in the coming season; Mayor White complies with the request.

July 28, 1995: Secret negotiations begin between the Browns and officials of Baltimore aimed at enticing the team to re-locate to that city.

November 4, 1995: Modell admits to several sportswriters that he is planning to move the team to Baltimore, and also makes public his intention to move his home from Waite Hill to West Palm Beach, Florida.

November 6, 1995: Modell makes it official; in a televised news conference in Baltimore, with Maryland Governor Parris Glendening at his side, it is announced that the Browns will leave Cleveland and play in Baltimore beginning in 1996.

November 7, 1995: Cuyahoga County voters approve a "sin tax" to finance the building of a new football-only stadium.

November 24, 1995: Cuyahoga County Common Pleas Judge Kenneth R. Callahan issues a preliminary injunction that will bar the Browns from leaving Cleveland until their Stadium lease expires in 1998, and sets a February 12, 1996 trial date to hear the case.

February 6, 1996: John Thompson, a.k.a. "Big Dawg," testifies before a Congressional committee, urging Congress to intervene in Modell's intention to move the Browns to Baltimore.

February 8, 1996: NFL Commissioner Paul Tagliabue officially promises to deliver a new team to Cleveland in 1999 if the city builds a new football only stadium; he also ensures that the name, "Browns," the team's colors and history will remain in Cleveland; and the NFL advances the city up to $48 million for construction of a new stadium.

March 11, 1996: NFL owners ratify the agreement signed by Tagliabue and White promising to restore a team to Cleveland, and the city agrees to drop all litigation against Modell and the league.

New Browns timeline

April 23, 1996:   The city of Cleveland agrees to build a new football only stadium at a cost estimated at $232.8 million.

June 7, 1996:   HOK, which designed Jacobs Field, is selected as the architect for the new football stadium, to be built at the site of the existing Cleveland Stadium.

June 26, 1996:   Bill Futterer is appointed by the NFL as president of the Browns Trust, and is charged with the responsibility to sell permanent seat licenses and luxury suites in the proposed new stadium.

September 21, 1996:   The "Final Play" is staged at the existing Cleveland Stadium and more than 50,000 fans attend the event, buying pieces of the building for souvenirs.

October 9, 1996:   The sale of permanent seat licenses, ranging in price from $250 to $1,000, and the sale of 108 luxury suites at the new stadium begins.

November 25, 1996:   Demolition of the existing Cleveland Stadium begins.

December 13, 1996:   The average price of season tickets - $42.19 – is announced by the Browns Trust.

December 17, 1996:   Eight thousand club seats are placed on sale.

January 24, 1997:   Tagliabue announces that Cleveland will get an expansion franchise rather than a relocated team

March 27, 1997:   The design of the new stadium is made public; it features a steel and glass exterior similar to the nearby Great Lakes Science Museum.

May 15, 1997:   Ground-breaking ceremonies for the new stadium are held.

May 19, 1997:   Officials announce that the estimated cost of the new stadium has increased to $247 million.

New Browns timeline

September 3, 1997:   Mayor White announces that overruns will drive up the cost of the new stadium by $12.8 million.

October 12, 1997:   The Browns Trust announces the receipt of 52,449 season ticket applications.

October 13, 1997:   The first concrete pouring for the stadium superstructure begins.

May 19, 1998:   NFL owners are unable to settle on a price for the new Browns franchise and decide upon a complicated bidding process that, in effect, will pit ownership applicants against each other.

June 2 – August 17, 1998:   Seven potential ownership groups are identified as applicants to the NFL to buy the Browns expansion franchise.

August 19, 1998:   NFL owners meet in Atlanta to hear the applications to buy the Browns expansion franchise.

September 8, 1998:   After nearly six hours of debate and four ballots Al Lerner is granted the Browns expansion franchise at a cost of $530 million, which includes $54 million earmarked for the new stadium.

September 9, 1998:   Lerner announces the new football stadium will be named Cleveland Municipal Stadium.

November 2, 1998:   Lal Heneghan, formerly with the NFL Management Council, is hired as the Browns assistant director of football operations/general counsel.

November 10, 1998:   Richard Bedell, formerly vice president of corporate financial affairs for International Management Group, is hired as the Browns chief financial officer.

November 12, 1998:   Lewis Merletti, formerly director of the U.S. Secret Service, is hired as a Browns vice president and director of stadium and security affairs.

November 30, 1998:   Dwight Clark, formerly vice president and director of football operations for the San Francisco 49ers, is hired as a Browns vice president and director of football operations.

New Browns timeline

December 4, 1998: The Browns are fined $10,000 by the NFL for Policy's public comments about the possibility of Mike Holmgren, then Green Bay Packers head coach, becoming available in the job mart.

December 14, 1998: Alex Martins, formerly director of communications for the Orlando Magic of the NBA, is hired as a Browns vice president and director of communications and public affairs.

December 16, 1998: Lerner rejects a request by several Cleveland City Council members to commit to pay for overruns if the cost of the new stadium exceeds $293 million (as Lerner and Mayor White previously agreed to a deal that calls for Lerner and the city to split any overruns if the project exceeds $283 million, or goes as high as $293 million).

December 22, 1998: The Browns sign their first players: street free agents Corey Bridges, a wide receiver; David Conner, a linebacker; Corey Dowden, a defensive back; Bill Duff and Albert Reese, defensive tackles; and John Dutton, a quarterback.

December 28, 1998: The Browns are given permission to begin interviewing other NFL assistant coaches; Brian Billick, offensive coordinator of the Minnesota Vikings is the first to meet with Policy and Clark.

December 29, 1998: The Browns interview Denver Broncos offensive coordinator Gary Kubiak.

January 6, 1999: Kentucky quarterback Tim Couch announces he will enter the NFL draft and publicly states it would be his dream to play in Cleveland and be the first pick of the Browns.

January 18, 1999: Policy eliminates Billick as a candidate to coach the Browns.

January 19, 1999: Oakland Raiders defensive coordinator Willie Shaw interviews with Policy.

January 21, 1999: Jacksonville Jaguars offensive coordinator Chris Palmer is hired to coach the Browns.

January 25, 1999: Bob Slowik, formerly with the Chicago Bears, is named defensive coordinator of the Browns, and Clarence Brooks, also formerly with the Bears, is named defensive line coach.

January 26, 1999: William D. Squires is named director of stadium operations by the Browns.

New Browns timeline

February 2, 1999: Billy Davis, Carolina Panthers outside linebackers coach, is named defensive quality-control coach, Tony Sparano, University of New Haven head coach, is named offensive quality-control coach, and Keith Kidd, Arizona Cardinals personnel assistant, is named pro personnel director of the Browns.

February 4, 1999: Jerry Holmes, West Virginia University assistant coach, is named defensive backfield coach, and Dick Portee, North Carolina State assistant coach, is named offensive backfield coach of the Browns.

February 5, 1999: John Hufnagel, head coach of the Arena Football League's New Jersey Red Dogs, is named quarterbacks coach, and Ken Whisenhunt, Baltimore Ravens assistant coach, is named special teams coach of the Browns.

February 8, 1999: Ray Perkins, former Tampa Bay head coach, is named tight ends coach, and Tim Jorgensen, formerly with the Atlanta Falcons is named strength coach of the Browns.

February 9, 1999: The first five players picked by the Browns in the expansion draft are Detroit Lions guard Jim Pyne, Dallas Cowboys defensive lineman Hurvin McCormack, New England Patriots guard Scott Rehberg, San Francisco 49ers center Steve Gordon, and Cincinnati Bengals return specialist Damon Gibson; the 37th and last player claimed is former Browns cornerback Antonio Langham from the San Francisco 49ers.

February 11, 1999: Jerry Butler, former Buffalo Bills wide receiver, is named receivers coach, and Mark Michaels is named quality control coach for special teams by the Browns.

February 12, 1999: The Browns make their first trade, getting San Francisco defensive end Roy Barker and tight end Irv Smith for "past considerations," for taking Langham's big contract from the 49ers in the expansion draft.

February 14, 1999: The first unrestricted free agents signed by the Browns are New England Patriots center Dave Wohlabaugh ($26 million over five years) and Chris Gardocki ($6 million over five years).

New Browns timeline

February 15, 1999:   The Browns sign two more free agents, Baltimore Ravens tackle Orlando Brown ($26 million over six years) and Minnesota Vikings cornerback Corey Fuller ($20.6 million over five years, and also acquire Buffalo Bills linebacker Chris Spielman in a trade for "past considerations."

February 22, 1999:   San Francisco quarterback Ty Detmer is acquired, along with the 49ers' pick in the fourth round, 27th overall, in the 1999 NFL draft, in exchange for the Browns first picks in the fourth and fifth rounds of the draft, and Detmer signs a new contract calling for $14 million over seven years.

February 25, 1999:   Chicago Bears free agent defensive end John Thierry is signed to a $1 million, one year contract with the intention of switching him back to his natural outside linebacker position.

March 4, 1999:   Arizona Cardinals free agent tackle Lomas Brown is signed to a $10.5 million, three year contract, and San Francisco free agent defensive back Marquez Pope also is signed for a $5 million, two year contract by the Browns.

March 27, 1999:   The Browns conduct their first practice to start three-day mini-camp.

April 1, 1999:   The NFL releases the 1999 schedule with the Browns opening the season on the night of September 12, against Pittsburgh at the Stadium; the "old" Browns (Baltimore Ravens) are scheduled to make their first appearance in Cleveland on November 7.

April 17, 1999:   Browns select quarterback Tim Couch of the University of Kentucky with their first pick in the NFL draft, and he immediately agrees to a $48 million, seven year contract, which includes a $12.25 million signing bonus. Other players selected by the Browns in the draft: Round Two – wide receiver Kevin Johnson, Syracuse, and linebacker Rahim Abdullah, Clemson; Round Three – defensive back Daylon McCutcheon, USC, and safety Marquis Smith, California; Round Four – linebacker Walt Rainer, Virginia; Round Five – wide receiver Darrin Chiaverini, Colorado; Round Six – defensive tackle Marcus Spriggs, Troy State, linebacker Kendall Ogle, Maryland, and tight end James Dearth, Tarleton State; Round Seven – running back Madre Hill, Arkansas.

'I expect to win Super Bowls'

The first step toward what the new Browns hope will be the Super Bowl was taken by Dwight Clark and Coach Chris Palmer on April 17, 1999, when they selected quarterback Tim Couch in the NFL-college draft.

Tim Couch

Couch, from the University of Kentucky, the first player picked overall, was chosen over two other highly-rated players, quarterback Akili Smith of the University of Oregon, and Heisman Trophy winner Ricky Williams, a running back from the University of Texas.

Couch, 6-4 and 220-pounds, was thrilled to be selected by the Browns and quickly signed a contract said to be worth $48 million over seven years. Included was a signing bonus of $12.25 million. Both of the dollar figures were said to be records for an incoming rookie.

The money, however, was not what thrilled Couch the most, he said. "I'm not a guy who wants for a whole lot. When I was a little kid dreaming, I didn't dream about making the big bucks. That tingle in your belly is about making the NFL … about playing in Super Bowls."

In his introduction to the Cleveland media, Couch further endeared himself to Browns fans by saying, "This is where I wanted to be from Day One," and that he reportedly had instructed his agent to "do what ever it takes to get me to Cleveland."

In that respect Couch reminded the fans of another quarterback who, fourteen years earlier, also wanted desperately to play for the Browns, then did everything possible to make it happen, and became an instant and longtime favorite – Bernie Kosar.

Based on the statistics he compiled in his three seasons at Kentucky, it would seem that Couch is not only capable of doing all that Kosar did on the field, but hopefully even more.

Couch took over a Kentucky team in 1996 that had gone 1-10 the year before he arrived from high school in Hyden, Kentucky and turned it into a winner.

In his 2 ½ seasons as the Wildcats' starting quarterback – he opted to enter the NFL draft a year early – Couch completed 67.1 percent of his passes, 795 of 1,184 for 8,835 yards, and 74 touchdowns with 35 interceptions.

According to one scouting report on Couch: "He is smart and tough, skillful, has a live arm, is capable of throwing all the passes, is patient and waits for receivers, leads receivers and hits them in stride, always tries to make something positive happen, senses pressure and is elusive, throws well on the run and his passes have speed, throws tremendous corner routes, putting air underneath his passes, places them where only the receiver can make the catch, makes good decisions, improved his ability to read defenses, and is a real leader."

It's no wonder that Clark, the director of football operations, and Palmer, a former quarterbacks coach for several NFL teams, consider that the choice of Couch is the first step toward the Super Bowl.

Couch promised he'd do everything possible to make the dream come true.

"I'll be the hardest working player on the team," he vowed. "That's what's going to make me successful. I expect to go to Super Bowls, and I expect to win Super Bowls. That's all I care about."

Which makes him a perfect fit for the Browns.